BLENDING GENDERS

Gender blending, or transgenderism, is at the cutting edge of contemporary debates about sex, sexuality and gender. The term 'transgender' includes transvestites, transsexuals, drag queens, gender benders and all gender blenders, whether straight or gay, who in their cross-dressing and sex-changing 'transgress' the binary divide between the sexes. *Blending Genders* is concerned with those who attempt to blend various aspects of genders, either in respect of themselves or others. The book describes the personal experiences of those who cross-dress and sex-change, and details how they organise themselves socially – in both 'outsider' and 'respectable' communities. The authors consider the dominant medical framework through which cross-dressing and sex-changing are predominantly viewed. A comprehensive treatment is afforded to gender blending in literature, the press and the recently emerged telephone sex lines. The book concludes with a discussion of the lively debates that have taken place concerning the politics of transgenderism in recent years, and examines its prominence in recent contributions to contemporary cultural and queer theory. *Blending Genders* is the first comprehensive treatment of the social aspects of cross-dressing and sex-changing and, as such, can rightly lay first claim to an emerging field of transgender studies.

Contributors: Dwight B. Billings, Neil Buhrich, Peter Farrer, Phaedra Kelly, Roberta Perkins, Janice Raymond, Mark Rees, Carol Riddell, Thomas Urban, Terri Webb and Stephen Whittle.

Richard Ekins is Senior Lecturer in Social Psychology and Psychoanalysis at the University of Ulster. **Dave King** is Lecturer in the Department of Sociology, Social Policy and Social Work Studies at the University of Liverpool.

BLENDING GENDERS

Social Aspects of Cross-Dressing and Sex-Changing

Edited by

Richard Ekins and Dave King

London and New York

First published 1996
by Routledge
11 New Fetter Lane, London EC4P 4EE

Simultaneously published in the USA and Canada
by Routledge
29 West 35th Street, New York, NY 10001

© 1996 Selection and Editorial matter, Richard Ekins and Dave King.
Individual chapters, the Contributors.

Typeset in Times by
Florencetype Ltd, Stoodleigh, Devon

Printed and bound in Great Britain by
Biddles Ltd, Guildford and King's Lynn

British Library Cataloguing in Publication Data
A catalogue record for this book is available from
the British Library

Library of Congress Cataloguing in Publication Data
A catalogue record for this book has been requested

ISBN 0-415-11551-5 (hbk)
ISBN 0-415-11552-3 (pbk)

CONTENTS

v

PLATES

THE CONTRIBUTORS

Dwight B. Billings is Professor of Sociology at the University of Kentucky. He is a specialist in the critical theory tradition in sociology and engages in historical and comparative studies of social inequality in the United States.

Neil Buhrich is Clinical Director of the Inner City Mental Health Service, Sydney and Director of HIV Psychiatry at St Vincent's Hospital, Sydney. He has a conjoint appointment as Senior Lecturer in Psychiatry at the University of New South Wales. He has published widely in the scientific literature on aspects of gender identity.

Richard Ekins is Director of the Trans-Gender Archive and Senior Lecturer in Social Psychology and Psychoanalysis at the University of Ulster at Coleraine. He has published widely on various aspects of trans-gender and is co-author of *Centres and Peripheries of Psychoanalysis* (1994). His book *Male Femaling* is to be published by Routledge.

Peter Farrer, formerly an inspector of taxes, is currently a freelance writer and publisher. He has worked on aspects of transgender for over forty years. His books include *Men in Petticoats* (1987), *In Female Disguise* (1992) and *Borrowed Plumes* (1994).

Phaedra Kelly is the alternate personality of gender transient Bruce Laker. She is the founder/director of the International Gender Transient Affinity, the first working world-wide transgender human rights organisation. She has published numerous articles on various aspects of transgender.

Dave King is a lecturer in the Department of Sociology, Social Policy and Social Work Studies at the University of Liverpool. He has been researching and writing in the area of transvestism and transsexualism for a number of years. In addition to several articles, he has written *The Transvestite and the Transsexual: Public Categories and Private Identities* (1993).

Roberta Perkins is a Senior Research Officer in Sociology at the University of New South Wales. She has worked in the area of transsexualism and prostitution for fifteen years and has published a number of books and articles based on her findings. *Working Girls* (1991) deals with female prostitution, and *Sex Work and Sex Workers in Australia* (1995) includes observations on transsexual prostitution.

Janice Raymond is Professor of Women's Studies and Medical Ethics at the University of Massachusetts, Amherst. She is the author of a number of books including *The Transsexual Empire: The Making of the She-Male* (1994).

Mark Rees is a local councillor and celebrated campaigner for transsexual rights. He is the founder of Press for Change. He is the author of numerous articles on transsexualism and his autobiography, *Dear Sir or Madam,* is published by Cassell, 1996.

Carol Riddell, a former Lecturer at the University of Lancaster and author, with Margaret Coulson, of *Approaching Sociology*, joined the Findhorn Foundation in N.E. Scotland in 1983 and wrote a book about it, *The Findhorn Community*. She still lives in Scotland and is interested in questions of spirituality. Her latest book is *The Path to Love*, Findhorn Press, 1995.

Thomas Urban is Professor and Chair of Sociology at Teiko Post University, USA His research at Yale University led to an unpublished monograph on 'sex change' clinics. He is the author of the two-volume *Anti-Primitivism and the Decline of the West* (1993).

Terri Webb was born an apparently normal male child but remembers transgender feelings from the age of six. She underwent medical treatment leading to sex-reassignment when aged forty. She worked for many years as a housing officer with the London Borough of Southwark and as a councillor in Lambeth. She is now a continental truck driver.

Stephen Whittle is Lecturer in Law at Manchester Metropolitan University. He has published widely on various aspects of transgender and is co-author of *Transvestism, Transsexualism and the Law* (1994) and editor of *The Margins of the City: Gay Men's Urban Lives* (1994).

FOREWORD
Genders in question

Ken Plummer
Professor of sociology, University of Essex

Gender is a Janus idea: strong, clear and bold whilst also shifting, ambiguous and fleeting. It is at once both one of the surest of all ideas in the modern world and also one of the most contested.

Thus, every reasonable member of society believes in the binary gender split! Everyone knows that there are two genders: men and women, and that indeed throughout the natural world of plants and animals there are also two sexes: male and female. Nothing could be clearer or firmer. Freud comments on the obvious: 'When you meet a human being, the first distinction you make is "male or female"? and you are accustomed to make the distinction with unhesitating certainty.'[1] Walk into any space and test yourself: however fleetingly, the first way in which people are identified – be it oh so tactily – is by their gender. We scan the world and divide it into boys and girls, men and women, masculine and feminine. And the world of science reinforces this commonsense view at every stage. Biologists can classify the hormonal, chromosomal and reproductive differences. Sociobiologists can define man as the promiscuous hunter and woman as the reproductive nurturer. Psychologists can locate the differences in personality, skills, even moral development. And even in the more humanistic worlds of arts, literature or drama, the powerful metaphors of gender are everywhere to be found. To deny the centrality of the organising power of gender to social life would seem futile.[2]

And yet . . .

Gender is also one of the most contested of concepts in the social sciences and in contemporary political struggles. What many take for granted is seriously questioned by some. Anthropologists have long been able to demonstrate the cultural relativities of genders – that men can be like women; that women can be like men; and that often there are no differences.[3] They have also shown many cultures where categories of androgyny, hermaphroditism and variations of all degrees can appear and even be institutionalised. Likewise, historians have suggested that our current views of two genders have only clearly emerged in the modern world. We have only recently 'made sex' in the way we take for granted, and prior to the eighteenth century, the worlds of men and women were not so tightly drawn.[4] Sociologists have also shown how gender gets socially constructed and socially organised through material and cultural conditions – shifting quite dramatically between different groups so that working-class masculinity in late nineteenth-century England is very different from middle-class masculinity amongst 1950s Italian men, which in turn is very different from the Latino male youth culture of Los Angeles in the 1990s. Gender in this view is something socially achieved, dramatically performed, a set of culturally produced practices of daily life which are open to much change and variability. An important idea to emerge in this book is that gender is a process and not a product. People achieve their masculinities or femininities. For Ekins, there is a basic process of 'male femaling' at work – there are the ideas of 'femaling' and 'maling' social life at work here on a wider level.

This book demonstrates an array of contrasting voices around gender that certainly do not see it as a simple unproblematic idea. The essays in this volume all demonstrate in contrasting ways that many people in the modern world do not find themselves comfortably slotting into the pre-ordained gender patterns that we are commonly supposed to hold. People cross gender lines for all sorts of reasons: entertainment, medicine, politics, play, sexual satisfaction, art, prostitution. Here are the voices of men and somewhat fewer women who like to attire themselves in the clothes of the opposite sex – with many different styles and for many different reasons. There are strippers and prostitutes, fetishists and sado-masochists, straights and gays. There are people who join clubs, others who become members of social movements, still others who have their experiences in isolation. Here are portraits of people entrapped by a medical profession that seeks to ensure people are placed firmly in one or other of the two main gender categories and not left hanging around the margins! For them it is a world of 'gender identity disorders'. But here also is a world of politics: of 'transgender' and 'queer' activism. Here are tales of cross-dressers who infuse their activities with political meanings, and others who locate themselves within much more medical frameworks. And here are the voices of change: late nineteenth-century cross-dressers, Porchester Ball 'elegance' and modern radical TVs.

The book falls into five parts. The first sets the scene by examining a series of accounts of gender blending – with Richard Ekins placing the development of such experience within the valuable framework of a theoretical model of 'careers'. This is a most useful concept that helps locate the stages through which many people pass in the development of their gender identity. The second part looks at three contrasting patterns of the ways in which 'transvestism' has come to the socially patterned over the past few decades – the slightly raunchy scene of drag performers (in Australia), a club of transvestites who exclude gays from their membership and a rather extravagant 'drag ball'. These are only three slices of very many 'scenes' organised around gender blending, and others await further exploration. A third section looks at the intrusion of the medical profession into gender blending this century. The process of medicalisation is now widespread: almost every 'problem' of the twentieth century has been taken into the realms of medical work – and problems of gender have often been to the fore. Here are two accounts providing a history and analysis of the workings of medicine around transvestism and transsexualism. Gender blending becomes 'gender identity disorder' and 'gender dysphoria'. The fourth section examines the ways in which the media has presented some of the gender confusions over the past few decades, as well as illustrating the development of a newer form around 'telephone sex'. TV/TS have indeed become popular fodder for the media – not just as key 'sexual stories'[5] around which debates galvanise, but also as classic reference points: *Some Like It Hot, Cabaret, Dressed to Kill, The Rocky Horror Picture Show, Tootsie, Victor/Victoria, Yentl, La Cage aux Folles, Mrs Doubtfire, Priscilla, Queen of the Desert, The Crying Game, Ed Wood* – all these highlight gender blending and have been major cultural top sellers. Their enormous popularity speaks of a fascination abroad in the wider culture with gender blending. A final section displays some of the growing political concerns over gender blending. At one end, gender blending is itself seen a radical act – because it threatens gender assumptions at the core. At the other end of the spectrum, there is the feminist charge made originally in the 1970s that transsexualism is indeed a reactionary movement: placing men in women's positions – ultimately to conspire against them.

There is much food for thought in this important and ground-breaking selection of articles. As well as combining a range of voices, it also combines an array of registers. Some voices speak in a popular everyday language, others speak in the rhetoric of politics, whilst still others provide a scientific discourse.

The theme of 'blending' raises important issues. It suggests a mix or a harmonising – but it can imply something that pre-exists, waiting to be blended. Herein are problems for any analysis – for once again the Janus face of gender is raised. 'Gender blending' – or even 'bending' – might imply that a core gender exists that can then be mixed, merged and matched. In this case, it poses little threat to the gender order at all, since it reinforces the notions of gender very strongly. Men who copy the dress codes of conventional heterosexual women, or men who simply wish to be really just like other women, blend conservatively. Their message seems to be that whilst anomalies of nature may happen, they can ultimately be located on one side or the other of the gender divide. Medical diagnostic categories or media stereotypes may work to co-opt them in some way. Much of the book shows this pattern at work. But, by contrast, there is also a much more culturally challenging form at work – the 'blenders' who transcend, transgress and threaten. The newly emerging 'queer theory' is an attempt to get beyond the gendered and sexed practices of the social world, yet it constantly harks back to the very categories it seeks to undo: male, female, gay, straight, bisexual. What seems to be sought is a world of multiple gendered fluidities – a world at home in a postmodern cacophony of multiplicity, pastiche and pluralities that marks the death of the meta-narratives of gender which have dominated the modern world. The claim, as Whittle so precisely puts it in his telling contribution to this book, is to live 'outside of gender'[6]. These are the 'gender outlaws'. We shall have to see if this is possible.

The books sets important parameters for debate. New areas now await enquiry. There is a curious widening definition of 'gender blending' taking place – a point highlighted in Stephen Whittle's 'queer' contribution (Chapter 14). This stretching was dramatically presented in the film *Paris is Burning*, where gendered notions of race and class became the key to understanding the 'blending' of some poor New York youth, camping up around the sleazy drag scene.[7] And it can be stretched elsewhere. Mark Simpson, for example, has recently suggested that there are 'male impersonators' who are men 'playing at men' – the gay world, he suggests, is full of such icons: from Marky Mark, Robert Bly, Clint Eastwood – three wildly different forms of playing being at men – and on to a whole world of sportsmen, body builders, porn stars, rock stars and the like.[8] And this is not new: think of Liberace, Elvis, Valentino. Add Quentin Crisp, Prince, Michael Jackson. And likewise, there are 'women impersonators' – just what Madonna is up to in a gendered world has been the focus of much debate (and much of it carrying academic tittle tattle to impossible extremes!). But then there is Shere Hite, Camille Paglia, k. d. lang? And then age, race, class and nationality can cross the gender lines in curious ways. Dare it be suggested that the *Black and White Minstrel Show* can now be read as a form of drag? And if so, where is its politics?

This book is the first wide-ranging collection of essays around gender blending. It covers a wide spectrum of experiences, provides an array of key questions and speaks in a number of different voices. As awareness of the contested nature of Janus gender grows, these essays will provide an important bench-mark of change.

NOTES

1 See Sigmund Freud, 'Femininity', reprinted in Freud, *The Essentials of Psychoanalysis* (1986), Pelican, p. 413.
2 A persuasive account of the power of the gender metaphor may be found in Helen Haste, *The Sexual Metaphor* (1933), Harvester Wheatsheaf.

3 See for instance Walter L. Williams, *The Spirit of the Flesh* (1986), Beacon Press. Williams is currently in the chair of the newly emerging 'Transgender Studies' at the University of California at Los Angeles.
4 See for instance Thomas Lacqueur, *Making Sex* (1990), Harvard University Press.
5 See my *Telling Sexual Stories* (1995), Routledge, for an account of such tales and the role they play in social life. There is some discussion of 'TV' and 'TS' stories in this book.
6 See also Kate Bornstein, *Gender Outlaw: On Men, Women and the Rest of Us* (1995), Routledge.
7 See the short discussion by Jackie Goldsby, 'Queens of Language', in Martha Geyer, John Greyson and Pratibha Parmar (eds) *Queer Looks* (1993), Routledge, pp. 108–15.
8 See Mark Simpson, *Male Impersonators*, (1994), Cassell.

ACKNOWLEDGEMENTS

The editors would like to acknowledge *Sociological Review* for 'The career path of the male femaler' by Richard Ekins; Avebury for extracts from *The Transvestite and the Transsexual: Public Categories and Private Identities* by Dave King; Allen & Unwin for 'The "drag queen" scene: transsexuals in Kings Cross' by Roberta Perkins; Phaedra Kelly and *Chrysalis Magazine* for the text and photographs of 'London grandeur: the Porchester Ball'; *Australian and New Zealand Journal of Psychiatry* for 'A heterosexual transvestite club' by Neil Buhrich; *Social Problems* for 'The socio-medical construction of transsexualism: an interpretation and critique' by Dwight Billings and Thomas Urban; Carol Riddell for 'Divided sisterhood: a critical review of Janice Raymond's "The Transsexual Empire"'; Loren Cameron for his self-portrait; and Teachers College Press for 'The politics of transgenderism' by Janice Raymond.

Thanks are also due to Wendy Saunderson of the University of Ulster for helping to bring this project to final fruition.

BLENDING GENDERS
An introduction
Richard Ekins and Dave King

Blending Genders is a collection of writings by a number of authors interested primarily in the social aspects of gender blending – an umbrella term we use to include cross-dressing and sex-changing and the various ways that such phenomena have been conceptualised. It provides a benchmark for those interested in exploring the complex issues concerning social and cultural constructions of gender raised by cross-dressing and sex-changing.

In making our selections for the volume we have sought to pay the proper respect to the full range of personal accounts and analytic writing from the mid-nineteenth century to the present day. The majority of the chapters have been written especially for the volume. These have been supplemented by a number of previously published, but important and often inaccessible writings.

We do not wish to appeal only to those interested in social science as an academic discipline. For that reason, in addition to historical, sociological and political analyses, we have included a number of descriptive accounts. Firsthand knowledge of the area is so sparse that these should be particularly welcome to the newcomer. Further, we believe that the time has now come to lay down parameters for a new field of enquiry. To this end, we have divided the contributions into five parts which, when taken together, lay claim to an emerging field of transgender studies. We have sought to emphasise the variety of styles and discourses, as well as the vehement disagreements, that mark the area. The polyvalent stance of the volume makes it eminently suitable as a first reader in a new field of study.

Gender refers to 'the culturally established correlates of sex' (Goffman, 1979: 1). Gender is attributed to social actors by self and others (Kessler and McKenna, 1978) and is a fundamental element in the everyday presentation of self (Cahill, 1989; Goffman, 1979). Various non-human animals, material objects, times and places may also be 'genderised' (Herdt, 1981). In countless small, seemingly natural actions, one of the most fundamental structural properties of our society is daily reproduced.

1

Blending has two basic meanings – to mix or combine, and to harmonise. This book is concerned with those who – in both senses – attempt to blend, or succeed in blending, various aspects of the culturally established correlates of sex, either in respect of themselves or in respect of others.

Once a gender attribution has been made, expectations follow that an actor will display the 'correct' blend of such things as dress and demeanour, sex object choice, occupation, leisure-time activities, and so on. In theory, the whole of social life could be dichotomised by gender, but in practice, a lot of 'incorrect' elements are allowed into the blend, particularly on an occasional and trivial level. More sustained and more fundamental blending of the elements threaten the gender categories themselves. In most cultures this is problematic, although some authors argue that in certain societies, such as that of the North American Indians, a third gender category exists (Kessler and McKenna, 1978; Herdt, 1994). Connell (1987: 76) argues that some transsexuals who live openly as such in contemporary society may be seen in similar ways, as a 'third' gender category.

Gender blending[1] in the first sense – the mixing of various aspects of male and female gender – has been seen in contemporary industrial societies as a pathological phenomenon, properly apprehended within a medical discourse, or as a source of amusement to be conceptualised as entertainment. Gender blending in the second sense of harmonisation is, arguably, a psychological and cultural imperative. Thus, in their accounts, individuals seek to bring harmony to otherwise disparate elements (Ekins, 1993; King, 1993). Medical and other interventions in cases of trans-sexualism or intersexuality seek to harmonise gender identity, gender-role, social status, the body, and so on. Media representations of transsexualism can be seen to be mainly concerned with the symbolic maintenance of the gender dichotomy (Pearce, 1981; Silverstone, 1982).

The body of academic literature on this topic, mostly North American in origin, is now a large one (Denny, 1994). It is, however, dominated by medical and psychological perspectives, with the vast majority of this work being broadly set within the 'medical model' (Ekins, 1993: 3–5). Writers and practitioners working within this approach are concerned with the collection and examination of biographical and in-depth psychological data, which they follow with classification, diagnosis and etiological theorising. Practitioners concern themselves with the treatment and management of what is most usually seen as a 'pathological' condition. The gender blender as subject becomes the embodiment of a diagnostic category, as well as a patient or client.

Academics working outside the medical model have taken various alter-native approaches. Garfinkel (1967) and Kessler and McKenna (1978) have examined the area from the standpoint of ethnomethodology. They show

how study of the sex-changer illuminates the normal features of 'gender work'. There have been a number of studies of transvestites and transsexuals from the perspective of the sociology of deviance. Sagarin (1969), Feinbloom (1976) and Talamini (1982), for instance, view transvestite and transsexual groups as deviant subcultures. Kando (1973) focuses on problems associated with the management of stigma. From a different perspective again, Raymond (1980) and Billings and Urban (1982) consider transsexualism in the light of the medicalisation of gender-roles drawing, respectively, on feminist and critical theory. Woodhouse (1989) considers male transvestism from a feminist position. Newton (1979) researches the world of female impersonators (male entertainers who cross-dress) using descriptive and unstructured methods to 'tell it as it is'. This is traditional anthropological fieldwork in an urban setting.

Most recently, cross-dressing and sex-changing have been approached from the standpoint of cultural criticism (Garber, 1992; Epstein and Straub, 1991). In particular, conceptualising gender in terms of 'performance' (Butler, 1990) – as opposed to category or identity – places cross-dressing and sex-changing (now theorised as transgenderism) at the forefront of contemporary challenges to gender oppression (Bornstein, 1994; Segal, 1994).

All of these works, however, are texts on gender blending set within particular specialist frameworks. Whereas there are a number of comprehensive books summarising the arena for those working within the medical model (Green and Money, 1969; Steiner, 1985; Bockting and Coleman, 1992b), there are no equivalents for those working within alternative approaches. This book is designed to meet that need.

The first part of the volume deals appropriately with the experience of gender blending from the standpoint of cross-dressers and sex-changers themselves. Peter Farrer provides the historical and descriptive dimension with his treatment of the personal confessions of male cross-dressers as revealed in the correspondence columns of a number of nineteenth- and early twentieth-century British newspapers. Mark Rees, a female-to-male transsexual, gives his own personal account of the various facets of his journey to 'become a man'. Richard Ekins provides the theoretical contribution to Part I by examining what he calls 'male femalers' in terms of a phased ideal-typical career path.

Increasingly, since the 1960s, cross-dressers and sex-changers have formed their own groups. Part II deals with the different aspects of this social organisation of gender blending. Roberta Perkins focuses on a group of male-to-female transsexuals living and working in the Kings Cross area of Sydney, Australia. Neil Buhrich provides a description of a club for heterosexual transvestites, of a type to be found in many countries throughout the world (Roberts, 1995). Finally in this part, Phaedra Kelly gives an insider's picture of a drag ball in London. Again, such events are widespread across the world, providing, as they do, festive occasions for the display of flamboyant gender blending.

Part III considers the dominant frame through which gender blending is viewed in modern societies – that of medicine. Dave King documents the history of medical ideas about gender blending and the use of medical technology in this area. Dwight Billings and Thomas Urban argue that transsexualism is constructed by the medical profession operating within a capitalist and patriarchal society.

Modern technologies of communication from the printing press onwards have provided the means of disseminating ideas and images of gender blending to millions of people who otherwise would have been unaware of its existence. In Part IV, Peter Farrer provides the historical and descriptive dimension to this aspect of gender blending in his review of the depiction of male cross-dressing and sex-changing in English and American literature since the mid-nineteenth century. Dave King examines popular press reports of both male and female cross-dressers and sex-changers, and considers their impact on a mass readership. Richard Ekins considers the latest use of technology in this field – that of telephone sex lines.

The political aspects of gender blending are the subject of Part V. Janice Raymond's influential book *The Transsexual Empire* is subjected to a powerful critique by Carol Riddell. Terri Webb focuses on transsexuals as a minority group and considers what rights they should be pursuing. Stephen Whittle reviews the recent work on gender blending and cultural criticism from the standpoint of contemporary queer theory. Finally, Janice Raymond considers the political significance of the new focus on transgenderism.

NOTE

1 The term 'gender blending' was first used, in an academic context, by Devor to refer to females who 'have clear female identities and know themselves to be women concurrently with gender presentations that often do not successfully communicate these facts to others' (1987: 12). As we make clear in this introduction, we are using the term in a much broader way.

Part I

EXPERIENCING GENDER BLENDING

INTRODUCTION

Prior to the categorisation and medicalisation of sexual 'perversions' in the latter half of the nineteenth century, gender blending could be written about in terms of simple descriptions of enjoyable experience and preferred behaviour. Medicalisation, however, brought with it new 'conditions' and the emergence of new identities. Increasingly, gender blending experiences and behaviours were made sense of in terms of the categories of 'science', most notably those of the 'transvestite' and the 'transsexual'. The recent emphasis upon the transgression of gender boundaries and on performance rather than identity, marks a return to experience and behaviour. In such writing, however, the experiences and behaviours are made sense of in terms of the deconstructions of postmodernist cultural theory rather than from the standpoint of the experiences of cross-dressers and sex-changers themselves. In consequence, these writings have yet to make a substantial impact on the subjective experience of gender blending.

Part I approaches the subjective experience of gender blending from three very different angles. Firstly, Peter Farrer opens up a new resource for historical research on gender blending and alerts us to a time before men who enjoyed wearing female attire came to be known as transvestites. In consequence, the experiences he features have a particular flavour of innocence. Secondly, Mark Rees details his own personal experiences as a modern female-to-male transsexual. His quest to 'become a man' is shot through with the paraphernalia of modern medicine. And thirdly, Richard Ekins provides the analytical and sociological framework from which to view various experiences of gender blending.

For over forty years Peter Farrer has ploughed a lonely furrow. Throughout the period, he has systematically and single-handedly built up a collection of books, magazines, press cuttings, and photocopied or written extracts covering all aspects of the frocks and costumes of the small boy; boys playing girls' parts in plays or masquerades; boys dressed as girls for punishment; female impersonation by men; and male cross-dressing in fact

5

or fiction, for any reason, and at any period or in any culture (Ekins, 1992b). For the most part he eschews theorising and critical comment, preferring to document the personal experiences of others and to unearth little-known sources and descriptions (Farrer, 1987; 1992; 1994). In Chapter 1, he provides a fascinating glimpse of the personal experiences of male cross-dressers as described in the correspondence columns of a series of British newspapers between 1867 and 1941.

As Farrer points out, the letters are anonymous, and it is, therefore, impossible to verify the extent to which they document fantasy or reality. All or part of each letter might be the inventions of editors or jokers, or the letters might merely be the fantasies of cross-dressers. The sceptical reader, with no knowledge of these things, may well find it difficult to accept them as descriptions of actual events. However, many similar accounts have been verified. The contemporary subcultural magazine, *International TV Repartee*, for instance, features a regular column entitled 'Pampered in Panties', which details similar confessions from elderly cross-dressers. We, the editors, have verified some of these narratives ourselves. In an area where fact is so very often stranger than fiction, we incline to Farrer's view that 'the majority are probably true. There is the sheer quantity of letters and the long period over which they have accumulated. There is the variety of circumstances and incidents described, the diverse nature of the periodicals used and the differing style and status of the correspondents.'

In Chapter 2, we turn to the experience of the female-to-male modern-day transsexual. Although there have been many biographical and auto-biographical writings on male-to-female gender blending, there have been remarkably few on those blending from female to male. Ekins (1989) provides the most comprehensive – though by no means complete – listing, but of the eighty or so publications detailed by him, only eleven refer to female-to-male writings. Subsequent writings covering biographical data on female-to-male cross-dressers include Dekker and van de Pol (1989), Devor (1989), Epstein and Straub (1991) and Wheelwright (1989), but these include very little information on sex-changers.

Female-to-male transsexual autobiographies remain a rarity. The auto-biography by Martino (1977), *Emergence: A Transsexual Autobiography* – arguably the most detailed available – was billed as 'the only complete autobiography of a woman who has become a man'. The autobiography of Chris and Cathy, the 'first transsexual parents', appeared in 1982 (Johnson and Brown, 1982). Both Chris and Cathy were sex-changers who achieved a certain notoriety by planning the birth of their child before they both changed over. Of the biographies published since 1989, Liz Hodgkinson's *Michael née Laura: The Story of the World's First Female-to-Male Transsexual* (1989) is worthy of special note, not least because back in 1948 the British subject Michael Dillon was able to amend his birth certificate from female-to-male (Hodgkinson, 1989: 63).

None of these biographical writings achieve the range and candour of Mark Rees' Chapter 2. Rees is particularly well qualified as a contributor. He has been writing about transsexuality for over fifteen years in various contexts – initially under pseudonyms ('John', 1977; Mason, 1980, 1980b), and more recently under his own name (Rees, 1987, 1993a, 1993b). His autobiography is forthcoming (Rees, 1996). For Chapter 2 we asked him to write about 'becoming a man'. We suggested the various headings he has used, but those apart he was given a completely free hand to write what he chose. The result is a moving and courageous account.

Whereas Chapters 1 and 2 remain largely at the descriptive level, Chapter 3 turns to the theorising of the experience of gender blending. Ekins utilises the concept of the career path, a concept that is widely used in sociological writings as a means of imposing an analytic order on experiences, actions and identities over time (Abrams, 1982). Its value lies in its incorporation of the ideas of movement, of development, of becoming and of personal history. Furthermore, as Goffman (1968: 119) points out, it 'allows one to move back and forth between the personal and the public, between the self and significant society', and is, therefore, peculiarly sociological.

Transsexuals were looked at by Driscoll (1971), in terms of career paths, and Buckner (1970) did likewise for transvestites. Levine, Shaiova and Mihailovic (1975) do not use the term 'career', but recount the transsexuals' progression through a series of stages or 'role transformations' marked by a mixture of general life-cycle periods, changing self-conceptions and involvement in particular subcultures. Ekins' use of the methodology of grounded theory (Ekins, 1993) leads him to reconceptualise the research arena of male cross-dressing and sex-changing in terms of the basic social process (Glaser, 1978) of 'male femaling'.

Chapter 3 considers the major modes of male femaling within a phased ideal-typical career path of the 'male femaler' and indicates oscillations between the major facets of sex, sexuality and gender frequently confronted in each phase. This approach enables the proper respect to be paid to the processual and emergent nature of much cross-dressing and sex-changing phenomena. In particular, the approach facilitates an exploration of neglected interrelations between sex, sexuality and gender with reference to the differing modes of femaling; to the categorisations of 'transvestite' and 'transsexual'; and to the constitution of 'femaling' self and world as variously sexed, sexualised and gendered.

7

1

IN FEMALE ATTIRE

Male experiences of cross-dressing – some historical fragments

Peter Farrer

INTRODUCTION

> One evening at the tea table my sister read from a periodical called *Modern Society* about a young man dressed as a girl ... Later I had the paper to myself, and, enjoying tremendous excitement, read a page or two of readers' correspondence on "effeminate men" ... By the time I was fourteen I had got hold of another periodical, *Photo Bits*, which devoted itself almost entirely to encouraging this trait and the pleasures of birching.
>
> (Ellis, 1928: 54)

These remarks were made by Havelock Ellis's subject 'D.S.' and were recorded by Ellis in his study of what he called 'eonism'. No one involved in the professional study of cross-dressing seems to have thought it worthwhile to follow up the references to *Modern Society* and *Photo Bits*. In fact, there is a whole series of English newspapers and periodicals from the middle of the last century to *London Life* in 1941 in which such correspondence appeared to a greater or lesser degree. It is the purpose of this chapter to introduce this neglected confessional material.

In the period under consideration it was the British habit to write to the newspapers about intimate matters of dress and domestic behaviour. Corporal punishment and tight-lacing were favourite subjects for discussion in letters to the editor. The background to, and the nature of, this material has been well documented (Kunzle, 1982; Steele, 1985). What has been overlooked, however, is the extent to which an element of cross-dressing crept into the correspondence. On the one hand, one of the methods of punishment which came to be discussed was dressing boys as girls. On the other hand, some male correspondents not only wore corsets but other items of female clothing, or full female attire.

THE ENGLISHWOMAN'S DOMESTIC MAGAZINE, 1867–73

In January 1867 Samuel Beeton, husband of the famous but recently deceased Mrs Beeton, and editor of *The Englishwoman's Domestic Magazine*, deliberately expanded the correspondence columns of the magazine to encompass a wide variety of subjects in some depth. In doing so Beeton introduced a new policy for handling the letters that came in. He gave his correspondents considerable latitude and allowed to appear in print frank expressions of sensual pleasure in such things as tight-lacing.

From November 1867, his new 'Conversazione', as he called it, included letters from men. Initially, these letters concerned men who told of the great pleasure they, too, derived from wearing corsets. Letters then began to appear that extolled the virtues of other female garments. By 1870 letters on 'petticoat punishment' were appearing. The first example I give describes the pleasures of wearing ladies' boots. The second example is from the first account of a petticoat punishment. It was printed in the Supplement from April to December, 1870 which was devoted entirely to correspondence about corporal punishment. 'Etonensis' wrote opposing physical punishment. In its place he proposed 'love' and 'shame'. He had experienced 'love' in the kindness shown to him by a master at Eton, and shame when his governess dressed him in his sister's clothes for failure to learn his geography lesson.

Example 1

Robin Adair – *The Englishwoman's Domestic Magazine*

Having myself a small and rather ladylike foot, I got Mr. Nicoll to make me, as an experiment, a pair of fashionable ladies' boots, with heels 2½ inches high. I was astonished to find how delightfully easy they were to walk in, and how much smaller and neater my feet appeared than in my own more clumsy foot-gear.

(September 1870: 190)

Example 2

Etonensis – *The Englishwoman's Domestic Magazine*

Stays were easy, but now came the fight again. The first petticoat I clutched hold of, and I think for ten minutes I held on, till at last that too was accomplished ... They now easily accomplished the rest; shame overcame my courage, and I had no strength. My trousers were now entirely removed. I was made to stand up, under more slaps and thumpings and threatenings of birch, while my dressing was most leisurely completed with a stiff starched petticoat, a blue frock down nearly to my feet, stockings and sandal shoes ... I know not if this punishment is more cruel than the birch; this I do know, that it put an end to it at home. The mere threat, the 'shall I send for some petticoats for you?' – always set me to work.

(Supplement, April 1870: 2–3)

THE FAMILY DOCTOR AND PEOPLE'S MEDICAL ADVISER, 1885–94

The Family Doctor and People's Medical Adviser, which began life on 3 March, 1885 was intended to give practical medical advice to families and it printed articles attacking the practice of tight-lacing. It also opened up its correspondence pages to opinions on a variety of subjects, including arguments for and against corsets. From 1886 men were writing letters describing their pleasure in wearing entire outfits of women's clothes. The first example I give appeared in 1888 and is from a man who has adopted female attire permanently. His letter was a reply to one from 'Misfit' (9 June 1888: 234), a female who wore male clothes and offered to send an 'entire outfit' of female clothes to any man who would show himself in the full dress of a woman in Regent Street at a pre-arranged time. The second example is from a married man who wishes to tell people about himself and encourage others to write to *The Family Doctor*.

Example 1

Josephine (formerly Joseph) – *The Family Doctor*

I have always suffered from a weak throat, and during a great part of the year am obliged to keep my neck and chest well wrapped up. Returning home rather late once, a lady friend lent me her fur boa. I found so much comfort in its use that I decided to get one. I did this, and wore it, with the result that I became an object of ridicule. I then reasoned that if so much comfort was to be obtained from one article of female attire, how much might I expect from assuming such entirely? I tried it, and was more than satisfied, and decided for the future to discard male dress.

I confessed my feeling in the matter to a friend of mine, an elderly lady, who approved of my plan. For the last four years I have been living with her as her niece, a quietly-dressed and modestly-conducted young lady.

(7 July 1888: 295)

11

Example 2

A would-be Petticoat – *The Family Doctor*

Some time back, when so much talk was made as to whether woman's dress was healthful and convenient, I determined to practically test the fact for myself. I accordingly encased myself in lady's full costume for one month, at the end of which time, whenever an opportunity presents itself in the privacy of my own home, I don female attire. In order to gratify my wish I have a complete lady's wardrobe of my own, of which I am very particular, especially of my under-clothing, which I cannot have too nice; although when fully dressed it is not seen, still the consciousness that it is there is a source of great pleasure to the wearer, a statement many ladies, I know, will endorse.

(19 August 1893: 396)

SOCIETY, 1879–1900

Another periodical to give space to the corset controversy was *Society*, which ran from 1879 to 1900. This was the sort of society newspaper typical of the time. There was a large section devoted to news of society, about the gentry, peerage and royalty of Britain and the world, set out in a series of miscellaneous paragraphs. In addition there were reviews of the arts, books and theatre and a fashion column, perhaps also some business and financial news. Most of these newspapers printed readers' letters. *Society* had letters about corsets in 1893–1894, 1899 and 1900. I cite parts of five examples. The first correspondent was pressed into service as a brides-maid when his sister was ill. He continued to wear female clothes thereafter. The second found corsets useful for support. His sister persuaded him to go further. The third could not find a job, while the fourth was the victim of an extraordinary caprice. The mother of the fifth ran a girls' school so he had to be one. These letters are among the best written and most unusual of the whole series.

Example 1

Dublin – *Society*

On rising in the morning (if my sisters desire me to accompany them in female rigout) I wear thin silk 'combinations', over which the corset is laced fairly tight. Coloured silk lingerie and a soft morning gown complete the outfit. After breakfast a few hours of recreation follow, and then we retire to our rooms, mine being that occupied until lately by my married sister. Once there, the maid comes round to each, and the silken corset laces are drawn to the extreme of tightness, nineteen inches never being exceeded. The silken under-garments are supplanted by white lawn, smothering with frills and laces, and each emerges from the room looking delightfully comfort-able and happy.

As I am writing this, I am arrayed in a grey tweed dress, having been out walking. At every movement of the body I hear the fasci-nating creak of a new satin corset, every movement of my limbs is followed by the swish of silken garments, a delicate perfume comes from the pink satin with which the skirt is lined, and when I cross my feet in true 'tomboy fashion' I can see a filmy cloud of white lace hovering over high heeled Parisian shoes.

(18 August 1894: 664)

Example 2

Satin Waist – *Society*

My sister and I live in a very quiet place, and a great deal of my days are spent in looking after stock, etc. Very often I am on my feet all day, and come in at night fagged and footsore. It is then that the real comfort of a satin corset fitting like a glove is experienced. At first I merely wore the stays under my ordinary clothes, but, after a while, my sister decided that it would be much better to complete my outfit, and I was forthwith initiated into a bewildering mass of lace-trimmed undergarments.

Now when my day's work is over, I have a hot bath, and come down to dinner feeling a different being, and enjoying myself thor-oughly, generally wearing a plain, tight-fitting costume in black satin.

(23 September 1899: 1871)

Example 3

Tablier Blanc – *Society*

I have lived as a woman for the last two years, and am doing so still, so it may interest your readers if I give you a glimpse of my expe-rience.

I have always had a great penchant for dressing in girl's clothes – many of your correspondents appear to have the same – and one evening my sister suggested to me that I should apply – as a girl – for a vacant situation as a barmaid at the restaurant where she was employed. This I secured, and, thanks to a slim figure, small hands and feet, and dark curly hair, I do not think my sex has ever even been suspected.

(31 March 1900: 203)

Example 4

Martyr – *Society*

I was adopted, when young, by a lady of considerable wealth, who was devoted to dress and fashion. I was just fourteen when this lady – who, in a year's time was to travel abroad – decided, partly, I think, out of caprice, partly for convenience sake, to take me with her, disguised as a girl. I dare say she was influenced by my effeminate appearance and complexion, and slender, slight figure. A fashionable dressmaker was consulted, and I was furnished with a large outfit of garments of the latest fashion and most dainty cut and material. In particular, great care was taken over my figure.

I had, of course, to wear false hair, until my own grew long, and I was most carefully instructed in ladylike manners and deportment. When we went abroad, my dainty complexion and hands, very smartly-shod feet, and extremely slim waist, and well-moulded figure, were the objects of much admiration and envy. There was not the slightest danger of anyone suspecting that the pretty, well-dressed girl, apparently, of about sixteen, was really an unfortunate boy. I had to endure three years of this bondage, and became so soft and effeminate that, when the death of the lady who adopted me made me independent, I went back to the garb and habits of my own sex with reluctance and difficulty.

(21 April 1900: 263)

Example 5

F.B. – *Society*

My father died when I was two years old, and my mother purchased a small young ladies' boarding school in a country town, and, acting under advice, she determined to bring me up as a girl, until circumstances made it possible for her to do without the aid of the school.

I was dressed and brought up in the same way as the boarders of the school, except that I slept in a small room opening out of my mother's, and that I mixed with the girls as little as possible.

This went on until I was nearly seventeen, when a legacy enabled my mother to sell the school and leave the town, and it was not until then that I was dressed in male attire. For some months I felt so uncomfortable that, whenever my mother and I were alone, I would resume my female dress, and have never discarded the underclothing; but even now, although I have been married [to one of his fellow pupils] three years, I still continue to do so beneath my ordinary attire.

(21 April 1900: 263)

MODERN SOCIETY, 1880–1917

Modern Society ran from 1880 to 1917 on much the same lines as *Society*, except that towards the end of 1909 there was a change of ownership and a deliberate attempt to create a correspondence column. A series of letters headed 'Slaves of the stay lace' ran from 13 November 1909 to 8 January 1910. The next important subject was effeminate men, which was current when D.S. (Ellis's informant) got hold of the paper. The example I give is probably one of the letters which D.S.'s sister read out.

Example 1

Jupon – *Modern Society*

I cannot agree with 'Happy Sister' that a young man can be feminine and not effeminate. Like her brother, I was persuaded one day five years ago, when a boy of fourteen, by the two older sisters with whom I lived, to dress as a girl. They were so delighted with my appearance that they insisted on my doing so again and again; and in time it became a custom that I should make a full feminine toilette every afternoon. I disliked it at first, but my prejudice disappeared with experience. Although pretty tightly laced, my corsets were extremely comfortable, and petticoats I found the most enjoyable garments in the world. I do not regret it; but I frankly admit I am thoroughly effeminate. Indeed, one cannot be manly in a dainty prison of lace and silk underskirts; one must bow to one's environment.

(19 February 1910: 26)

PHOTO BITS, 1898–1912

The periodical *Photo Bits* is entirely different from the kinds of paper or magazine so far considered. Founded in 1898 and classified as a 'comic' paper in the press directories of the time, it was in fact Britain's first pin-up magazine. It comprised a serial story, two or more shorter stories, miscellaneous comic pieces, and many photographs, drawings and sketches of theatrical stars and showgirls in various styles of dress and undress. In addition there was a weekly article in the centre pages dealing with some aspect of show business. At first these were unsigned, but from 11 January 1908 'The Amorist' wrote the articles until he was replaced by an American, who called himself 'Cosmopolite', on 23 July 1910.

'The Amorist' had already introduced the subject of tight-lacing and high heels. When 'Cosmopolite' took over he deliberately invited his readers to write to him about their particular 'fetish'. In this connection he claimed that he had read Krafft-Ebing's work (Krafft-Ebing, 1894), but he saw nothing harmful or wrong in having a 'fetish'. It was in response to 'Cosmopolite's' approach that the following example was contributed. Consequently, the writer talks quite freely about his 'fetish' The example is also interesting as showing how the whole household accepts and takes part in 'Pinafore's' game.

Example 1

Pinafore – *Photo Bits*

I am approaching middle age; and, to the outer world, I appear to be a rather unapproachable man, engaged in very dry literary work. I reside in a quiet London suburb – in one of those old houses with large gardens, which still survive the encroachments of the jerry-builder. My household consists of an elderly Scotch housekeeper and her two daughters, who do all the work of the place, thus ensuring me the perfect privacy that enables me to live my own life.

Those who know me in my public capacity would be infinitely surprised to learn that I spend several days in every week dressed and living as a woman! During these periods, it is always understood that 'Mrs. Mac' – my housekeeper – is the absolute mistress of the house, and that I, as well as her daughters, have to submit to her rule in every respect. My own peculiar 'fetish' is that of not only delighting to see women and girls compelled to wear large, sensible white aprons and long plain pinafores, but also to be dressed as a woman – and forced to wear aprons and pinafores myself! As I write, I am dressed entirely in feminine attire. My 'undies' are as fresh and dainty as you will find anywhere, and I am wearing a dark-blue linen frock with a 'Quaker Girl' collar. Over this, I have been compelled to put on a long, plain, white diaper pinafore; and the feeling of delicious humiliation entailed in being forced to wear a pinafore is more exquisite than I can describe! I never get tired of it, although I have experienced it constantly for some years past.

(18 November 1911: 7).

PHOTO FUN TO *BITS OF FUN*, 1906–20

The character of *Photo Bits* changed early in 1912, ostensibly because the writer of the serial story, Derk Fortesque, died and 'Cosmopolite' left the paper. Meanwhile, in 1906, another 'comic' paper had started publication, entitled successively, *Photo Fun, New Photo Fun, New Fun, Fun* and *Bits of Fun*. Although the word 'photo' occurred in the earlier titles there were never many photographs included in these 'comics'. The paper as a whole had less to offer cross-dressers than *Photo Bits*, but it had one claim to fame: its column headed, 'Confidential Correspondence'. This began on 12 November 1910 and continued right through the Great War until 1920. As distinct from *Photo Bits* there was no editorial intervention in the letter page, except for a very occasional comment.

From the hundreds of letters available, I include parts of six examples. 'Grateful' came to enjoy the punishment imposed on him. 'Alfred' was caught trying on his aunt's clothes, but she encouraged him and so does his wife. 'A Boy who is a Girl' had feminine tastes early on and was confirmed in them by his guardians. The war made no difference either to the letters or to the attitude of the correspondents. 'Subaltern' dressed up for the last time before going to the front. 'Teddy' was forced by a friend to get the 'kink'. Again, nothing untoward or undesirable is seen as attaching to the 'kink', and the friend's three sisters and servants all accept it. 'Cap and Apron' does, however, have some reservations about his behaviour. Like 'Alfred' he tries on the female clothes available in the house, but he meets with a very different reception. He seems to recognise that he is under a compulsion to try on women's clothes and he asks his landlady for help. It is obvious that the women rather enjoy inflicting the punishment they thought up.

Example 1

Grateful – *New Photo Fun*

The novel punishment of petticoat discipline is a most fascinating subject, and one that I, as a former victim, never tire of reading about.

To dress a boy in the daintiest of girlish clothing completely in every respect is to inculcate habits of gentleness and tidiness that will never be forgotten; and although the boy may chafe at, or even be ashamed of his silken bondage at first, he soon succumbs to the witchery of frills and flounces, and willingly conforms to the rules and regulations laid down for him. And many a boy has lived to be grateful for the petticoat punishment, and learned to love his silken fetters.

I was fourteen years old when I was introduced to this form of discipline, and my mother was persuaded to adopt it by a friend who had found it very successful with her boy, who like myself, was an only child. I fancy my mother had always wished that I had been a girl, which made the suggested regime even more acceptable to her.

Anyway she ordered a complete outfit of girlish clothing for me, and one morning I was told to put on the frilliest of dainty white underclothes beneath the plaid kilt which was my ordinary costume. With boyish prejudice I thought it was a degradation and refused.

17

My mother was determined, and as a punishment for my rebellion decided that I should wear the full costume of a girl.

In spite of my struggles and resistance I was forced into the expensive elaborately frilled and beribboned lingerie, laced up tightly in the shapely stays, and then beflounced petticoats and a dainty frock, pretty shoes and stockings completing my costume, and my mother was charmed at the result.

In a month I was resigned to my fate, and ceased to beg my mother to release me. I began to take pride in my dainty clothes, to be interested in my lessons, my needlework and dancing and deportment.

At the end of a year my mother took me to Paris to perfect my French and six months later to Berlin for my German. My skirts were lengthened, my corsets laced in tighter, and I often quite forgot my lost boyish freedom.

It came quite a shock to me when on my eighteenth birthday my mother decided I must resume masculine attire once more. I begged her to reconsider her decision, but she pointed out the wisdom of it. Finally it was decided that I could continue wearing girls' clothing and corsets, but that my outer clothes would have to be those of a young man, and with this I had to be content.

We returned to England. I had now become a tall, slim young man, devoted to my mother, who had made it possible for me to taste such happiness, and who had by her strict petticoat punishment so changed my character.

(15 June 1912: 15)

The editor made the following comment: 'We have published this letter as it is a typical one, but personally we think it not only cruel but wicked, to alter a boy's disposition, in such a manner. If there is one thing worse than a masculine woman, it is an effeminate man.'

Example 2

Alfred – *New Fun*

My passion for female attire commenced some sixteen years ago, when, as a lad of fourteen, I went to live with an aunt, and as I was mostly her sole companion, on special occasions I used to help her dress, and her dainty corsets and other attire so attracted me, that whenever I had a chance to be alone, I couldn't resist the desire to get into them myself. After doing this some time quite secretly, my aunt one day came home unexpectedly and found me playing my violin and dressed in almost complete female attire. To my surprise, she was quite pleased with me, and as it was wet weather and a bank holiday, she persuaded me to wear the clothes all day, and after dinner she changed her corsets for her best and smallest pair and I was dressed in a quite complete outfit, finishing with a pretty evening frock and a dainty little Swiss apron and high-heeled shoes.

I shall never forget the sensation; it was simply superb. After that I very often had a full evening with my aunt in her attire, and on two or three occasions went for a little work [sic] out with her after dark.

I am now a happy married man, and my liking for pretty feminine attire has grown even stronger. My wife's clothes with the exception of her gloves, fit me beautifully, and I can dress myself quickly and perfectly in them. She wears a 21 in. corset (I could really wear a 20), No. 5 shoes, and everything is of the daintiest, the underclothing particularly so. I seldom go more than two or three days without having a complete change of clothes, and it is my constant delight, after a heavy day at the office, to get home, have a bath, change into female attire, and have tea.

(21 November 1914: 10–11)

Example 3

A Boy Who is a Girl – New Fun

As a boy I was noted for my good looks, and at the first school I went to I was known as 'Kate'. I had such a bad time of it that the connection by marriage with whom I lived took me away, and decided to have a governess for me. I was at this time (now eight years ago) fourteen. Soon afterwards my mother's cousin by marriage took me and the governess to live in Paris. The governess was a pretty, and rather lively, girl of nineteen and encouraged me in my 'girlishness'. Once or twice, when Cousin Adela was away for a day or two, Miss F. dressed me up in her things. How I delighted in the masquerade! She used to lace me into a 19 in. corset which she had got for me.

In the end she persuaded Cousin Adela (I begged her to listen to Miss F.'s plea) to let me dress and be brought up as a girl. I was always much more interested in girl's pursuits – such as needlework, housework, piano-playing, and painting – than in boy's hobbies or pastimes.

My feet and hands were exceptionally small; I only took 6¼ in. gloves and could wear ladies' 3's in shoes. And my figure was most carefully, and even rigorously, trained. By the time I was sixteen I was transformed into a really pretty girl; slight and tall. My complexion had been so well cared for that it was quite of the 'milk and roses' type. I made up, too, and I used to evoke the most outspoken admiration when walking or riding. My bust, with the carefully cut corsets and constant massage, became almost as full, and with the same contours, as that of a girl and my hair, allowed to grow and stimulated, soon reached my waist.

I always wear the most exquisite French lingerie and the smartest shoes, stockings and gloves. I have been in England nearly two years, and since last Christmas have been living in my own flat (my Cousin Adela died three years ago) with a girl chum. I go about nearly everywhere, to the theatres, music halls, Hurlingham, and at homes, and my sex has, as far as I know, never ever been suspected – certainly it has not been challenged.

When I glance in the shop windows in Regent Street I see the reflection of a very pretty girl of about twenty, dressed in the height of fashion, with a remarkably good figure, and a 'silhouette' that any woman might envy.

(25 July 1914: 11)

Example 4

Subaltern – *New Fun*

I am just writing this to say good-bye to you. I have always enjoyed your 'Correspondence' page very much indeed. I have been home on four days' leave, and am tomorrow rejoining my regiment and very soon proceeding to France. I have always been very fond of dressing in girls' things, and am indulging my desire for perhaps the last time. My cousin, who is exactly my own age, twenty-two, and who lives with us, is leaning over me as I write. Without her I should not have had half such a good time as I have. She buys all my things for me ... I am completely dressed in girl's clothes as I write ... We often go out together dressed as we are now when my people are out or away, and have had many adventures together.

(21 November 1914: 14–15)

Example 5

Teddy – *Bits of Fun*

But what I want to tell you is an experience that happened to me while on leave at a friend's house in town a short while ago. This friend said many times what a fine girl I would make, and said he was determined to see me as a girl, as he possessed the 'kink' and I had no desire then to don girl's clothes. But on the first day at his place I was made to dress as a girl, as I will show you. He has three sisters, one just my build, and on waking up I found to my horror that all my clothes had gone, and in their place was a full rigout of female attire, and silk stockings, and about six pairs of boots and shoes, and a wardrobe of dresses and costumes and everything girls wear, and a note on the dressing table telling me to get the 'kink'. There was a beautiful brown transformation, earrings, etc., but nothing masculine but myself. At first I did not like the idea, but there was nothing else to do but dress myself in the clothes I had, and after a struggle I got into the corsets, etc. and the silk under-wear felt lovely after wearing khaki so long. I selected out of the wardrobe a lovely tight-fitting dress and high-laced boots, and looked at myself in the glass, and was amazed at the difference. Well, without wearying you further, I spent all my leave as a girl, and wore evening dress at dinner, and I had a splendid time, and I now possess the 'kink', and I suppose I will now all my life.

(7 September 1918: 10)

Example 6

Cap and Apron – *Bits of Fun*

Since my guardian's death I have lived as a paying guest with various friends and acquaintances. It was just previous to the war that I was spending a long holiday, as a boarder, with some friends of my late guardian at a country house near Cambridge, and one day I dressed up in the housemaid's clothes, complete black frock, cap, apron, etc.

She was naturally surprised and indignant, and after a struggle I got her to promise secrecy, although I had to pay a stiff price for what I was wearing (she refused to have them back) and had to buy her a present as well.

Even this did not cure me, for a week or so after the landlady and her elder daughter being out for the day, and the younger at school, I took the liberty of going through their wardrobe, and dressing myself up in the daintiest lingerie I could find, including a beautiful pair of corsets. After trying on various dresses, I put on the younger daughter's best frock, and after a struggle hooked it up at the back. It was dark velvet, and fitted me well, except that it was inches above my knees. I also found a nice white pinafore, and had just put this on when in walked my hostess with her daughter.

They both stared at me dumbfounded, then their eyes wandered around their bedroom taking in the open drawers and attire littered about everywhere. 'What on earth are you doing?' 'What is the meaning of all this?' 'What an unwarrantable liberty?' and so on. The daughter after a time began shrieking with laughter, until her

21

mother ordered her downstairs. I then explained the reason for my conduct, and begged for her forgiveness, at the same time asking her to cure me of my weakness. I felt too ashamed to look at her, and I was left uncertain as to my fate, except that I was startled to hear the key turn in the door as she went out.

An hour elapsed, when the key was turned, and the mistress came in with the eldest daughter. Before I knew what had happened my hands were severely tied behind, and a small fancy apron tied over my head. I was then led downstairs, and stood on a chair in the drawing room. The servants were called in (the housemaid had told of my previous escapade after hearing of my doings that day), and I then heard my fate, viz., one month as a maid and one month in the clothes I was wearing. The alternative was that my friends (male and female) would be wired for, and would see me as I was. I accepted the former, needless to say, with the stipulation that no one outside those present would see me under this punishment.

I am afraid this letter is too long now, or I would give you many details of my ordeal. I actually spent nearly two months as a servant; the slightest complaint from the cook was an extra day, and probably an additional humiliation in the evening, such as brushing the daughter's hair for an hour, or an hour's drill on my knees manicuring their hands, etc.

The daughter especially enjoyed my humiliation. My blushes were not spared, and even my hair, which was long, was curled and false hair added. With all this, except for the humiliation, I was sorry when I again donned male attire, and to this day I occasionally dress up in the clothes they insisted on my taking with me on leaving.

(15 March 1919: 8)

THE SUNDAY CHRONICLE, 1927

In the summer of 1927, the Sunday paper, *The Sunday Chronicle*, printed a few letters suggesting that women's lighter garments were equally suitable for men. As a result they received what the editor called 'a remarkable flood' of letters about the subject, and they printed many of them over a few weeks. As coming from a far wider public and from a different editorial source they can be seen as corroborating the authenticity of the other letters. I give three examples. 'Envious' received a punishment like the last correspondent and enjoyed it. The second correspondent, like 'F.B.' in *Society*, went to a girls' school and also married a pupil. 'A Contented Typist' lives and works as a girl, like 'Tablier Blanc'.

Example 1

Envious – *The Sunday Chronicle*

As a penalty for former pranks, I was forced by girl friends to wear their fashionable clothes throughout the whole of my summer holidays, and I can testify that the dress of Miss 1927 is without question the sanest, most comfortable, and thoroughly practical attire yet adopted by either sex.

(14 August 1927: 9)

Example 2

Reader from Ross-on-Wye – *The Sunday Chronicle*

Sixty years ago, I was met in London on my arrival from Jamaica by the two sisters of my mother. I had been sent home after the death of my father and mother. My aunts were the proprietors of a large, fashionable girls' school in Devonshire, and they were much concerned about what to do with me.

When they saw me I was about seven years old, and, as was the custom then, still wore a frock. My hair had grown long on the passage home. Thus the bright idea struck them to keep me for a while as a girl.

Accordingly I was fitted out in London with girl's clothes throughout, and charged, under all kinds of pains and penalties not to let anyone know that I was not a girl. They called me Georgie instead of George.

I was kept thus until I was just sixteen, and was always the most fashionably dressed 'girl' in the school. Those were the days of small waists and large crinolines, and I was considered a pattern for the other girls to dress up to. I overheard my aunts say once that there was a mile of crinoline wire in her school room. Tight lacing was normally disapproved of, but on Sundays and evenings 'young ladies who so desired might lace in'.

At sixteen I went to Rossall (an English public school – eds), and, of course, had to give up nice frocks. My aunts cried when the change was made, and I acknowledge I felt like it. I afterwards went out to Jamaica and there met a lady who had been at my aunts'. We became engaged. I then told her of my school days. She was six years my junior, and told me how she and others envied my figure and dresses.

After we were married, when we were packing for a holiday, she, without telling me, packed a complete replica of her underwear for me. I have adopted that style ever since, and must say that ladies' underwear is far more comfortable than men's. I would not on any account do without my corsets.

(21 August 1927: 9)

Example 3

A Contented Typist – *The Sunday Chronicle*

It is just over two years ago since, partly for business reasons, I decided to adopt girl's attire, and I have never repented doing so. I was very nervous when I went to apply for a job as a typist and was delighted when it was taken for granted that I was Mrs. 'X'. After work hours I find something to look forward to when I don delightfully light clothing and a smart dress.

(28 August 1927: 7)

LONDON LIFE, 1923–41

Bits of Fun ceased publication in 1920. It overreached itself. It tried to circulate by post a collection of letters only. It was prosecuted and fined for sending indecent material and the letter page ceased. The name was changed once again – this time to *Little Bits of Fun* – but without the letters the paper died. Meanwhile the owners of *London Life* had already acquired the ailing *Modern Society*, and *Photo Bits* had ceased publication altogether. *London Life* now became the sole purveyor of this sort of material. In general it was a popular illustrated weekly newspaper. There was gossip, short stories, a considerable amount about films and film stars as well as showgirls and a small amount about fashion. The owners were, however, very slow to launch a correspondence column. Gradually letters began to appear in 1923 and 1924, until by 1927 two pages were required. Then, as the popularity of the column grew, readers' letters multiplied to an enormous extent in the bumper issues from the late 1920s. The subjects covered were the same as in its two predecessors: punishment, fetishes and cross-dressing. Arguably, however, the quality and substance of the letters did not justify the space given to them. An element of overt fantasy and of verbosity creeps in. Many letters describe brief episodes of fancy dress parties or theatricals, or dressing up at home, but nothing more substantial. I have found only one example comparable to those already cited: namely a narrative in the first person describing a lengthy period of cross-dressing. This letter is from a man, who like 'Tablier Blanc' and 'A Contented Typist' was unable to get a job.

Example 1

Anonymous – *London Life*

As a last resort, I asked my mother, who was a widow, if there was anything I could do to help her run her business as a high-class ladies' outfitter, as I felt I must do something. She was against my entering the shop, as she did not consider that the presence of a young man was desirable, while at the same time she wanted me to know how to run it, so that I, being her only relative, could carry on with the business should anything happen to her. However, after a lot of discussion she got me to consent to put myself entirely in her hands, when she would see what she could do for me.

All my male attire and belongings were confiscated, and I was completely dressed in the fashionable clothes of a young woman. Special attention was paid to my figure, and I was compelled to wear corsets day and night. For about two months I was kept at home, during which time I was thoroughly initiated into feminine ways and habits and made to always pay particular attention to my appearance, so that it became quite natural for me always to appear immaculately dressed for all occasions.

I became accustomed to wearing high-heeled shoes, and had been taken out at night several times to get me accustomed to appearing in public as a girl. At first I was very shy and embarrassed, as I thought everyone was staring at me; but I was soon cured of this by being made to mix with women on every occasion, so that I quickly assumed all their mannerisms and learnt to repair my complexion in the approved style without arousing the least suspicion.

As 'Marie', the shop assistant, I now commenced my duties and became quite popular with all our clients and the girls in the shop. Though it may appear strange, my mother preferred that I should act as mannequin instead of the other girls, so with this end in view I had been made to practise lessons in deportment for several hours a day, with the result that I became quite a passable mannequin. The customers who saw me display the latest things in gowns, undies and coats little knew that I was a young man.

For over two years I lived as a girl, and made many friends whose friendship I found hard to break when I again resumed my duties in my proper sphere.

(30 November 1929: 45)

London Life survived a bombing on 30 December 1940, but not some sort of official intervention a year later. Exactly what happened I have not been able to find out, but after 4 October 1941 the size, style and contents of the paper changed completely. Never again did such correspondence appear in a British newspaper catering for the general public.

CONCLUDING COMMENT

What value do these letters have? Are they true? As anonymous letters printed sometimes in disreputable publications, some would say they are not worthy of serious consideration as reports of authentic experiences. After reading thousands of these letters, my feeling is that the majority are probably true, especially the earlier examples. There is the sheer quantity of the letters and the long period over which they have accumulated. There is the variety of the periodicals used and the differing style and status of the correspondents.

I believe that the bulk of the letters exemplify the need for people to confess, to disclose or even to boast about a bizarre or embarrassing aspect of their past. The letter to the editor provides a convenient opportunity. These people want to tell someone, but often not their immediate family or friends. Lord Curzon left a short memoir for posthumous publication, about the extraordinarily cruel regime of the family governess, Miss Paraman. In the mid 1860s, Miss Paraman made all the children make and wear long petticoats of red calico as penitential garments and show themselves to the servants and villagers so attired (Rose, 1969: 19–27). The regime would probably have been disbelieved if he had printed it as an anonymous letter when he wrote it. He wished to record that aspect of his life. Presumably he did not feel able to reveal it in his lifetime, so he left the memoir for posterity to read in his more recent biographies.

It seems to me, therefore, that this series of letters represents a body of evidence about cross-dressing which stands alongside and supports the case histories reported by Hirschfeld (1910), Ellis (1928), Henry (1941) and Cauldwell (1947a; 1947b) over a similar period. It could also be said that those case histories authenticate the letters. We may assume, perhaps, that most of correspondents felt no need to seek medical help and therefore did not come within the purview of the medical gaze. For that reason, if no other, the reports provide an important source of data for the comprehensive history of cross-dressing that remains to be written.

2

BECOMING A MAN

The personal account of a female-to-male transsexual

Mark Rees

BACKGROUND

My parents were married in 1938. Mother was a secretary in a City of London firm and my father was in the Merchant Navy. For a couple of years they lived in London but in 1940 my mother's firm was evacuated to Rusthall, a village near Tunbridge Wells in Kent. My mother moved with her widowed mother whilst my father sailed to places unknown – wartime security meant that his whereabouts could not be revealed, even to his family.

I was born in December 1942, the survivor of two-month premature non-identical twins. My sister, Carol, died five days after birth due to 'prematurity'. I was a weakly child and succumbed easily to illness, which meant much missed schooling. A younger sister, Rosemary, was born in 1946. She was much more robust than I had been and sailed through her schooling, passing the eleven-plus scholarship examination, which I did not. Rosemary went to the local grammar school, a privilege denied me, but ultimately my academic achievements were greater, if considerably belated. Although the move to Rusthall had not been my parents' original plan, both of them spent the rest of their lives there and became greatly liked members of the local community. At the time of writing my sister lives in Tunbridge Wells, a couple of miles distant, whilst I remain in Rusthall, which has been my home all my life.

BECOMING AWARE – CHILDHOOD, ADOLESCENCE AND ADULTHOOD, BEFORE MY ROLE CHANGE

My childhood was better than people imagine. Life for the potential female-to-male transsexual is undoubtedly easier than for the male-to-female. Tomboys, even in the 1940s and 1950s when I was a child, were acceptable and treated with good-humoured tolerance, whilst feminine boys known by the more derogatory name of sissies were – and remain – subject to derision.

My younger sister and I played with both boys' and girls' toys but once I had my own pocket money and was able to buy my own playthings, masculine toys predominated. In spite of playing with toy soldiers and trains my sister did not become a transsexual, whilst I, in spite of the dolls, did not become a normal woman. Our friends were of both sexes. My best pals were a boy (whose electric train I shamelessly coveted) and an assertive and confident girl. I never cultivated the friendship of 'frilly' girls.

For most of my school career I was at all-girl schools and lived with my sister, mother and grandmother – even the cat was female! My father was in the Merchant Navy for most of the time, so female influence was strong and male influence correspondingly weak. My condition could not therefore be ascribed to a lack of female environment. My mother was the closer parent and remained so for the rest of her life, but it was my father who was my role model – I adored Mum, whilst wanting to be like Dad.

It did not occur to me that my female peers didn't want to be boys, nor did I consider that I was destined for womanhood myself. This was totally outside my childish scheme of life, wholly detached from my thinking, as inconceivable as the notion of becoming a giraffe. I was therefore, until puberty, happily unaware of the problems to come.

Yet others, even if they did not verbalise it at the time, sensed that all was not as expected. When I was a small child my mother consulted a doctor, because she was concerned that my clitoris was larger than normal, but was reassured. Much later, both she and a close family friend were to make independent statutory declarations to the effect that I had been masculine from a very early age, both in looks and in behaviour. The friend added that I looked like a boy even when wearing the dresses mother put on me. Few friends and neighbours were surprised when I eventually changed roles.

The realisation of puberty was one of the most terrible traumas of my whole life, before or since. My peers were all more advanced than me so for a while my hopes were raised. Perhaps it wouldn't happen to me and I would change into a boy? But at fourteen I started having periods. I was consumed with anger, despair and anguish. My body was repugnant, something alien, almost a deformity, although as far as breast development was concerned, that was never very great – but sufficient to cause me abhorrence.

It was paradoxical that whilst supposingly passing into womanhood I was apparently becoming more ambiguous, judging by the number of mistakes made about my sex, not to mention the deliberate jeers. Even when I was wearing ostensibly female attire people thought me male. The caretaker at my new college tried to allocate me a locker in the boys' cloakroom, irrespective of the fact that I was dressed in a skirt and nylons at the time – a somewhat embarrassing encounter since it took place in front of several other students. Such mistakes were bad enough, reinforcing my sense of being an oddity, but less forgiveable were the thoughtless remarks from people who should have known better. 'He, she or it?' sneered a friend of my parents in my presence.

Little sympathy was forthcoming from my family over such incidents. Wasn't I inviting such remarks by my behaviour? Didn't I make matters worse by walking like a boy? I was accused of being abnormal, especially because I refused to wear a bra. I was seen as awkward. No one seemed to understand that I hadn't set out to be awkward but was just behaving in a way which seemed natural.

Had it not been for the feeling of shame and guilt over my problem I might have sought professional help sooner than I did. It took the combined efforts of my 'assertive and confident' childhood friend and a sympathetic college tutor to get me to see a doctor. I expected to be told to pull myself together – hadn't others said as much? – but Dr G. took me seriously and was very sympathetic. She referred me to a psychiatrist.

The psychiatrist offered to admit me into hospital. By now almost unable to cope with all the taunts, I accepted and became the hospital's youngest patient. I was seventeen. It was a refuge but little else. I certainly wasn't 'cured'. When I was discharged the lady psychiatrist said: 'Good-bye my dear, enjoy being a woman'.

I was now blighted with a psychiatric history. It prevented me from succeeding in my efforts to enter either the police or the Women's Royal Air Force (WRAF). The WRAF rejected my application on the grounds of 'temperamental instability'. Eventually I was given a chance by the Women's Royal Naval Service (WRNS) which accepted me after writing to Dr G.

By now, convinced that my conflict of mind and body and the accompanying isolation from normal society could never be resolved, I decided to cope by acting out the female role as far as dress was concerned – no further would I have gone. I donned a dress and court shoes and ventured forth, hating every moment.

'My God', exclaimed one of my WRNS friends, 'You look like a bloke in drag!' That's exactly how I felt. Nor were my superiors fooled by my role-playing: 'Tell me, Wren Rees,' asked my divisional officer, 'Why are you so mannish?'

As if that was not enough, I fell in love with a fellow Wren, although I didn't want a relationship with her as a woman myself. I thought I must be homosexual – there seemed to be no other label to give to my undiagnosed and apparently unique condition, but I was very uneasy with it. When later I met lesbians my uneasiness was confirmed. I wasn't one of them but very much heterosexual, although afflicted with the wrong genitalia.

29

There followed a very stressful period after my fellow Wren discovered my feelings for her and threatened to report me to the Commanding Officer. Not long afterwards I was given a medical discharge with the diagnosis of 'homosexual tendencies'. I knew this was wrong, but what was I?

By now life was barely tolerable. I avoided social gatherings and tried to bury myself in study. Contact with doctors and clergy proved unhelpful. The doctors told me I would grow out of it (at 25?) and would have to learn to live with it. A clergyman told me that one could live a fulfilling life as a non-practising homosexual!

In 1969, four years after my WRNS' discharge, I chanced to see an article in *The Times* of London which described the condition of transsexualism. It was a moment of enlightment; at last it all fitted into place. I was transsexual. It was a year or more before I managed to find a specialist and heard the words I never believed possible: 'I can help you live as a man'.

Having gained some 'A' levels since leaving the WRNS I was about to embark upon a degree course in dental surgery at the University of Birmingham. In theory it seemed wise to complete the course before changing roles, but in reality life was intolerable for me in the female role. I was acting out a part which was alien to me, suppressing my sexual feelings and suffering a perpetual onslaught of comments and mistakes about my sex. I decided to change roles as soon as possible.

My consultant agreed and prescribed methyl testostrone. I knew that the process would be long and arduous, but once I'd taken the hormone the depression which had hung over me since puberty lifted. I felt a new person, both mentally and physically. At the age of 28 I was about to start living.

BECOMING A MAN – PHYSICALLY

Practically and emotionally, becoming a man, physically, was the least difficult part of my role reassignment. It was, however, the most frustrating because it was only a compromise. I knew that, however good the treatment, I'd never be fully male, functionally, anatomically or chromosomally; but to be accepted socially as such was a tremendous release, a miracle.

The action of the hormones was almost immediate. A couple of weeks later I had my last period and within a month or so people began to notice a change in my voice. (Since I was still living as a woman, I told enquirers that I had a heavy cold!) Although the growth of my facial hair took much longer, I was surprised by the rapidity of the changes generally. How much the lifting of my underlying depression was due to the hormone intake, and how much to the relief of knowing that at long last I was being enabled to change roles, I do not know.

My superficial veins especially in the forearms, became more obvious as the subcutaneous fat decreased. This decrease was most obvious around the breasts, hips and thighs. There was an increase in muscle development with a corresponding weight increase, redistribution and increase in body hair and clitoral enlargement. After six months I was able to live successfully as a man.

In retrospect, whilst very grateful at the time, I realise that my treatment was somewhat arbitrary. The 'gender identity clinic' I attended seemed to consist solely of one psychiatrist. I had no physical examination or biochemical tests. It was the psychiatrist, not an endocrinologist, who prescribed the hormone preparation which was later found to put the liver at risk of cancer. Once this was known I was submitted to a liver scan, but otherwise did not receive any form of physical monitoring. All hormone treatment was stopped for six months during this period. Then, when I expressed concern about this – chiefly because I had lost all my chest hairs – another oral preparation was prescribed. It is now understood that these oral preparations and long periods without any hormone replacement therapy (HRT) render one prone to osteoporosis, a condition which has been diagnosed in some female-to-male transsexuals. My recent – and first – density scan showed a below average reading but 'acceptable' unless a continuous loss is observed.

It was not until just before surgery, in 1974, that I received any form of physical examination, and it was eight years after my first hormone tablets, when I had transferred myself to another gender clinic, that I was examined by an endocrinologist and biochemical tests carried out. An appropriate dosage was prescribed and later intra-muscular injections replaced the more risky – and less effective – oral preparations. My 'defection' meant that I have been monitored ever since, not only for osteoporosis but also signs of cardio-vascular disease. I see an endocrinologist annually and the practice nurses who administer the injections keep a check on my blood pressure and cholestrol levels.

I recently opted to reduce my hormone intake from monthly injections to about three or four annually, but began to feel less than fully fit, slightly depressed and lethargic, and experienced a return of a certain amount of subcutaneous fat. To avoid these eunuchoid symptoms I returned to a monthly regime, so far with no adverse effects.

Surgery is often depicted, especially by the more ignorant members of the media, as the sum total of a 'sex-change'. A man goes into hospital and comes out a woman, or vice versa. I find this utter nonsense. It is but part of a process which can take months, probably years. Alone it would achieve little. For myself the most wonderful thing was being enabled to live in the male role. This was achieved by the hormones, not by the scalpel. I had been living as a man for nearly three years before undergoing a bilateral mastectomy. This was straightforward and relatively painless. Prior to the surgery I had imagined that once relieved of what seemed like unnatural appendages I would go into paroxysms of delight, but this was not so. To discover myself with a flat, barely scarred chest seemed so absolutely normal; my previous form seemed a bad dream, something from another life.

The hysterectomy and oophorectomy (removal of the ovaries) a year later was less easy; I developed a massive haematoma which necessitated blood transfusions. I felt unwell and wondered if I'd been right to voluntarily undergo surgery on an otherwise healthy body, although medical friends had advised it, fearing the risk of cancer in the unused organs. None the less I felt guilty because of the bother caused to the medical and nursing staff and, not least, the anxiety undergone by my mother and friends. These qualms were finally laid to rest by a visiting friend who firmly told me that the treatment had been justified. As my friend put it: 'You were only half a person before, now you are whole.'

As time went on adhesions developed in my chest and rather unslightly concavities appeared. The surgeon who had carried out the mastectomy advised rubbing the affected parts with cold cream. This proved a totally useless exercise. By now I had 'defected' to the new clinic and its plastic surgeon performed corrective surgery in February 1985. To date there have been no problems since. None the less I remain somewhat apprehensive about being seen without a shirt. The possiblility of liposuction was discussed with the team, since large hips are as much a bane to the female-to-male transsexual as the presence of breasts, but I decided that I would be foolish to undergo the risk of surgery unless it were absolutely necessary. Besides, surgery could not alter the underlying bone structure. Bearing in mind that in my former role my sex had been questioned almost daily, whereas since my role-change it had been questioned only twice in some thirteen years, I felt such a procedure was not absolutely necessary.

A phalloplasty (the construction of a penis) is probably what most female-to-male transsexuals yearn for more than anything else, yet it is a most difficult, risky and unsatisfactory procedure. Had I been offered a phalloplasty when first changing roles it is possible that I may have accepted, but now, many years later and with considerably more knowledge, it is an operation I would not wish to undergo. Some techniques appear better than others but all involve considerable pain and scarring. Other areas of the body have to be mutilated in order to acquire tissue for the construction. The involvement of the urethra increases the risk of infection and the ability to micturate in a male fashion cannot be guaranteed. Indeed some patients are unable, after surgery, to pass water in either a male or female way. I met one who has to carry a jug everywhere he goes. Erection by natural means is, of course, impossible and no amount of surgery will render the female-to-male transsexual capable of fathering children. An added risk is the fact that the procedure often leaves the constructed phallus totally insensitive. Far from the phalloplasty being the philosophers' stone, it has instead made life worse, not better, for many of those desperate enough to undergo it.

Rather than enter the fraught area of phalloplasties, a number of female-to-male transsexuals have equipped themselves with very realistic looking prostheses, which can enable them to urinate in a male fashion if desired. I would not use one myself – they are expensive and add bother to life, both in the fixing and the cleaning. I suppose I feel, too, that their use is a little dishonest, which is illogical because a man with a false leg would not be so regarded.

Of course I despise my female body and the practical and psychological problems it causes. If some wonderful technique could be perfected whereby the hated vagina could be excised and a fully functional and aesthetically acceptable phallus constructed without the need for mutilation elsewhere, then I'd be as keen as any female-to-male transsexual to have it done. But, unlike some of my colleagues, I realise that maleness is not bestowed by genitalia alone. I have not needed a penis to be accepted as male. As Professor Milton Diamond says: 'The most powerful sex organ is between the ears, not the legs' (Diamond, 1982: 125).

BECOMING A MAN – SEXUALLY

It was during my teens that I discovered that women sexually aroused me, but it has been only recently that I came to the view that this experience was physically dissimilar from that of a normal woman, although our equipment was identical. Women, of my acquaintance, speak of an arousal which seems to be diffuse, whereas I had what I later recognised as a clitoral erection and this was over ten years before my hormone therapy.

I consider it impossible to become a man sexually as far as sexual intercourse is concerned. However good a phalloplasty, which they seldom are, no constructed organ will have a natural erection or impregnate a female.

Many female-to-male transsexuals do, however, have lasting relationships with normal, non-lesbian women, which include a sexual element. I believe that their partners do not see their lovers as women, but as men, albeit without penises and that many experience orgasms for the first time with these lovers. I am less certain of the satisfaction obtained by the female-to-male transsexual. One is in the unhappy situation of being stimulated by the same signals which would arouse a heterosexual genetic male, but having female genitalia which react in a way appropriate to a woman. Some may be able to cope with these unwelcome reminders of one's condition, but I find it difficult.

BECOMING A MAN – ADMINISTRATIVELY
AND SOCIALLY

Faced with all the documentation to be changed I decided that if there were any doubts about changing roles, this would be the point at which they would surface. I had none.

A change of name brings about an appreciation of just how many documents bear it. The initial deed poll on change of name was straightforward. 'Brenda' became 'Brendan' and 'Margaret' became 'Mark'. (Although not my intention at the time, a few years later I dropped 'Brendan' making 'Mark' (by which I'd been known socially) my first name.) My original change had been made in a way to ease life for those around me who found it difficult to use my new name – 'Bren' covered everything. Once established, I wanted to use a name which had no ties with the past. This undoubtedly had psychological benefits for me.

The university authorities were very discreet and helpful but there still remained much that I had to do. Names had to be changed on bank accounts, insurance policies, passport, driving licence, club membership, and on Department of Social Security, Department of Employment, Inland Revenue and medical records. The list seemed interminable. Some time later, when applying for another course, I discovered one omission – my examination certificates, so that required some explanatory letters to various examining authorities. All the official bodies with which I dealt endeavoured to be discreet and helpful. Bureaucracy had got a human face.

There was also the change of wardrobe, although having worn unisex clothes for some time this was less of a total change than an amendment. The few clothes I bought new were supplemented by gleaning from charity shops – I didn't want everything to look new! I took my feminine clothes back to the charity shops.

My father was dead by the time I changed roles, so it is useless to speculate as to how he would have reacted. Understandably, my mother found it hard, saying that she'd never realised my feelings. However, since all the neighbours had guessed, I suspect that it was a case of not seeing what was obvious because it was too painful. It was a very difficult period for all of us, but, as my sister predicted, once my mother realised how much happier I had become as a result, she was more able to accept it. We must not, however, underestimate the trauma families and close friends may undergo. There is a tendency, I believe, for transsexuals to be so wrapped up in their own problems that they do not see the anguish which those around them are also experiencing.

I found dealing with friends and acquaintances almost as fraught as coping with the family. Those who were close knew of my situation and were very supportive. I was in for some surprises from the others. My 'pious' and older friends, who I thought would be narrow-minded and condemnatory, turned out to be very helful and accepting; whilst my acquaintances in the WRNS, sure, I thought, to be broad-minded and understanding, were, with one or two exceptions, the least so.

Some people were surprised that I chose to remain in my home instead of 'vanishing', which seems to be a common transsexual practice. I saw no reason to do so. It was, admittedly, a little daunting to face the local community as 'Mark' after having been known as the rather ambiguous 'Brenda' for years. Of course, there was gossip, but it died down and now I am re-assimilated into the community, even singing bass in the choir where I once sang soprano! Twenty years on I can confidently say that my condition is not a barrier to social acceptance. In my experience, if one lives a normal life and makes a contribution to the well-being of the community in which one lives, then transsexualism is hardly worth a thought. This is borne out by the fact that recently I was invited to stand as a local candidate for the council elections and was duly elected.

BECOMING A MAN – PSYCHOLOGICALLY

For the transsexual, a change of role does not mean a change of personality, although that seems to be a popular notion. One relative suggested to me that I should take up pipe-smoking! I replied that I had no need of a nipple-substitute! The treatment may have changed the body and hence the world's perception of one, but the person is the same. It seems absurd to undergo all that a role-change involves in order to become a male (or female) stereotype. That would be as much of a prison as being trapped in the wrong body. Treatment has rendered my body as congruent as possible with my gender identity – my sense of myself as male.

There were changes, however. One of the most immediate was to be rid of my pre-menstrual depression. My change of roles enabled me to behave in a way which came naturally and no longer did I feel as if I were acting a role. As a consequence I became less self-consious, more relaxed, sociable and, so I am told, a more pleasant person. Psychologically, I did not 'become a man'. I became myself.

BECOMING A MAN – LEGALLY

The problems which would beset me as a result of the United Kingdom law were not uppermost in my mind when I initially changed roles. I knew that I could not change my name and sex on my birth certificate, the document being considered a record of fact at the time of registration. I knew, too, that the birth certificate was not technically an identity document, even though it might be used as such. What I did not bargain for, however, was how I would feel on the occasions when it was necessary for me to produce it. I deeply resented having to disclose my medical condition to people to whom it was not directly relevant and who may or may not have been sympathetic. I felt my privacy was being invaded.

I gradually realised that the legal situation had more far-reaching implications than I had originally thought. It was not just the birth certificate but the non-recognition of one's current status which placed considerable burdens upon the transsexual.

At that time, although a change of name was permitted on the passport, no gender prefix was allowed, a concession later granted. Whenever sex was legally relevant I was designated as a female and would be to the grave, since that is what should be recorded on my death certificate. I was barred from marriage with a woman, although not with a man!

I felt that my inability to marry a woman meant that it was unlikely that I would be able to adopt a child. Were a partner to have a child by artificial insemination I could not be recorded as its legal father. It was clear that not only transsexuals, but those closely associated with them were also adversely affected by the legal situation.

After years of solitary campaigning I took my case to the European Commission of Human Rights, spurred on not just by the bar to marriage but also because possible career prospects had been ruined. At that time, in 1979, I was just completing a degree course in religious studies and English literature at an Anglican College of Higher Education and was intending to be ordained as a priest. The Church deemed otherwise because I was legally a woman.

We sought to have my sexual identity as a man recognised for all legal purposes (Rees, 1984). We alleged that by its non-activity the United Kingdom government was in breach of Articles 8 (right to private life) and 12 (right to marriage) of the European Convention of Human Rights. The European Commission of Human Rights declared my application admissable and, following the refusal of the United Kingdom government to reach a friendly settlement, presented the case before the Court. Judgment was handed down on 17 October 1986. By twelve votes to three the Court ruled that there had been no violation of Article 8 and was unanimous in holding that Article 12 had not been violated (Rees Case, 1986). I was angry and shocked.

Now with support from many members of the public and the media, I battled on, but to little avail. A motion from the Committee on Petitions of the European Parliament calling, *inter alia*, for 'legal recognition; change of first name; change of sex on birth certificates and identity documents', was adopted by the European Parliament on 12 September 1989. The United Kingdom government has ignored it. The matter is under review! More recently, I founded the pressure group Press for Change (see Appendix II) which is seeking full legal recognition for United Kingdom transsexuals in their reassigned sex.[1]

At the time of writing progress towards reform seems slow. We need also to educate in order to gain support. With an increasing amount of backing from Members of Parliament, leading lawyers, medical experts, church people and the public at large, we are confident that change will come. For the present, our struggle will continue. One day I shall legally become a man.

CONCLUSIONS

'Becoming a man', physically, was apparently the most major and drastic part of my transition experience, but it was the process which brought peace of mind because at last society saw the outward manifestation of what I was within. After years of conflict between what I was inside and what I appeared outside, medical science had brought them into harmony. I was enabled to be true to myself. The discomfort of surgery and the risks associated with hormone replacement therapy were but a small price to pay for the reconciliation of my physical and psychological selves.

I feel I have always been a heterosexual male, psychologically. I did not 'become' one. The 'becoming' was the freedom to form relationships with non-lesbian, heterosexual women. Sadly, my experience in this area has been very limited, but enough to realise that women see me as a man in spite of my lack of male genitalia. My anxiety over this matter is not shared by women of my acquaintance. It is a far greater obstacle to me than to the women, especially now that my contemporaries are women who have finished child-rearing.

'Becoming a man', administratively, was tedious but not insurmountable, except for the wretched government's stance on legal recognition. Social acceptance was perhaps the easiest 'becoming' to achieve. That began immediately I changed roles, if not earlier. Paradoxically, this almost effortless 'becoming' was also the most important. By the same token, the 'becoming' which I have not yet attained and which would affect my daily life very little – legal recognition – is the one which has demanded the greatest effort, so far with apparently fruitless results.

For me, it is most important to become male socially. Without acceptance in my male role, life would be intolerable. Full legal recognition and miraculous surgery to construct almost perfect male genitalia would, without this acceptance, be worse than useless. People see a male or female person. They do not usually demand presentation of a legal document or medical examination of one's genitalia before deciding that someone is a man or woman.

Of course there are practical and psychological problems caused by my physical and legal situation, but they occupy a relatively minute part of everyday life. I have been indisputably accepted as a man socially. The world now sees me as I see myself. In its eyes I have become a man; in my own eyes I have become myself.

NOTE

1   The position of transsexual rights world-wide is outlined in McMullan and Whittle (1994: 104–17).

3

THE CAREER PATH OF THE MALE FEMALER*

Richard Ekins

Male femaling takes place in three major modes: body femaling, erotic femaling and gender femaling. These are broadly comparable with facets of sex, sexuality and gender, respectively, where 'sex' refers to the biological and physiological aspects of the division of humans into male and female; 'sexuality' to 'those matters pertaining to the potential arousability and engorgement of the genitals' (Plummer, 1979: 53); and 'gender' to the socio-cultural correlates of the division of the sexes.

Body femaling refers to the desires and practices of femalers to female their bodies. This might include desired, actual or simulated changes in both primary and secondary characteristics of 'sex'. Thus it would include chromosomal change (not presently possible), gonadal, hormonal, morphological and neural change, at one level (Money, 1969); and change to facial hair, body hair, scalp hair, vocal chords, skeletal shape and musculature, at another level (Lukacs, 1978).

Erotic femaling refers to femaling which is intended to, or has the effect of, arousing sexual desire or excitement. Although the term might be stretched to include femaling that is intended to arouse, or that does arouse, sexual desire or excitement in others, the particular feature of erotic femaling in cross-dressers is that the desire, or excitement, is aroused in the femaler himself by his own femaling and/or through the awareness of others of his own erotic femaling.

Gender femaling refers to the manifold ways in which femalers adopt the behaviours, emotions and cognitions socio-culturally associated with being female. Gender femaling need not be associated with erotic femaling.

In the process of femaling, persons (bodies, selves and identities), actions, events, and objects (clothes and the paraphernalia of femininity) are variously implicated. They are, or become over time, in varying degrees and with varying degrees of interconnectedness, sexed, sexualised and/or

* An earlier version of this chapter first appeared as part of 'On male femaling: a grounded theory approach to cross-dressing and sex-changing', *Sociological Review*, 1993, 41: 1–29.

gendered (SSG'D). Thus, in body femaling, for example, the characteristics of the genetic female's (sexed) body are taken on by the genetic male's body which becomes correspondingly sexed as female. Whereas in erotic femaling the gendered object 'petticoat' may become eroticized (sexualised). Again, in gender femaling the gendered mannerism sitting down in 'ladylike fashion' may be adopted by the gender femaler as a facet of his gendered presentation of self (Goffman, 1969; 1979). This is an exceedingly complex business, the components of which may be best illustrated with reference to the major phases in an ideal-typical career path of the male femaler that emerged from my analysis of the staged (Glaser, 1978: 97–100) male femalings of over 200 informants. The analysis reports the results of field work carried out in major British cities and life-history work with selected male cross-dressers and sex-changers, both since 1980.

PHASE ONE: BEGINNING FEMALING

In this first phase of femaling the emphasis is upon initial femaling behaviours – what deviancy theorists would call primary deviance.

An incident of cross-dressing occurs. It might occur by chance. It might be encouraged by others. It might take place in childhood, adolescence or adulthood. It might be more or less charged with affect. The cross-dressing incident, which I take to include the context and accompanying feelings and cognitions, may evoke varying degrees of certainty about its meaning. It could be remembered, re-experienced, or reconstructed as primarily erotic or sexual, especially when originally accompanied by perceived sexual excitement and arousal. It could be remembered, re-experienced or reconstructed in terms of fascination, sensuousness, mystery or awe. Further, the experience may be conceptualised in terms of the tactile, the visual or the olfactory, or any combination of them, and with varying degrees of focus and precision.

Typically, it is the untoward affect that leads to pondering the incident. 'What is the meaning of this pleasure, mystery or awe that I experienced?' 'What sort of person am I that could experience such a thing?' In short: 'what does it all mean?' Typically, in the 'beginning femaling' phase, the meanings are inchoate. In terms of the interrelations between sex, sexuality and gender, the feature of this phase is undifferentiation. There is undifferentiation because in this phase the untoward incident is dismissed, not taken seriously, or is seen as a temporary aberration and no subtle distinctions are made. There is also undifferentiation because the individual lacks not only the conceptual wherewithal, but also a sense of purpose, direction and volition, and, indeed, the means to gain them through interaction with others or relevant literature.

As likely as not, he will simply and inchoately conceive the incident in terms of 'something to do with sex'. Possibilities include variants of: 'I wish I was a girl' (inchoate as regards fantasy body femaling versus fantasy/acted-out gender femaling); 'I wish these clothes were part of my world. I wish I could be part of this world' (inchoate as regards gender femaling stress). Where the erotic looms large, beginning femaling might be seen in terms of the sexual (prehistory of erotic femaling), with the relations between the sexual and sex and gender obscure at this stage.

As regards the interrelations between the constitution of self and world as SSG'D, typically 'normality' reinstates itself after the incident. Nevertheless, thenceforth the meaning of female objects – clothes, for example – may well be different. In some more or less undifferentiated way they may be seen as charged, or capable of being charged with affect, which may be built on in a more or less cumulative fashion, pondered on and invested with new meaning. Likewise, new self-concepts will be rendered more or less negotiable, though typically, in this phase, the re-involvement within the meaning frames of 'normal' everyday life, following the cross-dressing incident, are such as to leave 'normal' self-concept and world more or less intact.

PHASE TWO: FANTASYING FEMALING

Fantasying femaling will frequently arise in tandem with 'doing femaling' (phase three), but in this phase the stress is on the elaboration of fantasies involving femaling. The fantasies may be more or less elaborate, scripted, adapted from incidents in 'real' life, innovative and imaginative. They might entail nothing more than fantasying the feel and texture of an imag-ined petticoat as implicated within a femaling episode (cf., fetishism unrelated to femaling). They might involve an elaborate script in which the boy child is taken shopping by his mother, has chosen for him all sorts of 'feminine' finery, and lives 'happily ever after' as an accepted girl child in the family.

In terms of sex, sexuality and gender and their interrelations, a number of possibilities arise. There may be quite unambiguous fantasies of being a girl or woman (fantasy body femaling). A common boyhood variant is fantasying 'waking up in the morning as a girl'. Many femalers who later conceptualise themselves as transsexuals and who are conceptualised as primary transsexuals within the psychiatric-medical literature (Person and Ovesey, 1974a) recall variations on this theme. For others, the fantasy femaling takes on a gender stress. Thoughts of male or female morphology do not arise. Rather, the emphasis is upon romantic fantasies relating to such things as dreamy dresses, ribbons, doll play, and the like. For still others, the emphasis is upon masturbatory fantasy cross-dressing in a range of variations.

There is a tendency in this phase for fantasies initially to cluster around certain themes, which develop only slowly. They may have a body/sex, gender, or erotic/sexual core, which may then be fuelled by one or other mode.

As regards the interrelations between the constitution of self and world as SSG'D, a number of points might be made. As with 'beginning femaling', there is a tendency for the meaning frames (Goffman, 1974) of everyday life to reassert themselves when the incident of day-dreaming or masturbation is over. However, in the case of erotic fantasy femaling, gendered objects are increasingly invested with potential affect, to form material for future masturbatory scripts. *Pari passu*, the environment is gaining potential for being increasingly eroticised/sexualised. Alternatively, there may be an increasing fascination with 'the world of women' (prehistory of gender femaling leading to gender femaling stress), with varying degrees of volition. As regards self and world, body femalers may become so preoccupied with their fantasying that their self-concepts as males become increasingly under threat; gender femalers, likewise, in more dreamy a fashion. More typically, however, there will be merely what might be termed incipient 'dual worlding'. An embryonic world will be constituted within which a femaling self and femaling related objects and practices are emerging, but which at this stage, the fantasying femaler keeps separate from his everyday world, thus keeping the latter more or less 'normal' and enabling its development more or less boundaried from the incipient femaling world.

PHASE THREE: DOING FEMALING

Although fantasying femaling is frequently accompanied by partial cross-dressing, doing femaling includes more 'serious' cross-dressing and acting out aspects of fantasy body femaling. The body femaler may, for instance, depilate parts of his body periodically. He may experiment with hiding his male genitalia ('tucking') and producing a simulated vulva. With, or just as likely without, body femaling variants, the gender femaler may well build up private collections of clothes and may experiment with more complete dressing using make-up, jewellery and accessories. All of these may, or may not, be built into masturbatory routines (erotic femaling), which may become more protracted.

In terms of sex, sexuality and gender, and their interrelations, it is as though the femaler is developing along clustered lines, without really quite knowing what he is doing. Cross-dressing is likely to play a major part in this phase whether the clusters follow sex, sexuality or gender patterns, but typically the femaler is not sure of the differences or where precisely he stands with regard to them. In this phase femalers become more knowledgeable about the gendered world of girls and women, about what dresses they like, about styles and so forth, this, in itself, giving pleasure. Others may place the emphasis upon increasingly elaborate masturbatory routines. Others may become more preoccupied with aspects of their morphology.

As regards the interrelations between the constitution of self and world as SSG'D, this is likely to be the period of particular personal confusion and of vacillation. Not only is the femaler 'betwixt and between' two worlds, but he has no clear notion of what he is doing or its likely outcome. His 'everyday' meanings in respect of his self and world are increasingly threatened by his developing 'doing femaling', but he is still not advanced in his conceptualisation of what he is doing and what it means. The femaler vacillates, for instance, between cross-dressing episodes, confusion about their meaning and, in many instances, repeated attempts to stop what he is doing, marked symbolically by frequent 'purges' – the periodic throwing away of offending collections of clothes, cosmetics, jewellery, and so on.

As 'doing femaling' becomes more frequent, the tendency to seek to 'explain' it may well become more pressing. The search for meaning is incipient. But unless the femaler chances upon, for example, media coverage of 'people like me', or comes across 'explanations' by others in scientific texts, he may well continue to think, as many do in this phase, that 'I am the only one in the world', 'I am a freak', ' I don't know why I do this', 'Where will it all end?'

PHASE FOUR: CONSTITUTING FEMALING

This phase marks the period where the femaler begins to constitute the meaning of his activities in a more serious and sustained way. As femaling experiences and activities increase many femalers are drawn increasingly to 'explain' themselves, to 'make sense' of themselves and their activities and to work out where femaling fits with the rest of their lives.

A number of possibilities are typical of this phase. The femaler may seek professional guidance – a 'cure' – having constituted himself as, for example, a pervert in need of help. He may in rare cases construct his own definition of the situation without access to literature or subculture. More typically, he will have chanced upon media references to 'people called transvestites (or transsexuals)', with whom he can identify. Many femalers, either through contact with subcultural literature or through their reading of the 'scientific' literature, begin to constitute a personalised transvestite or transsexual self-concept within a world of femaling, which is refined as they compare themselves with self-proclaimed transvestites and transsexuals they may meet in the subculture. Some definitions of the situation will be adopted 'ready made' as it were. Others are seen as inapplicable. More typically, the newly confronted constitutions are moulded to fit the particular self-concepts and understandings of self and femaling that the femaler has constituted thus far.

It is in this phase that meanings begin to crystallize around particular 'namings' (Strauss, 1977: 15–30), often quite discriminating namings having to do with psychiatric-medical conceptualisations as they have been absorbed into the subculture. Frequently, much thought and careful consideration is directed towards 'finding the label that fits'. Some come to label themselves as a 'true transsexual'; others as a 'TV (transvestite) with TS (transsexual) tendencies'; others as a 'middle-of-the-road transvestite'; while others, as 'primarily fetishistic'.

Having adopted a label, meanings can now be ordered and understood. Once the femaler has sorted out *what* he is (and this is where the emphasis lies), beginnings can be made towards understanding who he is, and towards understanding the meanings of objects to him as variously SSG'D. The emphasis in 'constituting femaling' does, however, tend to be on conceptualisations of self and identity. Once the label has been adopted, past identities are typically re-interpreted in the light of the newly discovered 'condition'. This is especially evident in the context of a consideration of the interrelations between sex, sexuality and gender, the modes of femaling, and the constitution of self and world as SSG'D. What had been a confusing *mélange* now becomes clear or clearer. Sally comments: 'I fought it for years, I realise now that I had been TS [transsexual] all along' (new-found 'sex', body femaling identity). Whereas for Annie 'it was always a sexual thing. Now I can meet partners and we can 'rub slips' together, I know that's where I'm at' (Erotic femaling identity, constructed around the sexual, with residual gender femaling).

The important and influential subcultural variant in which gender, and gender femaling is stressed – in many cases almost to the exclusion of sex, sexuality, body femaling and erotic femaling – is best seen with reference to the Beaumont Society.

The Beaumont Society is the largest and most well established society for transvestites and 'gender motivated transsexuals' in the United Kingdom (Alice, L100, 1991). It is an association for transvestites and 'gender motivated' transsexuals 'whose motivation for cross-dressing is primarily of a gender, rather than a sexual, nature' (Beaumont Society, 1983). In its texts, it conceptualises transvestism in terms of love of the feminine; the transvestite self in terms of 'full personality expression'. Moreover, the society, through its various activities in promulgating its ideas and in holding 'respectable' gender-orientated meetings at 'respectable', 'straight' venues, provides those identifying with it opportunities for managing the sexual stigma often attached to cross-dressing activities, both by cross-dressers themselves and the general public. Many of my Beaumont Society informants constituted their femaling selves and world in terms of 'the Beaumont' and would state publicly that their cross-dressing had nothing whatsoever to do with sex or sexuality. Privately though, many would say this was not the case.

PHASE FIVE: CONSOLIDATING FEMALING

This stage marks the period where a more full-blown constitution of femaling self and world is established. This will provide the individual with a more or less comprehensive and coherent framework within which to consolidate or develop his femaling self and world, and will also provide him with the means to relate these systematically to his 'everyday', non-femaling world, where this remains, as it normally will.

The consolidation may be centred around body femaling, erotic femaling or gender femaling, with the emphasis upon the corresponding features and facets of sex, sexuality or gender. Various combinations over time are possible, but, typically, having constituted self and world, 'consolidating' sees reconstructions of pasts, consolidations of presents and moves made towards intended futures, clustering around 'chosen' foci.

Thus, a consolidating body femaler having come to see that 'really' 'she' was transsexual all along (sexed identity), takes stock of 'herself' and embarks upon a programme of appropriate body feminisation, which may be seen as culminating in 'the op.', now defined in terms of becoming as near as is possible and practicable to what 'she' should have been all along. 'She' now dresses as a woman, because 'she' IS a woman. Her presentation of self is herself. As Carol puts it: 'Richard, this IS me!' 'She' is not merely expressing parts of 'herself', or play-acting. Thus, the meanings of what might have been conceptualised in terms of gender or sexuality are now redefined and may take on different career paths of their own, all, in a sense, as adjuncts to the major focus of 'her' femaling. As regards gender issues, 'she' develops 'her' personal style much as a genetic girl would have done – the difference being that 'she' is starting rather late, has to do it rather quickly, and is likely to be hampered by residues of 'her' maleness. As regards 'her' sexuality, as hormonal treatment continues, 'she' loses what male sexuality 'she' has, and is, in effect, desexualizing 'her' old sexuality concurrent with the construction of a new sex and sexuality.

The erotic femaler, having now consolidated his femaling around the erotic/sexual, may look to new ways to develop his erotic femaling. He may build up collections of subcultural literature and exotic paraphernalia. He may experiment with a view to finding what most 'turns him on' He may begin to conceptualise what 'turns him on' in a fairly fine-tuned way. His female style may take on sado-masochistic variants which would normally be considered fetishistic and which may take increasingly bizarre forms, for he is not so much interested in the subtleties of femininity as with his personal sexual excitement. The role and meaning of body and

gender femaling are redefined and clarified accordingly. Serious and sustained body femaling has no appeal at all. It would entail the loss of his
eroticism and his pleasure-giving penis. Likewise, orthodox gender
femaling may come to be seen as having prissy, drab or effete connotations.

Another approach lies in the developing of subcultural contacts that
will lead to a conscious celebration of the erotic. Erotic femalers may
advertise for partners in subcultural magazines such as *The World of
Transvestism* or *Transcript*. They may provide the magazines with
photographs, personal details and accounts of some of their sexual exploits
carried out with other 'TVs' (transvestites) or 'TV punters' (apparent
'straights' who fancy and hang around TVs and TSs) met through the
magazine. Many erotic femalers build up something of a cult following
through this procedure. Some may get further excitement from being
paid for their services. In this case the erotic femaler gets maximum
sexual excitement by becoming the stereotypical erotic female, the 'sexy
hooker'.

Embedded within the social worlds of cross-dressers and sex-changers
in Britain are a number of sometimes overlapping and interrelating
social circles (Simmel, 1955; Kadushin, 1966) of erotic femalers. Entry into
these social circles is often instrumental in consolidating an erotic femaling
identity.

The gender femaler, on the other hand, tends to move in the opposite
direction. Residual fetishisms may erode. Now his fascination with the
whole world of the feminine knows no bounds. He wants to look like and
behave like a 'real' woman (as he sees women), not some stereotypical
male fantasy of one. This may entail the steady development of his femme
self with 'her' own personality, tastes and enthusiasms. Many will model
themselves on admired 'RGs' (real girls); others will study deportment,
voice production, fashion, make-up and the like.

Body femaling and erotic femaling are now re-defined in terms of the
gender foci. It is not necessarily true that there is no body femaling. In
fantasy there may be much of it. Similarly, the gender femaler may adopt
every bit of the sex-role paraphernalia his ingenuity can dream up. He
may, for instance, insert tampons in his fantasied vagina (rectum), or occasionally 'go on the pill'. But he does these things 'because that is what
RGs do', not because he thinks he is one, or is becoming one, or because
of any very obvious erotic kick he gets out of doing it. ('That wouldn't
be feminine'.)

Typically, his relationship with the erotic is likely to be ambiguous. While
there are gender femalers who are asexual, or who increasingly become
so and who female for 'reasons of tranquillity' or even aesthetic reasons,
the eroticism is more likely, perhaps, to be attenuated and dispersed, and
may indeed become increasingly so. We might say eroticism is adjuncted

to gender femaling in these cases. For some, with increased gender fine-tuning an ever-increasing number of objects in the world of women become mildly eroticised. But, at the same time, their own sexuality becomes increasingly genderised. This can lead to a distaste for sexuality except as expressed in gender form. Sexual intercourse, for example, is fantasied in terms of gender femaling role-play. Another possibility is that past gender femalings which were not erotic femalings at the time, come to form material for erotic scripts in subsequent episodes of fantasy femaling (see Chapter 11).

CONCLUDING COMMENT

Grounded theory work with cross-dressers and sex-changers enables the ordering of a mass of what Herbert Blumer would have called 'intimate detail' (Anselm Strauss, personal communication, 1994). In particular, consideration of this detail in terms of the basic social process of 'male femaling' has a number of advantages. It enables the proper respect to be paid to the processual and emergent nature of much cross-dressing and sex-changing phenomena. It facilitates the generation of a number of categories which highlight facets of male femaling hitherto unstudied. Finally, it provides the framework for a rigorous examination of the various shifting interrelations between human sex, sexuality and gender which feature in a phased male femaling career path. All too often these complex inter-relations are conflated or ignored.

Use of the concept of the career path is sometimes said to impose too much order on lives which, both to outsiders and to those who have lived them, may appear to have 'been much more confused and chaotic' (King, 1993: 160–1). It should be remembered, however, that the phases do not delineate fixed sequences and stages through which male femalers move from less serious to more serious involvement in femaling in the way sometimes suggested for deviant careers (Lemert, 1972: 79). Not all male femalers get beyond the early phases of male femaling. Rather, it is the minority who proceed through all the phases of male femaling to a 'consolidated' end state. Most male femalers will circle and cycle all or parts of the phases again and again. They may stop off at different points, and for different periods, on different occasions (see Chapter 11).

Part II

THE SOCIAL ORGANISATION OF GENDER BLENDING

INTRODUCTION

Under certain conditions, subcultures or communities develop around shared spheres of activity.[1] When that sphere of activity is considered deviant and is thus both unexpected and without moral sanction, there are additional pressures towards subcultural or communal formations. When an activity is deviant, engaging in it carries additional problems such as those concerning access, secrecy and guilt. A subculture can thus be seen to provide solutions to some of these problems.

Deviant activities, to varying degrees, provoke a hostile response from others. Such condemnation can further contribute to the emergence of subcultural forms by reinforcing, alienating and segregating deviant groups (Plummer, 1975). The men discussed by Peter Farrer in Chapter 1 who wrote to various publications about their experiences of wearing female clothing in the later years of last century and the early years of this, appear, in the main, to have pursued their activities in isolation from other men who were similarly engaged. The other people who appear in these accounts are usually involved in aiding or witnessing the cross-dressing rather than cross-dressing themselves.

There is some evidence that around this time a number of informal networks of cross-dressers were emerging but it was not until the 1960s that these became more formalised and extensive (King, 1993: Chapter 5). The male femalers who provided the material on which Richard Ekins' analysis is based had available a wide range of organisations and settings in which to pursue their activities along with others in similar situations. By contrast, there has been little available to the 'female maler', who has often been forced to carve a small niche in the world of the male femaler. This is reflected in the literature, which is only concerned, therefore, with male femalers. In that literature we can discern two types of community.

The first type of community covers a range of small communities which

49

seem to be centrally concerned with doing rather than being, with celebrating and enjoying the artistic possibilities and the pleasures of cross-dressing and its associated sexual and other activities. In some cases such communities may be occupational ones concerned for example with prostitution (Perkins, 1983) or female impersonation (Newton, 1979). Some may be geographically located in those areas associated with deviant sexuality which are to be found in most large cities – Soho in London, Kings Cross in Sydney, the Tenderloin in San Francisco.

The members of these communities are full-time 'outsiders', living out their gender 'deviance' in 'deviant' ways – stripping, engaging in prostitution, performing as female impersonators in bars and night-clubs (Driscoll, 1971; Kando, 1973). They may also be involved in drug use or petty theft. This type of community is not consciously organised as such, although particular aspects of it will obviously require organisation of some kind. It depends primarily on face-to-face contact and is not literate in the sense that its members are concerned more with enjoyment, expression or practice than with analysis or remote communication. The 'outpourings' of such a culture are in the form and language of art – the photograph (Goldberg, 1993; Kay, 1976; Kirk and Heath, 1984; Berg, 1982; Mark, 1982; Newman, 1984); the novel (Marlowe, 1969; Rechy, 1964).

Chapter 4 is an extract from Roberta Perkins' book, *The 'Drag Queen' Scene*. It provides an excellent example of this first type of community. Despite the title,[2] this is actually a serious sociological study of a community of transsexual showgirls, strippers and prostitutes in the Kings Cross area of Sydney in the early 1980s. 'The girls on the street no longer work in the same area and are now overrun by transient cross-dressers. The strip clubs have fewer "trannies" and those who do work are now identified as "transvestites"' (Perkins, personal communication, 1995). The chapter does, however, give a particularly sophisticated account of that period of transition when closeted 'trannies' are no longer prepared to be subsumed within the gay subculture but are not yet ready to come out in the open everywhere.

The second type of community is that described by Feinbloom (1976), Talamini (1982) and Woodhouse (1989). This is not delineated by a geographical area and its members are not full-time 'outsiders'. They come together because they feel they share a common problem, one which is often hidden from the members of the other social worlds within which the major part of their lives is lived. If and when their lives do become organised around their gender deviance, this happens still within 'respectable' worlds, not the 'underworld' of prostitution or stripping. This community is more centrally concerned with individual being or identity. It has been consciously engineered in relation to the terms supplied by modern medicine. It is a literate community, since one of its central characteristics is the production of written accounts of its aims, policies and activities. It does not depend on face-to-face contact (although this does, of course, take place), since membership depends not on doing but on identity. It is possible to live in remote parts, never meet another member, yet to feel a part of a community to which one is linked by the written word. Such a community is thus less locally based than the first type and its potential membership much larger. It forms a national and even international network of those who identify with the terms 'transvestite' or 'transsexual'.

In Chapter 5, Neil Buhrich provides a detailed illustration of this second type of community. He describes a club for heterosexual transvestites, which is centrally concerned with fostering a particular and 'respectable' conception of transvestite being or identity. The club promulgates its viewpoint to the general public and professional bodies, and is affiliated to a world-wide network of similar organisations, which grew initially from the seed of Virginia Prince's Foundation for Full Personality Expression (FPE) organisation in North America.

In Chapter 6, the self-proclaimed 'gender transient' Phaedra Kelly gives an insider's view of a drag ball at London's Porchester Hall. Such events provide occasions when members of the two types of community which we have described may come together. The chapter sets forth a particularly vivid series of vignettes depicting the many facets of gender blending on public display at drag balls of this type.

NOTES

1 Hooker defines a community as, 'an aggregate of persons engaging in common activities, sharing common interests and having a feeling of sociopsychological unity' (Hooker, 1970: 118).
2 An inter-library loan request for this book by one of the editors was returned with a note saying that the service could not be used for books such as this. A copy was obtained when the serious and non-pornographic nature of the book was explained.

4

THE 'DRAG QUEEN' SCENE
Transsexuals in Kings Cross*
Roberta Perkins

THE TRANSSEXUAL COMMUNITY AND SUBCULTURE

The transsexual community in the Kings Cross and Darlinghurst area is divisible into four subgroups: the showgirls, the strippers, the prostitutes and the girls who pick up men in bars. While there is some overlap, and some girls have belonged to all four of these groups at different times, by and large they operate as separate social entities. The base on which each subgroup is structured is economic in that the girls tend to interrelate with one another as an extension of their working lives. The 'activities' and 'territorial spaces' (Clarke et al., 1976) are distinctive for each subgroup. For showgirls these are activities connected with 'female impersonation' entertainment and with the customers after the show. In addition, they tend to socialise with each other at parties, when going out and by visiting each others' flats. 'Territorial spaces' are more or less fixed upon the places where they work and meet. Much the same can be said of the strippers, whose activities and spaces centre on the strip clubs in which they work. In the case of the prostitutes and bar girls, however, whose activities are a little more fluid and spaces less fixed in that working together is a less cooperative activity, each girl is not bound to a specific corner or street, bar or hotel, although waiting for a client or a pick-up is something they all do in common.

Despite these differences I consider the transsexual community to be a single subculture. For one thing 'material artefacts' are the same in all the subgroups. These are the dress and make-up fashions which are borrowed directly from the wider culture. There is no particular style of dress that is peculiar to either the subgroups or subculture, as in so many youth cults. 'Values' also tend to be emulations of the wider culture, although these often tend to be exaggerated and stereotyped norms of bourgeois

• This chapter first appeared in *The 'Drag Queen' Scene: Transsexuals in Kings Cross*, Hemel Hempstead: Allen & Unwin, 1982, pp. 21–31.

behavioural patterns. Both the artefacts and values are selected to suit a narrower set of tastes than that of the cultural source, which is probably due to close contact and influences between members of the same subgroup.

There is an acceptance of, if not a strict adherence to, bourgeois ethics and values within the transsexual community. These are assumptions which are rarely questioned in the subculture and, quite unlike the counter-cultural reactions of the various 'beat' generation subcultures to middle-class values or gang rebellion as a protest against working-class oppression, the girls generally strive for approval by adopting middle-class standards. Although most of the girls come from working-class backgrounds (the showgirls are predominantly middle class) their links with middle-class values have evolved because of day-to-day contacts with middle-class men, clients and show patrons. The subculture, or rather its standards, are derived from a middle-class 'parent' culture. Money and material possessions have high places in the value system, as has work as 'an achiever', although the one exception here might be the methods employed in acquiring money by many of the bar girls who make a living out of socialising in hotels. The methods of interacting with men, in particular, mirrors the attitudes of the middle class, for example, by following the behavioural patterns of heterosexual niceties over a drink.

The transsexual subculture is not simply 'loosely defined strands ... within the parent culture' and it has a 'distinctive world' of its own. Yet it follows no strict code of ritual and symbolism of the sort that marks the relatively closed youth cult communities. Nevertheless, it does possess a recognisable style rhetoric and set of mannerisms that may be loosely termed the 'symbolism' of its members, and which sets it apart from other subcultures. This gives it an identity, although it may not be immediately apparent to the outsider who walks into a 'drag' bar without prior knowledge.

On the other hand, the subculture is not 'tightly bounded' in that outsiders are not entirely unwelcome. Men in general are indeed an essential part of it and boyfriends, gay men and others are not excluded. But these tend always to be marginal participants; the girls remain the core. To be one of the girls is not difficult for a male-to-female transsexual, so long as she is reasonably fashionable, reasonably 'passable' as a girl, sexually attracted to men and willing to mix with the other girls in her leisure time. Friendships between the girls come and go, and range from intimate to superficial. Close friendships tend to occur more often among the showgirls, and friendships are generally more fluid among bar girls. The prostitutes seem to develop close ties less often than the other subgroups. In all the subgroups the networks of friends and inter-relationships are never wide. In one sense there is support within each subgroup, especially when a girl is being threatened by an outsider, whereupon the others will rally around. But many of the girls complain of bitchiness within the group. With so much low self-esteem, insecurity and superficial props, hostility that is internalised as a result of individual sufferings, when it does surface, tends to be aimed laterally at one another, rather than vertically in the direction of the real source of their oppression. Perhaps each girl sees in the others a reflection of herself and a reminder of her guilt as the reason she has been made to suffer. It is this sort of divisiveness, along with a genuine fear of suffering further humiliation, that keeps the girls as a community from openly campaigning for legal reform and cultivating public sympathy and support.

The transsexual community is the common 'meeting ground' that loosely links the subgroups together. The similar personal experiences of each girl give her a unique 'sympatico' and sense of common suffering with every other girl of her subgroup or other subgroups. It was these experiences that drew transsexuals together in the first place, from which emerged the community as it exists today which acts as a haven and refuge from their individual isolation and felt oppression in the wider society. Many of these girls have been cast out of their parental homes or have left because of pressure from their families. However, rather than a community of supportive people cooperating to offer a united front and to close ranks against the oppression, what has occurred is a community of guilt-ridden, fearful and divided people, who can be scorned, laughed at and jeered at as one. Society's treatment of the transsexual community acts as a conspicuous object lesson to any male who expresses even the slightest dissatisfaction with the male sex-role. The community also serves as a sexual ghetto from which respectable suburban males can take their pick whenever they feel the urges of the 'natural male sexual impulse' coming on.

The transsexual community and subculture is a modern urban phenomenon which has developed since the reforming movements of the 1960s and the redefining of 'homosexuality' by the gay community, which has forced transsexuals to find their own point of reference outside gay lifestyles. In Sydney the community is centred in Kings Cross and Darlinghurst, but this is not to imply that it is the home of most of Sydney's transsexuals. Indeed, it probably represents less than half of Sydney's population of around 500 transsexuals. There are many transsexuals who live and work in the suburbs, undifferentiated from the general population and who have little affinity with the showgirls, strippers, prostitutes and bar girls of King Cross, apart from recognising them as transsexuals as they themselves are. Of Harry Benjamin's (Benjamin, 1966) patients, only ten were entertainers and three prostitutes, while the other thirty-eight worked as clerks, typists, hairdressers, housewives and other female-oriented occupations at the time of their sex-change operations. These figures would indicate that for a transsexual being a showgirl or hooker is not the most sought-after occupation in America any more than Australia. But it must also be pointed out that some girls, in or out of the community, reduce ridicule and the risks of violence by restricting themselves to a narrow living space of home, workplace and the corner shop.

HIERARCHY AND ORDER

It became apparent after a few interviews that some of the girls tended to see themselves as a part of a hierarchical structure ordered according to the status of each subgroup. But there was a lot of disagreement as to exactly how the structure was ordered. One of the showgirls saw it this way:

> I think the people you would admire – at the top – are the people you rarely see. They are the ones who live in the suburbs with super-straight jobs. Then, I would say, showgirls come after that. But there are different types of shows and these are ranked. If you've made it to one of the established shows people will say, 'Wow! You've really made it'. But if you're in a smaller show, just hitting the clubs and without the money to spend on costumes, that's another step down. Again, if you're accepted by the establishment showgirl, like the star, then you're looked up to, and this depends a lot on ability, beauty and intelligence. Girls who work in straight drag shows and those who work in gay shows are on the same level, but with all the girls it's a graduated scale with the stars and legendary figures up at the top, then people who are coming up and then the newcomers – kids who are trying to work their way up. After the showgirls come the strippers, and they are a world of their own. Then I'd say the parlour girls, followed by the street girls. But there is a whole hierarchy just among prostitutes. I think the girls who work from bars would follow the street girls. Then you get the weekenders who throw a frock on for a night and have a lovely time, but this depends on how good they look – and whether they are affected or outrageous decides how well they are accepted.

Another showgirl saw it quite differently:

> As a showgirl I don't think I am superior to a stripper or a whore. I can't put it into categories because each job is entirely different, yet within that job there are rankings – you're a good stripper or a lousy stripper, you're a good whore or a bad whore. The only hierarchy is within those segments because they are each aiming for something different, aren't they?

I asked a prostitute if she thought there was a hierarchy.

We're all transsexuals regardless of what we do for a living. But showgirls always like to think they are at the top, yet they forget that a lot of them have been out there on the street making it for a living. They look down on us with their tits and feathers, but we're the ones with the money. We can make in a night what they make in a week. The showgirls are the only ones who think there is a hierarchy. The strippers probably do too, but they don't look down on us as much as the showgirls, and besides many of them are lining up their next mug while they're stripping.

Another prostitute thought the hierarchy was based on how the girl conducts herself, and divided everyone into two basic categories.

Nobody looks up to anybody else – because she is a showgirl doing a glamorous job or a prostitute earning a lot of money. I mean, I don't look up to the showgirls, why should I? And they don't look up to me, and why should they? I think there are high-class showgirls and there are high-class prostitutes, and there are low-class showgirls and low-class prostitutes. Just because you work on the streets doesn't mean you can't be classy.

According to one girl who was working as a waitress in a place which ran a regular drag show, there is an order of succession to becoming a showgirl. It begins with a girl waitressing and, after a period of time, she graduates to a place in the show, beginning as just a chorus girl and ending up with a feature spot. But, according to this girl, it doesn't happen quickly enough. Once on the stage, the girls do not often leave as opportunities elsewhere are very limited. Whenever a vacancy does occur, more often than not it is filled by an experienced showgirl, so some of the waitresses who have been patiently waiting for the opportunity to move up become frustrated and leave. Thus, according to her, the 'floor to stage' progression is a carrot on a string which the management dangles before a whole line of starstruck girls. Since job opportunities for transsexuals are almost non-existent and given the constant fear of ridicule and rejection in the outside world, most of these girls have little alternative but to accept meagre rates of pay.

From what I could gather, a ranking order of subgroups was seen to exist by most of the girls, but it differed considerably depending on the criterion used. It might be seen in any of the three systems shown in the table overleaf.

The urban 'drag queen' scene consists of a number of components each coming together within the setting of Kings Cross and adjacent Darlinghurst. The transsexual subculture is the core component, with its transsexual community divided, as we have seen, into four subgroups – showgirls, strippers, bar girls and prostitutes – and with its 'marginal

According to prestige	According to financial gain	According to success at 'passing' as girls
Showgirls	Street girls	Strippers
Strippers	Call girls	Call girls
Call girls	Strippers	Bar girls
Bar girls	Showgirls	Street girls
Street girls	Bar girls	Showgirls

participants', such as boyfriends and other friends. More peripheral, but nevertheless essential, are the show patrons, strip club patrons, the male 'pick-ups' of bargirls and the clients of prostitutes. There are other components in the scene with an even more marginal position, and these include the police, residents and visitors to Kings Cross. Finally, there is the component of space, where the interactions between the different human components take place, such as the venues of the drag shows, the strip clubs, the hotels and bars, and the streets.

To most people who interact with the drag scene fleetingly, the nucleus of the community is seen as an image carried inside their heads rather than individuals with separate self-perceptions. This image is of a highly made-up tart who loves to 'put on a show' for everyone and spends every waking hour thinking of nothing but sex; a weak, simple-minded male, who can't cope in the tough world of manhood. Though far from the truth, none the less it is a common notion of the drag queen. She is a creature of the 'glittertown' atmosphere. She serves to titillate voyeurs, sexual fantasisers and an assortment of perverts, and she also provides a sexual outlet for frustrated males. But she is also seen as a threat to the ideals of masculinity and the gender dichotomy. Thus, by stigmatising her in the same way as gays, she serves as an example to males who might step out of line. This then pushes her into a position where she can best be an avenue for capitalist exploitation. If she attempts self-employment as a prostitute, she'll be subject to the financial demands of a pimp or a member of the local constabulary. She cannot avoid the constant demand for court fines, or an occasional term in gaol. She is often forced from the streets into the bars to work where a ready clientele is gathered and business booms for the proprietors. In this two-way enterprise everyone gains but the girl herself. At her slightest whimper of complaint she is met by a barrage of voices: 'Well, she's only a drag queen', and in this context the term means 'non-person'.

UP THE CROSS

Kings Cross beckons the visitor to Sydney from one end of the broad arm of William Street, which links it with the city centre. Affectionately called 'the Cross' by Sydneysiders, it is the metropolis's sexual playground; everything else that goes on there takes second place for the suburbanite and visitor. A stranger who stumbles into the area without prior knowledge of this is quickly made aware of it. Strip clubs, sex shops and street girls are the most conspicuous elements of the commercial end of Darlinghurst Road. And there, at the centre, in large neon letters above the street are the words 'Les Girls – World Famous All-Male Revue', the most popular drag show venue in the Cross.

I asked a number of visitors from Europe, America and interstate about their impressions of the Cross. Most agreed that the prostitutes are an important element, but others thought the buskers are important too, and still others considered the drag queens of equal importance. Here are a few comments on the latter:

'Drag queens are fun.'

'Drag queens are an important part of the Cross, part of anywhere.'

'Drag queens add to the colour.'

'Drag queens are the main attraction.'

'Drag queens are pretty weird. You see very few in Soho.'

Nearly everyone I spoke to thought that taken together the prostitutes, buskers and drag queens gave the place flavour, colour and personality. Almost every visitor I interviewed agreed that the Cross is expensive. 'A good place if you've got money', said one couple. One young man from Melbourne put it this way: 'It's a big rip-off'. General impressions varied:

'Good. Lively. There are things here you can't get in the country.'
'Great, love it. The Cross is unique. Lot's of action, crazy people.'
'Wonderful variety of people. Pros, drag queens, buskers, punk rockers, I think they're all wonderful. Reminds me a lot of 'Frisco.'
'Night life, fantastic. I lose track of time here after dark.'
'Exciting place. More laughs than anywhere else.'
'Shit-hot place. It's like watching a big TV screen.'

Some people were not so positive about the place.

'They're a lot of weirdos. Great place to visit, but not to live.'
'Some people look as though they're haunted.'
'Not as good as it used to be. A lot tougher now, not so eccentric.'
'It's a fucking hole. A good place to get crabs.'

Perhaps the general feeling about Kings Cross can be summed up in these three comments: 'It's the heart of Australian night life'; 'The Cross really opens your eyes to life'; 'I couldn't live here – there's just too many people'.

Just how many people? The Cross and including the adjoining inner suburban areas of Potts Point and Elizabeth Bay (although many residents of these two areas would deny they are associated with Kings Cross in anyway at all), covers some sixty-four hectares and, according to the 1976 census, had a residential population of around 11,000, which gives it an average density of 172 people per hectare. This is considered to be Sydney's most highly concentrated residential area. But this figure, by itself, does not account for the large shifting population that lives in one-room flatettes, in the backstreets of the Cross and in abandoned tenement houses as illegal squatters. These people are not hard to find. They include the derelicts who lie in the well-lit railway station entrance and sleep in darkened alleys; the kids who shuffle aimlessly from fun parlour to fun parlour; and the prostitutes who are conspicuous everywhere. They include, too, the relatively few young transsexuals who live semi-nomadic lives moving from flat to flat almost on a monthly basis.

To these people the Cross represents a light in the darkness of their everyday lives. To the derelicts it is the sound if not the touch of human life; to the youths cast out of unhappy homes, it is the comfort of others like themselves who are confused by the rigidity and lack of understanding of adults; to young transsexuals it is their place of reference in society, where at least there is a token acceptance. The Cross is a human collage, a meeting place of society's non-conformists, where non-conformity is accepted. But this acceptance exists only under the terms of exploitation, whether this be pushing drugs, the entrepreneurial activity of showgirls, sexual exploitation of prostitutes and strippers or visitors seeking the outlet of voyeurism in an effort to escape the mundane life of conformity. Those who live in the Cross as the non-conformists are inevitably at the end of a vast chain of exploitation, so that in order to survive they have to depend on degrading work, low-paying activities, hand-outs and socially disapproved methods of getting money.

There is, however, another important aspect of Kings Cross that is often less conspicuous than these non-conformists who roam the streets and frequent the bright lights of the commercial centre, and this is what one social worker who has been working in the Cross for twelve years describes as 'the silent majority; the marginal residential population who do not move about'. This includes the wealthy people who would vehemently claim they are not part of 'the Cross'. The Australian Bureau of Statistics give a population figure for 1981 of 16,740 for the total area of Kings Cross itself, Potts Point, Elizabeth Bay, Woolloomooloo and Rushcutters Bay, a large proportion of whom are the high-rise and waterfront apartment dwellers whose quiet, luxurious and established lives stand in direct contrast to the unsettled, shifting and uncertain lives of the conspicuous minority – the derelicts, the runaway kids, the prostitutes and the young transsexuals. Thus, the Cross is a microcosm of the socio-economic spectrum of Australia; two minutes walk away from each other one may see the inhuman shapes of the rich, plush apartment houses on the one side, and the gutter and sidewalk dwellers on the other.

Each of the various groups on the socio-economic scale in the Kings Cross area has its own social space. So far as the transsexuals are concerned the venues they frequent vary considerably, depending on the type of clientele, and the outsiders who come to these places for one reason or another. At the top end of the scale is one nightclub which caters for a mixed patronage of tourists and non-regulars, middle class in appearance and mostly in groups. The surroundings are fairly plush and the lighting soft. The interiors are neither showy nor glittery, but create an illusion of expense and exclusivity. The atmosphere is low-key, and there is usually a battery of bouncers, not inconspicuously dressed in dinner jackets and black tie, who make certain it stays that way. The costs of shows and dinner are built into the entry charge. Drinks are extra and more expensive here than in bars, but compare favourably with other clubs. The first show begins late at night while the third, and last, ends in the early morning hours, and then a songster and keyboard player take patrons through to dawn with a string of favourites and evergreens. The impression the place conveys is of giving good value for money and that the club represents 'the good life'.

At the other end of the scale is a sidestreet bar, where drinks are relatively inexpensive and the clientele is exclusively a cross-section of heterosexual males on the prowl. There is no pretence here, no attempt to disguise the true nature of the place. With its dim red and yellow lighting, jukebox disco music, scantily clad (and sometimes nude) girls parading, revealing their wares before the machismo onlookers – a definite 'see before you buy' approach – it simply oozes sex. The girls are on tap, rooms are provided, at a price, for any male who wishes to go the whole way with the girl sitting next to him without having to leave the premises. This is sexual exploitation at its most blatant.

In some of the places of employment wages are poor for transsexuals, as in the case of the waitresses who are waiting to move into stage performance. Job insecurity often creates tensions among the staff; as another waitress told me: 'I could get put off tomorrow and not get any pay in lieu whatsoever'. The prospects of finding work elsewhere for a transsexual are very limited. Life at the top is hardly any better, since the showgirls too are paid low wages for the long hours they work, and this payment does not include daytime rehearsals. In addition, there is the ever-present threat of dismissal, with a string of waitresses eager to demonstrate that they can do better. One club decided to alter its entire show format, dismissing its entire troupe at short notice. The retrenched girls were out of work for some months as the other drag shows had no vacancies and no new ones opened up. Job risk, insecurity and exploitation are part and parcel of the way of life for many of the girls in the Cross.

The Kings Cross area as a sexual playground caters mainly to middle-class male tastes and the men go there because sex is easily available. It attracts many suburbanites because it offers excitement and an escape from the boredom of outer-suburban life. They, may also come 'to see how the other half lives', or to watch the 'freaks in the human zoo'. But to many who live and work there the Cross is no carnival. It is a genuine refuge for the stigmatised and for the sexually frustrated.

The drag queen scene is only one of a number of scenes that are to be found in the Cross, but it is an important one, which for many people adds a definite colour and flavour to the area. Some passers-by refer to the girls within earshot as 'drag queens' or 'queers' or 'poofters' or 'sick' in such a way that they cannot miss hearing it. But, as every girl knows, those people who are loudest in their condemnation in the company of their peers are very likely to be the ones most enjoying their own voyeurism and the same men who, once alone, provide her with temporary sex liaisons.

5

A HETEROSEXUAL
TRANSVESTITE CLUB *

Neil Buhrich

HISTORY OF THE CLUB

In 1970, a founding member returned from the USA where he obtained knowledge of the American transvestite club, Full Personality Expression (FPE) founded by Virginia Prince in the early 1950s. He placed an advertisement in the *Daily Telegraph* seeking a response from 'T.V. enthusiasts who would like to meet and discuss more on the subject'.

Most of the replies were from people wishing to join a club for television enthusiasts. Several replies were from transvestites. The first meeting took place in a member's vacant flat in June 1971. Four people attended. Guidelines for the club were drawn up. It was

> dedicated to the needs of heterosexual transvestites who had become
> aware of the other side of their personality and sought to express
> it. We do not condemn or judge the areas of homosexuality, bondage,
> domination, or fetishism, these are left to others.

The club was named after the seahorse because it is 'a rather delightful creature, a trifle slow but with graceful movement and quiet dignity' and because of its 'combination, at times, of both gender-roles'. In February 1972 wives and girlfriends of members were allowed to attend club meetings. More recently children and parents have also been accepted. In August 1973 a branch of the club was founded in Melbourne. At present the club has over 250 members and branches in all Australian capitals. There are no female transvestite members in the club. The existence of female heterosexual transvestism has been questioned (Benjamin, 1967b).

The club's magazine, *Feminique*, was first published in March 1972. Editions are printed three or four times a year. *Feminique* contains letters

* This chapter first appeared as part of 'A heterosexual transvestite club: psychiatric aspects', *Australian and New Zealand Journal of Psychiatry*, 1976, 10: 331–5. The research was carried out while the author was a Research Fellow of the New South Wales Institute of Psychiatry. The project was supported by a National Health and Medical Research Council Grant. The assistance of Associate Professor Neil McConaghy is gratefully acknowledged. The author would like to thank the Seahorse Club for its cooperation.

to the 'editress', short stories by and about transvestites, advice on make-up, a list of shops where transvestites can buy clothes and information as to how transvestites can correspond with each other.

CLUB RULES

The magazine states the rules of etiquette for club meetings. Members are expected to cross-dress for meetings and changing rooms are provided for those who cannot arrive cross-dressed. Members are asked to cross-dress with taste.

> We all admire women and want to emulate them . . . your favourite thing may be a tassled stripper's costume, but do not expect much acceptance of this . . . observe the dictates of good taste . . . avoid extremes, do not display your lingerie. These rules should apply whether women are present or not.

CONFIDENTIALITY

Security is strict. Anybody can write and become an affiliate member. To become a full member one must first be interviewed by an executive member. If accepted, full name and address must be given for the club's files. At the meetings members address each other by their feminine names, both for reasons of confidentiality and for the pleasure of being addressed as a woman. The female name chosen is often a modification of their given name, e.g., Paul – Paula, Warren – Wendy. Hirschfeld (1938) has called this 'name transvestism'.

THE CLUB MEETINGS

Members meet once a month in one of the several members' homes. The homes are chosen for their seclusion. Curtains are drawn during the meetings. On entering, the first impact is somewhat startling. Large women, overdressed in evening gowns, are standing about as if at a quiet semi-formal cocktail party. On closer examination the more angular facial features, the large feet and hands with their prominent veins and the protruding laryngeal processes make it obvious that these are men dressed as women. This is confirmed when they speak using normal masculine voices. It can be quite disconcerting, having been introduced previously to a man with a man's name, to be then introduced to the same person dressed as a woman with a woman's name. If one mistakenly addresses the subject by his male name, one is quickly corrected: 'The name is Cathy not Chris'. In time it becomes quite easy to use the male or female name depending on how the subject is dressed.

Members may take up to three hours to dress for meetings. They look forward to them with enthusiasm. Beards are closely shaved or removed by applying melted wax which is pulled off when it has solidified. The most popular dress materials worn by members are satin, silk, nylon or other 'feminine' materials. Corduroy, leather and denim are almost never worn. For the uncertain, the club journal gives hints on what to wear to meetings: 'Terrace wear, patio gowns, the short cocktail dress or normal day wear. The gown or dress you will feel most comfortable and relaxed in is likely to be the best choice.' The members' ages vary from 20 to 70 years. Most cross-dress in clothes suitable to their age. Some members wear clothes which were fashionable in their youth and which now look out of date. Others favour a particular style, a mini skirt or somewhat tartish dress, worn with heavy make-up. In general, the clothes worn are sedate, semi-formal and expensive. All wear female shoes, a wig and make-up and have feminine accessories such as a necklace, bangle, brooch or wristwatch.

Although members speak in their normal masculine voices some attempt, by speaking softly, to sound more feminine. They may also, by looking directly at the person to whom they are speaking, increase the effect of cues such as hair and make-up and thereby distract attention from their deep voice. The pitch of the voice is never raised. One newly arrived member, initially speaking with a high-pitched voice, was most relieved when club members replied with their normal voices. Apart from this aspect of speech, an attempt is usually made to imitate women as accurately as possible. No members have a mincing gait or flamboyant gestures and no attempt is made to caricature film stars or ladies of high fashion. Sequins, coloured hair, tight low-cut dresses and silver eye shadow are not worn. The atmosphere is quiet and relaxed. Members maintain that they feel comfortable even though they admit that their shoes may be too tight or that undergarments are stretched tightly to diminish their waist size. Most sit with their legs together or stand primly holding a small glass of wine. A minority do not pose as women but sit or stand as they normally would as men. Although fetishistic aspects of transvestism are emphasised in the literature (Benjamin, 1967b; Stoller, 1971), the primary reason for cross-dressing reported by club members is not that it produces fetishistic arousal but that it makes them feel natural and relaxed. Conversation covers many topics and no pretence is made to camouflage masculine hobbies or occupations. Two ex-first-grade footballers regularly discuss games they have played. Another member relates how he ejected from his jet aeroplane during the Korean war and survived the dangers of the China Sea. Two members race sports cars, three others have aeroplane licences and one is a professional cyclist. All types of occupations are represented, with the bias towards those requiring higher education. None work in what are popularly regarded as occupations containing an unusually high proportion of homosexuals, such as hairdressing, window-dressing or acting.

Members frequently discuss their female clothes – where to buy them, how to make them and what they have purchased. Relating experiences which have occurred while cross-dressed in public are popular. The anecdotes are often told humorously. One member described his visit to a male toilet while cross-dressed. A man, on coming out of the cubicle and seeing the 'woman', was highly embarrassed and apologised profusely. (The decision whether to use a male lavatory is difficult for a transvestite. If caught by the police in either situation he may be suspected of a misdemeanor. Wanting to void is the explanation least likely to be accepted.) Another member described how a neighbour had often seen him leave the house cross-dressed. The neighbour eventually plucked up the courage to approach him. They discussed the weather, car engines and the cricket but the neighbour never enquired why this 6ft. 1in. man was repairing his car engine while dressed fully in women's clothes. On another occasion a member greeted a friend from the club in a department store. He was surprised to see his friend become very anxious, looking from side to side and obviously trying to escape. His friend had failed to recognise him in his male clothes. Transvestites report that it is especially pleasurable to be mistaken for a woman in public. The Abbé de Choisy, a transvestite, in his autobiography written in the seventeenth century (Scott, 1973) described the intense pleasure of being mistaken for a woman. Conversations are never sexually titillating and no attempt is made to appear seductive. There are no sexual innuendoes to conversation nor are sexual jokes made unless they are very bland.

Later in the evening members may dance. The transvestites dance with women. Women may dance with each other but the author has never seen a transvestite dance with another transvestite. This underlying acceptance of maleness can also be observed at restaurant outings, where the members, although dressed as women, alternate with their wives when sitting at the table. Meals are served and drinks poured in the sequence of women first, transvestites next and normally dressed men last.

Some sort of entertainment is often arranged for club meetings. A hairdresser or beauty expert may be invited to demonstrate his techniques to club members. A game, based on snakes and ladders is played. In this game a dice is thrown and depending on where the tor lands the player must give an explanation of such situations as 'You are in a train carriage in your negligee when the conductor comes in – explain'; 'You are trying on high-heeled boots in a department store when, on looking up, you see your boss doing the same thing – explain'; 'While fully cross-dressed you are stopped by a policeman and on getting out of the car your wig falls off – explain'. Club reviews are popular and these are arranged about three times per year. Considerable preparation is made for them. They are an excuse for members to dress up several times in the evening and act out the fantasy of portraying a favourite actress or interpreting a song. Licence is given for more daring costumes. The costumes, however, are not worn to seduce the audience but more for the narcissistic pleasure of the 'actress' to be acclaimed as a beautiful and successful star. There is an old-fashioned quality about the material used. Typical songs are those sung by Julie Andrews, Marilyn Monroe, Jeanette McDonald, Mae West and the Andrews Sisters. The songs are usually mimed.

Prizes are given for the best act and for the most convincing transvestite appearance. Movie film and photographs are taken. The film without sound may be shown at future meetings to the great interest of the participants.

Meetings often draw to a close in the early hours of the morning. Members are rarely intoxicated. Some members change before leaving, slipping their 'sister' back into their suitcase, while others more courageous leave cross-dressed, feeling somewhat exhilarated by the risk of being caught.

ACTIVITIES APART FROM MEETINGS

One restaurant is regularly frequented. A private room is booked. Members cross-dress carefully for the occasion, usually arriving in company of their wife or girlfriend. On other occasions three or four members eat in a more exposed restaurant. Here they may have sarcastic or jibing remarks directed at them. These they accept with amused tolerance and the experience may form the basis for future transvestite anecdotes. Group outings to theatre productions with transvestite themes are popular. Semi-public fancy-dress parties are used as an excuse to cross-dress, sometimes less sedately than at club meetings. They are aware of their motives for going and feel nothing in common with the 'drag queens' who are often present at these functions. If a man asks them to dance, they may consent but any sexual advances are sternly rejected.

AIMS OF THE CLUB

The club has several aims. Primarily, it gives members an opportunity to appear fully cross-dressed in a semi-public situation without fear of ridicule. Acceptance into the club does not depend on the 'ability to look like a beautiful woman – heaven help 75 per cent of the members if it did'. Inexperienced members are given hints on how to apply make-up or dress more convincingly. Information about techniques for removing facial hair and where to buy dresses is exchanged. Members travelling interstate are given contact addresses and welcomed to meetings.

Club members are aware that transvestism can be a great strain on a marriage. No attempt is made to dissuade members from cross-dressing.

Instead, their wives or girlfriends are invited to club meetings in the hope, often fulfilled, that they will establish friendships with other couples. Women are fully accepted in club activities, taking part in entertainment and outings. To cushion the impact of the first meeting, 'straight parties' are arranged for new members and their women partners. At these gatherings nobody cross-dresses. Club members' attire show no evidence of the care and effort made when they dress as women. Apart from long finger-nails members show no evidence of effeminacy. Compared to the monthly transvestite meetings, more beer is consumed. The topics of conversation tend to be the same at both meetings. Wives who feel too uncomfortable to accompany their husbands while he is cross-dressed often attend.

Another aim of the club is to disseminate information about transvestism to the general public and professional bodies. Articles are written for newspapers and magazines. Interviews are given on radio and television by those transvestites who are prepared to 'come out'.

SIGNIFICANCE OF THE CLUB

The rapid growth of club membership appears to be due to a number of factors. A large number of transvestites exist. Ellis and Abarbanel (1961) suggest an incidence of 1–3 per cent, but do not provide the data on which they based this figure. Transvestites find after a time that dressing alone is no longer sufficiently satisfying. Club meetings provide an opportunity to cross-dress and be seen by others. Transvestites have an urge to meet other people like themselves and come to a better understanding of their condition. Recent media coverage has made many transvestites aware of the existence of the club.

Most transvestites think their condition will disappear after marriage and do not inform their wives about it prior to marriage. In fact, many wives do not know of their husband's transvestism even after years of marriage. Transvestites who present for treatment have usually been coerced by their wives. They are ambivalent about being cured. The suggestion that they wear feminine-looking shirts or 'unisex' clothes holds no interest for them. To satisfy his urge the transvestite must fully and without compromise be dressed as a woman.

A few transvestites attend one meeting and find that they do not need to come again for many months. Many come regularly to monthly meetings and do not cross-dress at other times. However, it is not uncommon for them, on meeting transvestites with a more convincing appearance than themselves, to have their own transvestite urges reinforced. They may begin to dress more often at home or want to be seen publicly dressed as a woman. Whatever the outcome, the transvestites almost always report that they are happier, more relaxed and more able to accept their condition.

The outcome for the wife of the transvestite may not be as satisfactory. Many tolerate their husband's cross-dressing, lending him clothes, perhaps attending meetings or even accompanying him in public when he cross-dressed. Others cannot learn to accept their husband's femininity: 'I married a man and he wants to be a woman'. Even the knowledge that her husband cross-dresses somewhere else is impossible for some wives to accept. In these cases the transvestite very rarely feels able to cease cross-dressing altogether, and the marriage usually becomes strained.

A minority of couples have informed their children of the father's transvestism. The children have appeared either indifferent or accepting of it. The ease with which children overtly accept their father's transvestism depends on their pre-existing relationship. Their main concern is that other children may tease them about their father's behaviour.

Although transvestites greatly fear public exposure and ridicule, all those who have informed friends about their transvestism have found them to be intrigued but accepting of it.

Not all transvestites are suitable for referral to the club. Transvestites with a sociopathic personality or who are psychotic, 'drag queens' and most transsexuals are not accepted. Transsexuals have as their primary goal a change-of-sex operation. They aim to live permanently as women. Transsexuals who have attended club meetings feel that they 'do not belong'. They consider that, unlike them, club members are only 'playing at being women', that they overemphasize clothes and do not have a complete feminine gender identity. However, some transsexuals who have come to terms with their inability to have a change-of-sex operation, either because of refusal on medical grounds or family commitments, learn to enjoy club meetings and find in regular attendance some substitute for their real desire.

6

LONDON GRANDEUR
The Porchester Ball*
Phaedra Kelly

The Porchester Hall is a massive Victorian structure which dominates a quarter of the lower side of the aptly named Queensway, in the heart of Bayswater's embassy land – an area more famous for the violent siege that lead to the sniper killing of woman police constable Yvonne Fletcher. A few yards down the road is the embassy where hostages were dramatically freed by the SAS using stun grenades as they dangled from the roof on ropes, to the balcony below. Around the corner lives my friend Odette Tchernine, a frail elderly spinster of whom you would never guess that she was a legend of the Fleet Street newspaper world, poetess and author, fellow of the Royal Geographical Society and pioneer hunter of the Yeti and sasquatch.

In the streets outside walk the rich and famous, the obscure and eccentric, people of all races, creeds and colours. Artists display their work along four miles of park railings, and gays and transgenderists of all callings walk free. Here, is where comedians have said, half in truth, that a young man of modest means can live like a queen. Here is where a dashingly dark Arab may treat you like a lady in the evening, lay you like a racehorse all night and, at dawn, put £4,000 into your palm for taxi fare – nobody expects the recipient to leave a tip that big for the cabby.

It's little wonder that it's a target also for bands of skinheads and muggers. But on certain nights, such low-lifes dive for cover, for, as every skinhead has learned, one angry trannie fights like a one-woman army – half a hundred or more, just riot!!

These are the nights of the Porchester Balls. The Hall's exterior shows signs of modernisation, but the music-hall style of the inside remains quaintly Victorian. It is not the most plush nor the newest, the vague scent of architectural decay lingers amid the perfumes and powders, but it has a well-loved atmosphere to the imaginative. Envision regal post-apocalyptic sets like the ruined casino in Kubrick's *A Clockwork Orange*,

---

* An earlier version of this chapter first appeared in *Lady Like*, no. 3, 1988, pp. 20–5. All photos courtesy of Phaedra Kelly and Chrysalis Magazine.

or perhaps the surreal/medieval of a corner of *The Company of Wolves* set, plus its unusual inhabitants. The sound is of a panic in a large bird aviary, and the sight suggests that every bird in it is an exotically plumed tropical. The more nervously cerebral have said that it reminds them of a movie version of a Francis Bacon painting. Hieronymus Bosch, to the less pessimistic viewer.

But I took it from the start for what it was, a gathering of clans for a fun informal night. The 'Stately Queens' were as elegantly austere as ever, but not taking themselves too seriously as they smiled and joked in character – 'Are they really burning Atlanta?' quoth one to me. Feeling as much the Scarlet as she, I declined the feedline and left her to her hunt for a less feminine Rhett Butler.

Here too, were nervous first-visit transvestites, insular individualist gender benders, garishly coloured and moustachioed gays, some of them from political drag theatre groups, and the more complete young cabaret club circuit acts in *diamanté* and gold lamé, fur and feathers evening dresses. Some of these were just hard workers on the road to the top, a few are already celebrated performers, like 'The Pure Corn Company', rough drag 'let's all scream our tits off' kind of folk who dye their moustaches bright colours and pose for pics, mouths agape in Hollywood parody. Their shows get good reviews for their campy monologues and sketches, a field all its own.

Ziggie Cartier, a tall, elegant mature blonde, experienced of club cabaret and a sometime 'counsellor' to lonely gentlemen and inexperienced TVs via her contact ad in her role as a queen of exotic love. Ziggie lately works the piano bars, as a genial hostess and performer, notably the now very famous Madame Jo-Jo's Piano Bar. TSs are well represented, and as many of the less notable or notorious ones are just as beautiful, just as convincingly woman all over. There are some, like Rital, who are on the periphery of fame. Rital is an ex-officer in the Greek navy, with a very feminine, bubbly disposition. Its often hard to photograph her for the men that cluster admiringly around her. She too, runs and performs in a piano bar.

I have met at balls in the past, April Ashley, UK's first most famous TS, and Tula Cossey, our second top celebrity famed as the 'James Bond Girl' for her brief walk-on part in *For Yours Eyes Only*. I can forgive her, for she is lovely, but she knocked the glamour out of me when we first met. Also, on the same night, I encountered the late Vikki de Lambray, sometimes called TS though nobody knows for sure, nor will they now. Vikki was to die a month later, the victim of an overdose of lethal heroin which many say was forced upon her, since she was implicated (as much by her own design) in the controversial Spycatcher affair. Vikki's claim was that she would be the most famous transgenderist ever and die dramatically at the age of 30. The latter she managed, the former she held for a week, having rung at last in desperation not the police, but her press agent to say the now famous words, 'I have been killed'.

Borderline in the drag queen area are 'Rebel Rebel', a cabaret mime trio who disdain the ball gown for modern leather minis, oft of their own design. Hard to choose, but their slender sultry leader, known contrastingly as Butch, presents the most glam image. Theirs are regular faces at balls. One of a similar kind, who has now made the grade was Alana Pellay, who swapped her drag for gender bending in the 1970s to join a punk band, 'Spit Like Paint'. That went nowhere in itself, but lead her on to join 'The Comic Strip', a clique of alternative comedy writers and performers whose hit series of the same name dominated BBC Channel 4 television into the 1980s. Now a post-op TS, Alana did the unexpected in starring in her first full length film, *Eat the Rich*, not as the new woman she is, but playing the part of a man! A challenge for any actress.

Amber is a Scots-born gender bender living in London, who opts for full transformation (unlike most GBs who mix-match unisex) and adds to hormone induced breasts (*à la* TS) pierced nipples. He/she was the subject of one of the *Sunday Mirror*'s better features, and adorns the cover of Kris Kirk's *Men in Frocks*, a book which documents some of the London drag life.

A new woman now, but not then post-op, Lynda Gold is not just known for her page in the same book. Lynda is a vivacious blond cockney girl with a cute if pugilistic nose, a strong but shapely body and a flair for showing herself off to her best advantage – and why not, indeed! So we think, but the police did not. The law says that in instances of transgender a woman officer must be present at all times, but the Metropolitan force forgot that detail, and took advantage. An officer allegedly got too excited and let his hands stray when checking her gender out, in a manner against all the rules. Lynda doesn't take any nonsense, and the newspaper reported that it took some six big cops to hold her down and get her into a cell. She claimed that they had tried to rape her, but whatever, no charges were made. I rang Lynda the night she had just had the op, and spoke to her about her plans, while she was still groggy from the anaesthetic. 'Maybe the quiet life with the boyfriend', she said. She may have made it there by now, but before she vanished off the scene her new womanhood had one more outing in the press and police station. *En route* to a kissogram assignment in nothing but a fur coat, some cops wolf-whistled her, and, quote: 'I spied a handsome sergeant, so I gave him a kiss . . .' While locked in the embrace and enjoying it, an officer whispered to the sergeant 'the lady used to be a man' – then the fur and feathers flew again!

A quieter celebrity is Martine Rose, a TV from Sheffield famed for her parties. She comes up with unusual costumes every time and is often a winner in the parade at this predominately gay venue.

Ziggie Cartier, centre

Rital, a look-alike for Sophia Loren

Rebel Rebel, à la Bowie

Amber, in leather and nipple rings

Lynda Gold, in competition

Martine Rose, in a smashing red leather mini

Anne Downes, blonde on the left

'Pure Corn', gender bending at its best

Another cabaret troupe like 'Rebel, Rebel'

A Halloween Medusa

Anne Downes, another TV, is a lifer. She lives permanently in her female role while being hetero, and without drugs or surgery of any kind. Yet she is a happy, relaxed and attractive woman, as the picture shows. Anne's story was told on the BBC television programme *Phantom Ladies*, which featured three members of UK's Beaumont Society. She lives quietly in Portsmouth where she runs an antiques shop, having been caught out transforming in a car while still an officer in the British navy, forced through electric shock aversion therapy, eventually dismissed from the service and divorced from her wife. Anne is one of the quiet heroines of our gender.

Towards the end of the evening, as the live band followed by disco trails off, the well-used catwalk, in four wooden segments is laid out and there is a mad dash for number cards for all those participating in the parade. Celebrities, too, dash, some to the stage having already agreed to judge, others to the bar to hide from Dennis (Gilding) the Ball's host and director. Dennis is an affable, lovable, gay, middle-aged act agent, who will press into service as many 'names' as he can, and is very proud that Boy George once visited the Ball, and that Marilyn, his GB star contemporary, once won the Miss Drag International annual award when still just an also-ran nobody.

The competition is always a farce; the order dealt with wrongly, and nobody takes it at all seriously. Both gents and ladies toilets are crammed with people chatting (away from the music's blare) and making-up, but never a tear is seen, even after the annual competition at New Year. It's a fun, almost family affair, and as many ordinary heteros with wives or girlfriends as 'straight gays' are among the crowd and in whatever toilet, confusing the issue.

Mostly, we laughed at the poor celebrities, frantically trying to make some sense of the order, as some stoned drag queen and her assistant announced everyone backwards. Of the faces to be seen, only one may mean anything to you – the Streatham Madam Sin, as Cynthia Payne is known, on whose life the film *Personal Services* is based. Her head is up where others are down, busy marking points – because she has judged many a ball (and not just drag ones, either!)

Ah! but this was all last seen more than a year ago. There were two main balls at The Porchester: The Dennis Gilding and the Ronata Storme, the latter being a well-known drag queen. Ronie, as we call her, moved hers to another venue, the Tudor Lodge, but Dennis stayed and took in the refugees, when police crackdowns closed several hetero S&M clubs.

Suddenly the fun themes like 'Halloween', 'Hollywood and Films' started to go, replaced by 'Kinky Leather' this and 'Perverted Rubber' that. The S&M took over, until even the Miss Drag International competition was scrapped. Instead, 'dominants' (weekend minorities, unlike us) performed buggy races across the stage, whipping their submissive 'horses' in overtly fetishistic undress. Few trans and even fewer drag queens bothered to come, and the last ball was an open target for the cops, brim full of undercover 'pretty policemen' as they are known.

Inevitably, someone was caught naked in one of the Hall's many smaller rooms and the whole event closed – forever.

The Hall remains, as it houses a swimming baths, sauna, skating rink and several other venue rooms. I recall seeing children with skates come to the wrong door and stare in amazement, and once was myself mis-directed through a wrong door, when wearing a red lycra catsuit, red hair, five-inch-heel thigh boots and a whip. I entered to find a wedding recep-tion going on, at which all but one guest was deaf and dumb! Surprisingly, I was well received and considered an omen of good luck for the bride and groom. But no more will the building echo to the gaiety of transworld.

The good news arrived in early 1988. Announcing the Miss Drag International, back from obscurity – no longer at the cosy, well-loved crumbling Porchester Hall, but now at the glitzy modern Stringfellows, the place to be 'seen', the place that anybody in the London glitterati who thinks they are anybody goes to (but where those who ARE, don't). Stringfellows is all chrome and laser, and sports three toilets: men, women and transsexuals – few of whom use that one. It's back, our event, but can it ever be quite the same!?

Part III

THE MEDICALISATION OF GENDER BLENDING

INTRODUCTION

What ethnomethodologists call the 'natural attitude' towards gender (Garfinkel, 1967: 122–8: Kessler and McKenna, 1978: 113–14) assumes that all human beings will belong to one of two discrete gender categories permanently determined on the basis of biological ('naturally' given) characteristics. The latter is traditionally referred to as 'sex' and the former as 'gender' (Stoller, 1968: 9). Congruence is expected both within and between a person's sex and gender. Congruence is also expected between these two areas and a person's sexuality with the 'default' assumption being probably, even in the 1990s, that this will be heterosexual. These are expectations in both cognitive (this is how things are) and normative (this is how things should be) senses.

Any breach of these expectations is therefore a potential threat to this aspect of what constitutes our reality. In the face of threats such as these, societies:

> develop a conceptual machinery to account for such deviations and to maintain the realities thus challenged. This requires a body of knowledge that includes a theory of deviance, a diagnostic apparatus, and a conceptual system for the 'cure of souls'.
> (Berger and Luckmann, 1971: 131)

In contemporary industrial societies, the institution of medicine has assumed or been given the task of maintaining this aspect of our reality, just as many other phenomena have become 'medicalised' (Conrad and Schneider, 1980). The innocence with which the men discussed by Peter Farrer in Chapter 1 pursued their activities is now no longer possible. Medicine has provided us with a language through which the activities of such men are apprehended as pathologies which can be diagnosed, treated and, perhaps ultimately prevented.

So, now, medical perspectives stand out as the culturally major lens through which gender blending may be viewed in our society. Other perspectives must take medical perspectives into account whether they ultimately incorporate, extend or reject them. These perspectives present themselves against a backdrop composed of current medical knowledge in general and, in particular, that of psychiatry, surgery and endocrinology.

The history of medical intervention in this area stretches over little more than a 100 years. In Chapter 7, Dave King provides a historical account which is based, not only on a study of the literature but also on interview material with English practitioners covering the past forty years. This history discloses much controversy over the nature of 'transvestism' and 'transsexualism' and particularly over the appropriate methods of dealing with the latter. Since the late 1940s, when the endocrinological and surgical means to 'change sex' began to be more widely employed, transsexualism has dominated the literature, with some practitioners advocating physical or psychological methods directed at the removal of the transsexual's 'pathological' wishes and desires and others being willing to facilitate a 'change of sex' in what are regarded as appropriate cases. Both approaches can be regarded as seeking to restore harmony in a situation of discord. Both are, in different ways (and this is also true of the patients who seek out the practitioners of these approaches), seeking to ensure that identity, social status and biology 'match'. The end result is that the binary structure of gender is maintained.

The dominant medical position is that transsexualism is a 'given' disorder which has been discovered. Several critics (Birrell and Cole, 1990; Eichler, 1980; Raymond, 1980; Sagarin, 1978) have argued, in contrast, that transsexualism has been invented. The medical conception of transsexualism is, it is claimed, an illusion, a fabrication whose explanation must therefore be sought in terms other than the putative 'thing' itself. Once conjured up, legitimised and disseminated, this illusion has real social consequences through the actions of members of the medical profession, 'transsexuals' themselves and other members of society, all of whom have been seduced into believing in it.

Sagarin (1978) clearly distinguishes between 'real' diseases which medicine can discover and 'unreal' ones which are invented. He has no doubt that transsexualism is an invented condition whose incidence has been amplified as a result of its legitimision and dissemination. The 'real' disorders, he argues, are effeminacy, homosexuality and transvestism. Some who suffer from these disorders eagerly embrace the transsexual diagnosis because it removes the stigma from which they suffer by attributing their behaviour to a legitimise medical condition unamenable to psychotherapy (Sagarin, 1978: 250). Thus 'impressionable and susceptible' people 'flock to "gender identity clinics"' (p. 252) where they 'play the game' in order to obtain the surgery which medicine and the media have told them is the answer to their problems.

Raymond (1980; 1994), whose work is discussed in Chapter 12, has more fully than any other writer argued that transsexualism is not an individual condition, a personal problem for which changing sex is merely a neutral, technical method of treatment, but instead is a social and political phenomenon. She argues that not only does transsexualism reflect the nature of patriarchal society, but also that it is ultimately caused by it. Eichler takes a similar view: 'individual transsexuals are casualties of an overly rigid sex-role differentiation' (1980: 82). Both writers argue that transsexualism is not only caused by, and a reflection of, patriarchy, but also supports it by maintaining notions of 'appropriate' gender-roles, by deflecting attention away from the real cause and by defusing the potential threat which transsexuals represent. As Birrell and Cole put it, 'ironically the transsexual's personal relief reinforces the very system that produces transsexualism' (1990: 5).

Chapter 8 by Dwight Billings and Thomas Urban is another example of this approach. Their critical history of transsexualism in the United States characterises it as a socio-medical construction which serves the interests of the medical profession and a patriarchal and capitalist society. This is an important piece of work which has not received the attention in the literature which it merits, the only substantial discussion of it being in two earlier works by one of the present editors (King, 1987; 1993). It is important because, of all the critical approaches, it is the only one which seriously attempts to base its arguments on empirical research.

Ultimately, however, whilst these critical approaches question the reality of transsexualism and point to the functions it serves for men or capitalism, they leave untouched the basic gender division. Their sceptical approach to social categories is a selective one. This is the strategy of what Woolgar and Pawluch call 'ontological gerrymandering' in which 'some areas are portrayed as ripe for ontological doubt and others portrayed as (at least temporarily) immune to doubt' (1985: 216). Thus, as Woodhouse (1989: 80) points out, Raymond seems to be operating with an essentialist view of gender categories, challenging their hierarchical order but basically accepting a naturally given, culturally independent masculinity and femininity. Only the ethnomethodologists such as Kessler and McKenna, and the cultural and queer theorists discussed in Chapter 14, are radically challenging the gender categories themselves.

7

GENDER BLENDING
Medical perspectives and technology*
Dave King

INTRODUCTION

In their introduction, the editors point out that blending has two basic meanings – to mix or combine and to harmonise. Gender blending in the first sense – the mixing of various aspects of male and female gender – has been seen in contemporary industrial societies as a pathological phenomenon, properly apprehended within a medical discourse. The goal of medical and other interventions is gender blending in the second sense – to harmonise gender identity, gender-role, social status, the body, and so on.

In this chapter I discuss the development and changing nature of medical thought and practice with regard to cross-dressing and sex-changing based on a study of this literature and also (particularly for the period since approximately 1950) on interviews with some of the English medical practitioners involved (see King, 1986; 1993). I begin at the turn of this century with the emergence of the 'transvestite' through that of the 'transsexual' around 1950 to the recent condition of 'gender dysphoria'.

EARLY MEDICAL PERSPECTIVES

The latter half of the nineteenth century saw the beginning of what Foucault terms the 'medicalisation of the sexually peculiar' (Foucault, 1979: 44). 'There emerged a world of perversion. . . . a setting apart of the unnatural as a specific dimension in the field of sexuality' (Foucault, 1979: 39–40). And within this new world of perversion there was much to explore; new lands to discover, territories to be claimed, named and their boundaries marked. And so, just as the worlds of animals and plants had been elaborately classified, so too was that of the 'sexually peculiar'. It is during this period that we find a number of descriptions of cases which, with

* An earlier version of this chapter appeared as part of Chapter 2 in *The Transvestite and the Transsexual: Public Categories and Private Identities*, Aldershot: Avebury, 1993.

hindsight, can be subsumed under the modern terms 'transvestism' or 'transsexualism'. Pauly (1965: 172), for example, dates the entry of trans-sexualism into the medical literature as 1830 and Hoenig (1982: 171) dates it as 1853. In terms of conceptualisation and classification, the category of the transvestite was available around 1910 and the transsexual some forty years later.

Before 1910 a variety of terms were applied to cases in which cross-dressing in some form was involved (Ellis, 1928). Sometimes an already existing diagnostic term was used, perhaps fetishism or one of the many terms used to refer to what would later be seen as homosexuality, 'sexual inversion', 'contrary sexual feeling', 'homo mollis'. Sometimes cases were seen as combinations of various categories: 'effemination with fetishism', 'sexual inversion with complete sexual anaesthesia'. And there were also attempts to create new diagnostic categories, 'gynomania', 'psychical hermaphroditism', 'sexo-aesthetic inversion'. There seems, however, to have been little general agreement about the terms to be utilised or their definition. These terms can be seen as the beginnings of an attempt to impose a new form of order on the world.

Alongside and often intruding into the medical literature was the conception of masquerade, impersonation or disguise. At the end of the nineteenth century the biographers of the Chevalier d'Eon (Telfer, 1885; Viztelly, 1895) refer to his *masquerade* as a woman. In 1895, *The Lancet* published a series of letters recounting stories and biographical details of James Barry, a woman who lived as a man and who worked as a doctor. Barry is discussed as an interesting member of the profession and there appears to be no conception of him as a 'case'. An editorial response to one letter refers to 'the Chevalier d'Eon and others of the more notorious *impersonators* of sex' (12, 19, 26 October 1985; 16 November 1895). This theme dominated the popular literature and the press at least until the 1930s. A selection of the titles of this period is illustrative of the general theme: *Famous Imposters* (Stoker, 1910); *Men in Women's Guise* (Gilbert, 1926); *Venus Castina. Famous Female Impersonators, Celestial and Human* (Bulliet, 1928); *Women in Men's Guise* (Gilbert, 1932); *Mysteries of Sex; Women who Posed as Men and Men who Impersonated Women* (Thompson, 1938). This conception of masquerade returns again in feminist critiques of medical approaches to transsexualism (see Part V).

This conception focused on the act – the nouns referred simply to those who performed such acts. The new conception, the new order, looked behind the acts to the condition or the type of being which they presum-ably represented. Thus, it became possible to distinguish 'real' from 'pseudo' transvestism (Ellis, 1928: 14–15), a distinction which suggests that transvestism implied more than an action.

This new perspective was not peculiar to this specific area. Foucault notes that:

> Homosexuality appeared as one of the forms of sexuality when it
> was transposed from the practice of sodomy onto a kind of interior
> androgyny, a hermaphroditism of the soul. The sodomite had been
> a temporary aberration; the homosexual was now a species.
>
> (Foucault, 1979:43)

As this quote suggests, a common conception of the homosexual involved not only or not even the inversion of the preferred sex object but the inversion of those psychological (and often physical) characteristics presumed to be peculiar to the sexes. The 'transvestite' was not simply as Talmey put it, 'a new discovered anomaly' (1914: 362) but also had to be separated out from the homosexual, and many of the earlier writers were centrally concerned with this process. Foremost in the setting apart of transvestism from homosexuality were Havelock Ellis and Magnus Hirschfeld.

Ellis (1913a; 1913b; 1920; 1928) was one of several writers who, in the late nineteenth and early twentieth centuries, were seeking to normalise homosexuality. 'Ellis was striving to emphasize that "inverts" were essentially ordinary people in all but their sexual behaviour' (Weeks 1977: 63). In part, this involved a rejection of the view that a preference for sexual relations with members of the same sex is necessarily associated with the adoption of the dress, mannerisms and so on of the opposite sex. Likewise, he wrote that it is possible for a person, 'to feel like a person of the opposite sex and to adopt, so far as possible, the tastes, habits and dress of the opposite sex while the direction of the sexual impulse remains normal' (Ellis, 1920: 1–2).

Ellis originally used the term 'sexoaesthetic inversion' to refer to this because he saw its essence as:

> The impulse to project themselves by sympathetic feeling into the
> object to which they are attracted or the impulse of inner imitation
> (which) is precisely the tendency which various recent philosophers
> of aesthetic feeling have regarded as the essence of all aesthetic
> feeling.
>
> (Ellis, 1928: 28)

This term was later rejected because Ellis saw it as 'too apt to arouse suggestions of homosexuality', and he argued that just as, 'a large proportion perhaps the majority of sexual inverts have no strongly pronounced feminine traits', so, 'the majority of sexo-aesthetic inverts are not only without any tendency to sexual inversion but they feel a profound repugnance to that anomaly' (Ellis, 1928: 102–3).

Ellis's preferred term was 'eonism', coined from the name of a famous transvestite, the Chevalier d'Eon and designed as a parallel to masochism and sadism. This was the only alternative term to transvestism to enjoy any currency and has survived in some writings, being used to refer to what was later to be designated as transsexualism (Hamburger, Sturup and Dahl-Iversen, 1953; Meyer and Hoopes, 1974). Ellis stated that there were two main types of eonist:

> One, the most common kind in which the inversion is mainly confined to the sphere of clothing and another less common *but more complete* in which cross-dressing is regarded with comparative indifference but the subject so identifies himself with those of his physical and psychic traits which recall the opposite sex that he feels really to belong to that sex although has no delusion regarding his anatomical conformation.
>
> (Ellis, 1928: 36: my emphasis)

This distinction comes very close to the contemporary one between transvestism and transsexualism. Ellis seems, however, to regard this, 'less common but more complete' type as embodying the essence of eonism, and he objected to the term transvestism because it focused attention solely on the element of cross-dressing. He also objected to Hirschfeld's phrase 'impulse of disguise' because, 'the subject of this anomaly, far from seeking disguise by adopting the garments of the opposite sex, feels on the contrary that he has thereby become emancipated from a disguise and is at last really himself (Ellis, 1920: 3).

Ellis was mainly attracted by a biological theory of the aetiology of eonism, although he was rather vague as to the specific mechanisms involved:

> Early environmental influences assist but can scarcely originate eonism. The normal child soon reacts powerfully against them. We must in the end seek a deeper organic foundation for eonism as for every other aberration of the sexual impulse.
>
> (Ellis, 1928: 110)

He surmised that the 'real physical basis' of eonism was, 'some unusual balance in the endocrine system' (Ellis, 1928: 110).

The terms transvestism (more rarely, transvestitism) and transvestite are traced back to Magnus Hirschfeld and his book *Die Transvestiten*, first published in 1910. Carpenter (1911) seems to have been the earliest writer to employ the term cross-dressing as a translation of Hirschfeld's term. Hirschfeld defined transvestism as, 'the impulse to assume the external garb of a sex which is not apparently that of the subject as indicated by the sexual organs' (quoted by Ellis, 1928: 13). Transvestism, with the translation/synonym cross-dressing, became the accepted term, although Hirschfeld admitted that the term indicated only the most obvious aspect of this phenomenon. Like Ellis, Hirschfeld distinguished transvestism from homosexuality. He criticised Krafft-Ebing who, he said, remained ignorant of the true nature of the phenomenon:

He saw in it like most authors before him and after him nothing but a variant of homosexuality whereas today we are in a position to say that transvestism is a condition that occurs independently and must be considered separately from any other sexual anomaly.

(Hirschfeld, 1938: 188–9)

According to Ellis (1928: 110), in Hirschfeld's view, 'we may fit this anomaly (transvestism) into the frame of intermediate or transitional forms of the sexual disposition, and regard it as a form of feminism; though why the feminine strain should so operate', he remarks, 'that in one case hermaphroditism should appear, in a second gynacomasty, in a third inversion and in a fourth transvestism, at present escapes our knowledge.'

The main, indeed the only real, theoretical challenge to the views of Ellis and Hirschfeld came from the psychoanalysts. As Ellis saw it, they explained transvestism as, 'largely or mainly a disturbance in the psychosexual mechanism, due to influences traceable in early life, and involving a persistence into later life of infantile traits', thus, 'the anomaly appears on a normal constitutional basis and is completely explained by psychosexual disturbance' (Ellis, 1928: 16). Ellis was probably exaggerating the differences between his general views and those of Freud, and certainly the views of the latter on constitutional influences were more complex than Ellis implied (see Sulloway, 1980: 311–12). Fenichel certainly seemed to be allowing for constitutional factors when he wrote of a transvestite patient that, 'we must in any case assume that he had a special bisexual disposition, for otherwise the desire to bear children, for example, could never have acquired such importance' (Fenichel, 1954, first published 1930: 178).

Stekel, originally a disciple of Freud's but later splitting away, much to the latter's delight, apparently (Roazen, 1979: 224–34), challenged Ellis's and Hirschfeld's view that transvestism was a phenomenon separate from homosexuality. He took issue with Hirschfeld and wrote, 'I fail to understand the need of setting up beside the hetero and homosexuals, a third group, the so-called transvestites'(Stekel, 1934: 69), and 'it were [sic] nothing less than doing violence to facts to attempt to distinguish the transvestites from the homosexuals' (Stekel, 1934: 70–1).

By contrast, Fenichel, who was a more orthodox follower of Freud, argues that transvestism was, 'rightly, described by Hirschfeld as a specific form of perversion' (1954, first published 1930: 167). He noted though the similarities with homosexuality and fetishism remarking that, 'psychoanalysts will suspect ... resemblance in the fundamental unconscious mechanisms' (Fenichel, 1954: 168). The 'fundamental unconscious mechanism' involved here centres on castration anxiety; 'the transvestite ... has not been able to give up his belief in the phallic nature of women and, in addition, he has identified himself with the woman with a penis' (Fenichel, 1954: 169).

The approaches of Ellis and Hirschfeld, and of the psychoanalysts, were all influential but, laying as they did outside mainstream medicine, none of them became dominant, at least not in the literature available in English. Not that there was a large literature on the subject at this time. Even in the specific literature on 'sexology', transvestism received little mention. It was given only five pages out of Haire's mammoth, 647-page *Encyclopaedia of Sexual Knowledge* (1934) and found no mention in Walker and Strauss's *Sexual Disorders in the Male* (1939). Transvestism never seems to have been a central interest of the Sexual Reform Movement of the 1920s and 1930s (see Weeks, 1977; 1981) despite the involvement in this of Ellis, Hirschfeld, Benjamin (who only began to write on the subject in the 1950s) and Haire, who in addition to his *Encycopaedia of Sexual Knowledge* also wrote an introduction to the autobiography of Einar Wegener who changed sex in the early 1930s (Hoyer, 1933).

By the Second World War, though,transvestism seems to have become an established 'perversion', at least in the psychiatric field. As with other 'perversions', the question of aetiology was of paramount importance, and probably the most sophisticated attempts in this area were the psychoanalytic ones, the others being mainly elaborate *ad hoc* statements of common-sense ideas rather than being derived from any coherent theoretical framework. For example, transvestism was seen as resulting from the parental wish for a child of the opposite sex or from dressing a child in the clothing of the opposite sex as a punishment (see examples in Lukianowicz, 1959). The literature consisted mainly of additional case material. Often papers would consist simply of detailed case histories with a few comments (Horton and Clarke, 1931; Yawger, 1940; Olkon and Sherman, 1944). No one up to the early 1950s, with the exceptions of Ellis and Hirschfeld, seems to have seen large numbers of transvestites. So, although transvestism was a known 'condition' or 'perversion', there were still few if any generally agreed notions of its more detailed nature apart from cross-dressing and probably its separateness from homosexuality. The term was, however, used across the literature widely enough to encompass those wishing to change sex through to the 'automonosexual' fetishistic cross-dresser.

Although the language of pathology was almost universally used, by this time there were few reports of cures and even clear reports of attempts are rare. In one case ECT was used (Liebman, 1944), otherwise there are simply vague references like 'psychotherapy'.

During this same period, however, the basics of modern hormonal and surgical methods for what came to be known as 'sex-reassignment' were established and had in fact been carried out on some patients, although the few reports on these were confined to the continental literature.

SEX-CHANGE

Castration has a long history and was, during the 1920s and 1930s, popular in certain countries for the 'treatment' of sex offenders. According to Tappan, 'considerable interest was expressed in castration in Europe during the 1930s' (Tappan, 1951: 244). Switzerland, Holland, Germany, the three Scandinavian countries, Finland and Iceland all developed legal provision for castration during this period. Castration was also legitimate in certain American states. It was sometimes used not only for sex offenders but for others who might request it (Bremer, 1959: 30; Kinsey et al., 1953: 739).

Marshall (1913) dated the first recorded attempt to create an artificial vagina (for women) as 1761 and he cited several methods used with varying degrees of success. It was not until the 1930s, however, that an effective method was devised (McIndoe, 1950).

Although Benjamin (1969) said he first attempted to induce breast growth in a male patient by means of hormones in the early 1920s, it was not until the successful production of synthetic oestrogens during the 1930s that we find evidence of attempts at hormonal changes. As with castration, there was much interest in the use of oestrogens to treat sex offenders (Dunn, 1940; Foote, 1944; Golla and Hodge, 1949).

That some transsexuals (as we would now see them) were treated by these methods is not therefore surprising. At least two doctors involved in sex-change operations – Wolf (see de Savitsch, 1958 and Bremer, 1959) and Sturup (see Bremer, 1959 and Hamburger, 1953) – were also involved in the castration of offenders.

Pauly (1965) cited reports of twenty-eight cases of transsexualism published before that of Christine Jorgensen in 1953 (see below). Of these twenty-eight cases, sixteen had obtained some form of surgery. All sixteen had been castrated, seven had penectomies; in six cases artificial vaginas had been created (two in 1931, one in 1947, two in 1950 and one in 1952).

The actual condition of such patients (according to modern conceptions) is often unclear, however. Abraham's cases reported in 1931 (Pauly, 1965) were described as transvestites whereas Lili Elbe was described by Haire (introduction to Hoyer, 1933) as a case of 'sexual intermediacy', although Elbe is usually cited as an early example of a transsexual (e.g., Benjamin, 1966). It is also not always clear what the surgeons and endocrinologists thought they were doing when they changed a person's sex. Apparently, in Lili Elbe's case, surgical intervention was seen as rectifying an intersexual anomaly (although see my comments later on British plastic surgeons in the 1950s). A Swiss male operated on in the early 1940s was considered to be a constitutional invert, 'anima muliebris in corpore virili' (de Savitsch, 1958: 71). Surgery was justified on the grounds that it would aid his psychic equilibrium and the idea of becoming more socially useful was expressed, a point also made by several later psychiatrists and surgeons. Whatever the conceptions held, it is clear that by 1950 sex-changing was not unknown.

ENTER THE TRANSSEXUAL

Around 1950, the idea of sex-change begins to dominate the literature. A new term, 'transsexual', emerges to distinguish those seeking such a change from other transvestites and, intertwined with the spectacular reporting of some cases in the media, medical reports in English begin to delineate the boundaries of this new category.

The term seemingly first appeared in the literature as one of a number of terms applied to homosexuality and embodying an 'intermediate sex' conception of that phenomenon (Kinsey, Pomeroy and Martin, 1948: 612). It was used, more in line with today's meaning, by Cauldwell (1949c), but Benjamin, an endocrinologist with case experience stretching back to the 1920s, brought it into mainstream medical literature (1954).

Benjamin's first article on the topic (1953) began, 'this article is the result of the wide publicity given to the case of Christine Jorgensen'. The report by the Danish team involved (Hamburger, Sturup and Dahl-Iverson, 1953) also resulted from the same publicity (Jorgensen, 1967: 209–10) although it used the term transvestism. Benjamin argued that,

Transvestism ... is the desire of a certain group of men to dress as women or of women to dress as men. It can be powerful and over-whelming, even to the point of wanting to belong to the other sex and correct nature's anatomical 'error'. For such cases the term trans-sexualism seems appropriate. (1953: 12)

Cauldwell also used the term 'sex transmutationist' (1951). He regarded the transsexual as 'mentally unhealthy' (1949c), a product of an 'unfavourable childhood environment' and referred to the use of surgery as 'criminal mutilation'. He was more tolerant of transvestism, which he regarded as a 'personality quirk' (1949a: 6) or a, 'harmless pastime of a group of loveable eccentrics' (1949b: 20). Cauldwell (1897–1960) was a minor figure in terms of the professional literature but in the late 1940s and early 1950s (e.g., Cauldwell, 1947a; 1947b; 1949a; 1949b; 1950; 1951; 1956) he wrote several popular booklets on these subjects (and other forms of deviant sexuality) which were probably influential in enabling transvestites and transsexuals of the period (at least in the USA) to develop an 'understanding' of their 'condition'.

Unlike Cauldwell, Benjamin favoured a biological explanation of this phenomenon. Environmental influences are important, he admitted, but the genetic and endocrine constitution must provide a 'fertile soil' in order for them to have any effect; 'if the soma is healthy and normal no severe case of transsexualism, transvestism or homosexuality is likely to develop in spite of all provocations' (1953: 13). This seems a similar view to that of Ellis, who had written, 'the same seed of suggestion is sown in various soils; in the main it dies out, in the few it flourishes. The cause can only be a difference in the soil' (Ellis, 1928: 309–10).

During the following six to eight years or so the term 'transvestite' remained dominant, although with varied applications. Some writers recognised that the term covered, 'a wide range of cross-dressing and sexual behaviour and feelings' (Bowman and Engle, 1957: 583). Some used transsexual and transvestite interchangeably (Greenberg, Rosenwald and Nielson, 1960; Northrup, 1959). Exceptionally, transvestism was defined solely in terms of the desire to change sex:

> transvestites wish to assume the sex characteristics of the opposite sex and to wear its clothes, they feel as if mentally and bodily they belong to the opposite sex and look upon their sex characteristics as a contradiction to their 'real' sex.
>
> (Hertz, Tillinger and Westman, 1961: 283)

Others implied a progressive continuum of transvestite behaviour with the desire to change sex as its 'final expression' (de Savitsch, 1958: 17). Similarly, Benjamin (1954) and Lukianowicz (1959) regarded transsexualism as an extreme or rare form of transvestism.

Some writers did not use the new term at all but thought, as Ellis had done some thirty years earlier, that transvestism was an inadequate term to apply to those who requested a change of sex and wrote of 'genuine transvestism' or 'eonism' (Hamburger, Sturup and Dahl-Iversen, 1953; Armstrong, 1958).

However, despite the sensational publicity surrounding the Jorgensen case and that of Roberta Cowell a little later, the coining of a new term certainly did not produce an outburst of research and publications on the subject. Most of the literature of this period is discussed above. By the early 1960s the situation seemed little different from a decade earlier. Benjamin described the period thus:

> Few references to transsexualism could be found in the medical literature during the ensuing years. It seemed not only a terra incognita but also a noli me tangere. Undoubtedly in the minds of many in the medical profession, the subject was barely on the fringe of medical science and therefore taboo.
>
> (Benjamin, 1969: 5)

The concept of the transsexual seems to have been finally integrated into psychiatric thought by the end of the 1960s, albeit somewhat unevenly. According to Raymond (1980: 20), it was in 1967 that 'transsexual' was first listed as a subject heading by the *Index Medicus*. The *American*

Psychiatric Association's Diagnostic and Statistical Manual of 1968 did not list the term, however.

TREATMENT IN THE 1950s

Two contrasting cases illustrate the range of 'treatments' offered in the 1950s. In 1952 Roberta Cowell, whose birth certificate had been amended from 'boy' to 'girl' a year earlier, had an artificial vagina created in London by one of Britain's most distinguished plastic surgeons. This followed approximately three years' oral consumption of female hormones. Cowell was the son/daughter of Major-General, Sir Ernest Cowell and was 34 years old. She had married as a male and had fathered two children (Cowell, 1954).

In early 1953, George Jamieson, aged 17, was a patient in the psychiatric department of a Liverpool hospital following a suicide attempt. Jamieson, later to achieve fame as April Ashley, came from a Liverpool council estate. The doctors described him as a 'constitutional homosexual who says he wants to become a woman'. He was treated with male hormones and ECT (See Fallowell and Ashley, 1982).

Cowell was one of a small number of people who found their way to a small number of plastic surgeons and endocrinologists who were prepared to use their skills and knowledge to attempt to change the patient's sex. Cowell was not the only patient to receive this 'treatment' in Britain. Michael Dillon, an anatomical female, underwent a series of operations beginning in 1942 with a bilateral mastectomy (Hodgkinson, 1989: 61–2). A small number of other patients, male and female, received sex-change operations from the same surgeon (Hodgkinson, 1989: 66).

So, certainly before 1950, some people were undergoing physical attempts to change their sex. These included all the measures now in use: hormones, castration, penectomy, creation of an artificial vagina for males; hormones, mastectomy, hysterectomy and the creation of an artificial penis for females. By the early 1950s the conversion of a male-to-female was regarded as 'technically fairly straightforward' by one eminent surgeon involved (interview).

The use of such procedures, however, was surrounded by controversy. In 1950, the issue was debated in the German journal *Psyche* (Boss, 1950; cit. in Hoenig, 1972). The first appearance of the controversy in the literature available in English followed the report by Hamburger, Sturup and Dahl-Iversen (1953) of the Jorgensen case. This article had described transvestism as a symptom which may appear in a number of conditions. However, the authors distinguished a category of transvestic men which they thought justified the term 'genuine transvestism', 'psychic hermaphroditism' or 'eonism'. Believing the 'disease' to have a 'somatic' cause, and noting that attempts to cure it had proved futile they argued that, 'the object of the medical profession was to bring about ... by hormonal feminisation and operative demasculinisation ... conditions that may contribute towards the patient's mental balance and a certain sense of "purpose of life"' (Hamburger, Sturup and Dahl-Iversen, 1953: 393).

The only visible evidence of controversy, however, now appears to be two critical letters (Ostow, 1953; Wiederman, 1953). Either the issue did not spur medical practitioners to reach for their pens or publication of the controversy was editorially censored. In 1954 the case of Roberta Cowell was the subject of debate in the popular press but it received no explicit discussion at that time in the medical press. Later in the month in which Cowell's story was first reported in the press, however, *The British Medical Journal* (20/3/54) distinguished intersexuals from 'transvestists' and was somewhat less than enthusiastic about the use of surgery in the latter case. Letters by Allen and Cawadias in later editions of the journal (10/4/54 and 1/5/54) revealed two polar positions. For Cawadias, 'these transvestites are as much hermaphrodites as those designated with this term', whereas for Allen 'transvestism is a psychical disease'.

This brief exchange was the only visible sign of a medical controversy, but outside of the professional journals the arguments were apparently more heated (interview) and those who continued to operate on trans-vestites (some discontinued their involvement) felt themselves to be 'tainted' by this involvement, operating surreptitiously or at least without publicity or professional report. Transvestites requesting sex-changes were a professional headache:

> From the experience I have had, and I have had considerably more experience of them than I would have liked to have had, it is extremely difficult to know what to do with them. The plastic surgeons won't touch them and the psychiatrists, very often, are completely uninterested in them ... I think it would be a very good idea if the psychiatrists, plastic surgeons and endocrinologists got together and really tried to think what is the right thing to do with these people.
>
> (Bishop, 1958: 90)

Those involved were aware that their work in this area was regarded with some distaste by their fellow professionals who, in the words of one surgeon, 'thought we were just dealing with homosexuals and perverts' (interview). They were also wary of any legal repercussions, although there was no specific ruling on this. And so a number of common strategies evolved which were designed to maintain a low level of visibility and legit-imise the surgical intervention.

In some early cases after hormone treatment, the legal sex was changed, thus enabling plastic surgery to be justified as corrective. One doctor explained to the press that in Cowell's case the amended birth certificate was 'in the nature of a working certificate to enable the plastic surgeons to carry out their operations' (*Sunday Pictorial*, 14/3/54).

A particular fear was that the law of mayhem would be invoked in relation to castration. For this reason, some plastic surgeons would only become involved after castration. This also meant that they were only 'finishing off' and not beginning an irreversible process. Many British patients, I am told, went to Holland or France to be castrated, returning to Britain for plastic surgery, although in some cases it seems that the phrase 'castrated abroad' was a euphemism used to hide the identity of the surgeon concerned. One surgeon solved the problem by resiting the testes inside the body.

The terms used in hospital records were also deliberately vague or misleading in order to disguise the nature of the operations. Thus, the condition of a male-to-female transsexual might be described vaguely as 'genitalia' or more specifically (and truthfully if misleadingly) 'congenital absence of vagina'.

With these methods of deception going on it is difficult to be sure what those involved actually thought they were doing when changing a person's sex. From the information available it seems that they did not think that they were actually changing a person's sex. As Walker and Fletcher wrote, 'sex is genetically determined and what is altered by operations of this kind is not sex itself but its secondary characteristics' (Walker and Fletcher, 1955: 119), and this seems to have been the view of the surgeons involved.

Some, however, put forward the theory as we have seen (see also Hamburger, Sturup and Dahl-Iversen, 1953) that transvestism or at least 'genuine transvestism' was an intersexual variant of some kind caused by biological factors.

In this they can be seen as descendants of Hirschfeld and Ellis, although being predominantly surgeons and endocrinologists, it is unlikely that they were very conversant with the writings of their ancestors. Put simply (although these ideas were rarely expressed in a very sophisticated fashion), behaviour patterns or personality characteristics were seen to be dichotomised by sex in as clearcut a manner as the gonads, genital organs or other physical characteristics were supposed to be. Hence a 'male' personality with a 'female' body was as much an intersex mixture as breasts and a penis. Surgical and hormonal intervention in the case of transvestites, as in other intersex cases, was then seen to be concerned with restoring a natural harmony between the various (physical and psychical) sexual characteristics.

A few pages before describing the techniques for transforming the

genitalia of a 'female with male outlook' and a 'male with female outlook',
Gillies and Millard write:

> The physical sex picture does not always bear a fixed relation to the
> behaviour pattern shown by an individual. One or other hormone
> may determine an individual's male or female proclivities quite inde-
> pendently of the absence of some of the appropriate physical organs.
> It may be suggested, therefore, that the definition of hermaphro-
> ditism should not be confined to those rare individuals with proved
> testes and ovaries, but extended to include all those with indefinite
> sex attitudes.
>
> (Gillies and Millard, 1957: 370–1)

In 1958 in a presidential address to the Royal Society of Medicine's Section
of Endocrinology, Armstrong wrote that he regarded transvestism, 'as
being of a constitutional nature, doubtless on a genetic basis'. 'There is
no sound evidence', he wrote, 'for accepting the contention of psychiatrists that it is due to a castration complex or other environmental factors'
(Armstrong, 1958: 25).

These attempts to classify transvestism as an intersexual variant or to
invoke biological explanations for the patient's identification with the
opposite sex were clearly central to the task of justifying surgical and
hormonal intervention, not only by members of the medical profession
but also their patients (see Cowell, 1954). As Garfinkel remarked in respect
of the case of Agnes (presumed to be a case of intersex):

> It is not that normals and Agnes insist upon the possession of a
> vagina by females ... They insist upon the possession of *either* a
> vagina that nature made *or* a vagina that *should have been there all
> along*, i.e., the *legitimate* possession.
>
> (Garfinkel, 1967: 127; italics in original)

Whether or not an intersex theory was advocated, the appearance and
manner of some male transvestites evidently inspired the response 'they
should be women'. Randell who, in 1959, was generally not in favour of
the use of surgery nevertheless found two patients, 'so manifestly lacking
in masculine traits and so feminine in appearance, manner and speech
that this step [surgery] is logical' (Randell, 1959: 1449–50).

Apart from the intersex theory, surgery was also legitimised on pragmatic grounds. Walker and Fletcher for, example, argued that, 'conversion
operations when performed on suitable cases ... would appear to produce
better adjusted and reasonably contented "women"' (Walker and Fletcher,
1955: 199). By contrast, they also argued that psychotherapy was ineffective: 'in over thirty years of practice the writer [K.W.] has never seen
a well marked case of transvestism cured or even materially helped by
psychological means' (Walker and Fletcher, 1955: 197).

An alternative form of justification might have been available in some countries if the transvestite requesting a change of sex was conceptualised as homosexual. Apparently, Christine Jorgensen was originally seen as a homosexual by the medical team involved: 'his medical history recorded what was medically identified as homosexual drives and he wanted to live as a woman' (Sturup, 1969: 455). 'The patient was suffering from homosexual tendencies and the oestrogens were given partly therapeutically i.e., in order to suppress the sexual libido and partly experimentally' (Hamburger and Sprechler, 1951: 170). By 'experimentally' they are presumably referring to their general programme of investigating the endocrinological effects of administering various steroid substances (Hamburger and Sprechler, 1951: 168). Hertoft and Sorensen, having examined the medical records and interviewed Sturup, the psychiatrist involved, concluded that the medical team dealing with Jorgensen, 'were not aware of any independent nosological unity' (Sorensen and Hertoft, 1980: 62). The medical team, 'regarded Chris Jorgensen as a homosexual man suffering from his homosexuality and since he himself asked for castration, they would not deny him this operation' (Hertoft and Sorensen, 1979: 168). So castration and hormone treatment were originally employed, not with a view to changing the patient's sex but in order to treat homosexuality, and the legal permission necessary for the castration was obtained with this argument. It would appear, then, that the media deserve more credit (or blame) than the medical profession for the invention of transsexualism: 'Not until afterwards, when the press published the case, did the team behind the procedure accept it as a sex-change' (Hertoft and Sorensen, 1979: 168).

So, in the 1950s surgery was being used, somewhat surreptitiously, in a small number of cases. Those who were prepared hormonally and surgically to feminise their male transvestite/transsexual patients were in contact with one another and this informal network also extended abroad to Benjamin in the USA and to Hamburger's team in Denmark (interview). Where the use of surgery was legitimised theoretically, this was in terms of an intersex theory. In particular cases the appearance of the patient as someone who 'should' be a woman may have been crucial. Otherwise, it was legitimised on pragmatic grounds.

Probably more common, though, was an opposing view which saw transvestism (including transsexualism) as evidence of psychological disturbance (Gutheil, 1954; Worden and Marsh, 1955). Thus, as Allen argued, 'the abnormal minds should be treated in order to conform them with the normal body and not vice versa' (Allen, 1954: 1040). As in the earlier period, psychoanalytic approaches or (more usually) aspects of them predominate in such writings.

Less frequently found in the literature are reports of attempts to cure the transvestite or transsexual of his or her wishes by the use of physical methods. An early report on the use of ECT to treat a transvestite has already been mentioned (Liebman, 1944), another appeared in 1960 (Eyres cit. by Brierley, 1979: 160). One of Randell's sixty-one male patients and two of his sixteen female patients had been given ECT. In the cases of the two females this was given to relieve their 'severe depression' but we are not told the reason for its use in the case of the male patients (Randell, 1960). Given the popularity of ECT at this time it might be that this form of treatment was used more frequently than these few cases indicate.

There are no reports so far as I am aware of the treatment of male transvestites with male hormones (except for Ashley), but Benjamin (1954) and Randell (1960) had both used oestrogen, not as a prelude to surgery but to reduce the compulsion to cross-dress or seek sex-change.

At the end of the decade Lukianowicz concluded that, 'various kinds of treatment have been attempted in cases of transvestism, though none of them can claim to be really successful' (1959: 58).The decade had, however, brought the possibility of one form of 'therapy' – that of sex-change – to greater prominence. It was a therapy which some 'transvestites' would come to demand from the medical profession.

GENDER DEVIANCE

Between roughly 1964 and 1969, a mere five years, the old world of the transvestite was superseded by that of the transsexual. Germinated some fifteen years earlier, the concept suddenly blossomed forth to produce a new era of gender identity clinics and research programmes – at least in the United States! Experts in other countries could not fail to take note of these new developments, but the pattern would not necessarily be repeated elsewhere.

This was the period which saw the establishment of the term 'transsexual' to refer to those requesting sex-change and to distinguish them from transvestites, who merely cross-dressed. Accompanying this was the growth of literature on transsexualism emanating from the United States, especially in the second half of the 1960s. In particular, this period sees the emergence of publications by those who Raymond (1980: 187–8) sees as the 'Holy Trinity' in the field of transsexualism; Green, Money and Stoller. The three books which have probably been cited most often in the literature, Benjamin's *Transsexual Phenomenon* (1966), Stoller's *Sex and Gender* (1968) and Green and Money's *Transsexualism and Sex Reassignment* (1969), all appeared in this period. Also, several series of articles appeared in the late 1960s, in *Transactions of the New York Academy of Science* in 1967, in the *Journal of Nervous and Mental Disease* in 1968 and in the *Journal of Sex Research* in 1967 and 1969.

Moreover, this literature became dominated by the concept of gender. By the end of this period terms such as gender-role, gender identity, crossgender identification, gender incongruity, and so on, had become commonplace in the literature which by this time was dominated by American authors.

The gender terminology related primarily to a literature which, as far as the present discussion is concerned, is important for its stress on the independence of sex and gender identity and the immutability of the latter. Thus, it was no longer necessary to claim a biological cause of transsexualism in order to legitimise changing sex. If gender is immutable, even though psychologically produced, and if harmony between sex and gender is a precondition of psychic comfort and social acceptability, it 'makes sense' to achieve harmony by altering the body. (See Diamond, 1965 and Raymond, 1980).

Research on transsexualism and programmes of sex-reassignment involving teams of doctors began in gender identity clinics at 'respectable' medical centres, most notably the Johns Hopkins Hospital (Hastings, 1969; Money and Schwartz, 1969). This feature obviously was intertwined with the building up of a network of medical men involved in this field, the holding of conferences and the compiling of research findings.

In the literature and in the clinics the role of the psychiatrist (or less often psychologist) comes to the fore in this period as the organiser, the theorist and the gatekeeper to surgical facilities. Benjamin, by then a prominent figure, was nevertheless an anachronism, a throwback to the 1950s and earlier, when the surgeon or endocrinologist played a more central role.

Billings and Urban (1982) point to the role of the Erickson Educational Foundation in 'selling transsexualism' by disseminating information, giving grants for research programmes and providing advocacy and other services to patients. One example of its enterprising activities is to be found in its newsletter for Fall 1969 (vol. 2, no. 2) where readers were told that editors of 105 medical and lay dictionaries and encyclopaedias in America and Britain had been sent definitions of transsexualism and transvestism prepared by Money and Benjamin 'to update incorrect or obsolete definitions and to be included in revised editions where hitherto omitted'.

Over this period, the transvestite fades out of the picture somewhat. In the transvestism and transsexualism section of Bullough et al.'s, *Bibliography of Homosexuality* (1976) there are about 450 references. There are only eight references to articles on transvestism in the professional literature after 1965 and two books (which may be popular titles). There are also six references which include transvestism *and* transsexualism after 1965. This is tiny compared with the number of articles on transsexualism.

It is not surprising to find a number of reports of the use of aversion therapy in cases of transvestism during the 1960s. Commonly depicted as compulsive behaviour and often linked to fetishism (e.g., Randell, 1959), transvestism must have seemed to some ideally suited to this form of treatment. The reports to be found in the literature coincide almost exactly with the 1960s (see Brierley, 1979, Chapter 8 for examples), but the use of aversion therapy certainly continued into the 1970s (interview data).

Other forms of treatment in use at this time, again hardly documented, included various forms of psychotherapy, counselling, the prescription of oestrogens 'to reduce libido' and tranquillisers, and at least one patient (Hoenig, Kenna and Youd, 1971) had a leucotomy, possibly in the mid-1960s.

GENDER DYSPHORIA

During the 1970s, the literature continued to be dominated by writers from the United States, although it is equally clear that the term and concept of transsexualism had by this time been successfully exported to many parts of the world. It is also clear that the literature was no longer dominated by a small group of writers which suggests the more wide-spread nature of work with transsexuals. Overall, the rate of publications increased. Reports of single case studies were fewer during this decade; unless reporting on a particularly noteworthy case (e.g., Van Putten and Fawzy, 1976) articles routinely covered a series of patients.

Surgical sex-reassignment initially seems to have become accepted as the treatment of choice for transsexuals (American Medical Association, 1972, quoted by Lothstein, 1982) but by the end of the decade its usage was, if anything, even more hotly contested (Meyer and Reter, 1979; Bockting and Coleman, 1992b). By this time about thirty to forty gender identity clinics existed in the United States (*Transition*, no. 11, July 1979); in 1973 there were 'almost a dozen' (Edgerton, 1973a: 3).

The concept of the transsexual and its seemingly clear differentiation from transvestism and other 'conditions' as outlined by Benjamin and others in the 1950s and 1960s began to lose ground somewhat. Early in the decade the term 'gender dysphoria' appeared in the literature (Laub and Gandy, 1973) and quickly established itself as the dominant term, although transsexualism has continued to be used.

This was not just a case of one term beginning to replace another, however. Gender dysphoria was introduced according to its originator, Fisk (1973), to reflect the fact that applications for sex-reassignment came from a variety of persons, by no means all of whom fitted the classic picture of the transsexual. What they all shared was the fact that they, 'were intensely and abidingly uncomfortable in their anatomic and genetic sex and their assigned gender' (Fisk, 1973: 10).

Meyer and Hoopes, quickly taking up the term, wrote that it emphasises, 'the patient's difficulty in establishing an adequate gender identification, and the pain and conflict surrounding masculinity and femininity' (1974: 447).

By 1979 the term seemed to have become, as one report put it, 'the primary working diagnosis applied to any and all persons requesting surgical and hormonal reassignment' (Berger et al., 1979: 2). The American Psychiatric Association's *Diagnostic and Statistical Manual of Mental Disorders III* of 1980, however, used the term 'transsexualism' under the general heading of 'Gender Identity Disorders'.

Over the past twenty years 'gender dysphoria' has now become the preferred term used in the titles of conferences, associations, books and articles. There are a number of points to be made about the significance of this change in terminology.

Firstly, it underlines the element of gender and ties in to the whole family of gender concepts and terminology. It thus consolidated the trend begun in the 1960s with the work of Stoller, Green and Money.

Secondly, gender dysphoria turns the focus away from the actor and on to the condition and at the same time represents a reaffirmation of professional authority. The terms 'transsexual' and 'transsexualism' retained the 'intermediate sex' connotations with which they originated (Kinsey, Pomeroy and Martin, 1948: 612); they pointed to a state of being in between the two sexes. They, together with 'transvestite' and 'transsexual' fit best into the era discussed at the beginning of this chapter, the end of the nineteenth century, when various new sexual 'species' were being 'discovered'. As 'states of being', they also lend themselves to self-definition. By contrast, 'gender dysphoria' names a 'disease' (Fisk, 1973) and therefore presumably is the 'property' of the medical profession.

Thirdly, gender dysphoria also legitimised another pattern which existed prior to its inception; it freed the diagnosis from a specific form of intervention – sex-reassignment surgery. Some writers (e.g., Stoller, 1968; 1975) had defined the transsexual independently of the request for sex-reassignment and had argued that this procedure should only be offered to those who could be so defined. Probably, for most practitioners, however, referral to a surgeon was based less on reaching a formal diagnosis than on the success or otherwise of the patients attempts to live for a period of time in the other gender category. With the advent of 'gender dysphoria' this approach was legitimised. (See Berger et al., 1979; Fisk, 1974). Sex-reassignment could be considered as a possible treatment for 'gender dysphoria' instead of the inevitable outcome of a transsexual career. It is interesting that the interim report of a subcommittee of the American Psychiatric Association reviewing its *Diagnostic and Statistical Manual of Mental Disorders* suggested the elimination of the term 'transsexualism' in order to 'uncouple the clinical diagnosis of gender dysphoria from criteria for approving patients for sex-reassignment surgery' (quoted in Pauly, 1992).

Finally, gender dysphoria potentially widens the area of expertise of interest of the practitioner. No longer is he or she concerned only with a special type of person, the transsexual, but with all who suffer from gender dysphoria and potentially this includes not only transsexuals, transvestites and homosexuals but also those who are physically intersexual (MacKenzie, 1978), and indeed, possibly all of us suffer from it in a mild form (Fisk, 1974: 388).

Another feature of the 1970s was a renewed interest in transvestism. The American gender identity clinics seem to have attracted those who were diagnosed as transvestite as well as transsexual and this may have provided some doctors with the opportunity to gain experience in this area. The growth and greater visibility of organisations for transvestites during the 1970s (King, 1993) also provided some doctors with opportunities for research. (Brierley, 1979; Buhrich, 1976; Buhrich and McConaghy, 1977a; 1977b).

As with the transsexual, some subdivision of the category of the transvestite has taken place. A major focus of this has been on the gender versus the sexual aspects of transvestic cross-dressing. Those who have used non-clinical groups of subjects for their research have tended to stress the gender aspects (Brierley, 1979; Buhrich and McConaghy, 1977a; 1977b) whereas those who have based their work on their patients have favoured a sexual interpretation (Wise and Meyer, 1980).

During the 1980s and into the 1990s the conception of gender dysphoria remained the dominant one. This is evidenced in a *Lancet* editorial (7/9/91) in which, despite the heading 'Transsexualism', the language of gender dysphoria is predominant, and by the appearance of a new journal, *Gender Dysphoria: An International Journal of Gender Identity Disorders*. In the fourth edition of the *American Psychiatric Association's Diagnostic and Statistical Manual* (1994) transsexualism has been replaced by gender dysphoria.

The nature/nurture issue has continued to be debated (*Lancet*, 7/9/91; Tsur, Borenstein and Seidman, 1991). But there is evidence that, as Bockting and Coleman put it, 'today, more clinicians recognise that gender dysphoria is far more complex than previously assumed' (1992a: 133). This recognition, then, requires, at least for Bockting and Coleman, a range of treatment options rather than simply screening people for possible surgery. These writers also argue that their treatment model,

allows for individuals to identify as neither man nor woman, but as someone whose identity transcends the culturally sanctioned dichotomy. For example, for some of our male gender dysphoric clients, identifying as a stereotypical heterosexual woman is not a desired goal because they cannot identify with the rigid gender schema of western culture. The model also gives those pursuing sex-reassignment permission to be less rigid in their social sex-role expression.

(Bockting and Coleman, 1992a: 144–5)

At least some medical practitioners, then, appear to be operating with a more complex and less stereotypical view of gender than their feminist and other critics have charged them with.

CONCLUSION

In this chapter I have outlined the main themes apparent in the professional literature from the late nineteenth century to the late twentieth and have added to this such other information as I have been able to gather from interviews concerning the experience of the medical profession with those who cross-dress or wish to change their sex.

Perhaps the most important outcome of the thoughts, actions and writings of this relatively small group of members of the medical profession has been the creation of a discourse by means of which matters concerning cross-dressing and changing sex can be apprehended. Within this, ways of categorising the self and others have been created. The categories have never been simple and unambiguous, they have never been static. But they have allowed those who call themselves 'transvestites' and 'transsexuals' to emerge in our society.

8

THE SOCIO-MEDICAL CONSTRUCTION OF TRANSSEXUALISM
An interpretation and critique*

Dwight B. Billings and Thomas Urban

There is hardly a more dramatic instance of contemporary professional authority than so-called 'sex-change' surgery. Physicians perform cosmetic surgery yet certify that their patients have undergone a change of sex. Courts acknowledge this claim by allowing transsexuals to be issued new birth certificates in most states. Our study of sex-change surgery[1] reveals that these physicians heal neither the body nor the mind, but perform a moral function instead. After conducting a surgical rite of passage, physicians are accorded moral authority to sponsor passage from one sexual status to another. Public acceptance of sex-change surgery attests both to the domination of daily life and consciousness by professional authority as well as the extent to which many forms of deviance are increasingly labelled 'illness' rather than 'sin' or 'crime' (Freidson, 1970). Furthermore, and in a curious way, the stress by 'phallocentric medicine' (Wilden, 1972: 278) on the presence or absence of a penis as the definitive insignia of gender challenges the politics of the women's movement and the intellectual thrust of the behavioural sciences, which assert that anatomy need not define destiny. Sex-change surgery privatises and depoliticises individual experiences of gender-role distress.

We show that transsexualism is a socially constructed reality which only exists in and through medical practice. The problem of transsexual patients does not lie 'in their minds,' as sex-change proponent John Money (1972: 201) puts it. Money's statement typifies medicine's reification of transsexualism as a psychological entity. In contrast, we believe transsexualism is a relational process sustained in medical practice and marketed in public testimony such as Money's (1972: 201) description of the 'warm glow' of sexual fulfilment available through surgery. The

* Copyright 1982 by the Society for the Study of Social Problems. Reprinted from *Social Problems*, 1982, 29: 266–82. The authors thank Robert Goldman, William Lacy, and Al Reiss for their comments.

legitimisation, rationalisation, and commodification of sex-change operations have produced an identity category – transsexual – for a diverse group of sexual deviants and victims of severe gender-role distress.

THE SEARCH FOR THE TRUE TRANSSEXUAL

Naming the problem

The first reported sex-change operation took place in Germany in 1931 (Pauly, 1968) but the procedure was not widely known until Christine (George) Jorgensen's much-publicised surgery in Denmark in 1952. The desire to be a member of the opposite sex had previously been viewed in psychoanalytic literature as an undifferentiated perversion. In 1954, however, US endocrinologist Harry Benjamin asserted that Jorgensen's claim that he was a woman trapped within a man's body was indicative of a unique illness distinct from transvestism and homosexuality, perhaps conditioned by endocrine factors, and not amenable to psychotherapy. He named this non-psychopathic sexual disorder 'transsexualism'.[2]

Benjamin's (1954; 1966; 1967a; 1971) discussions of diagnosis, etiology and treatment provoked hostile reactions from psychoanalysts (Greenberg, Rosenwald and Nielson, 1960; Gutheil, 1954; Lukianowicz, 1959; Northrup, 1959; Ostow, 1953) who charged that it is one thing to remove diseased tissue and quite another to amputate healthy organs because emotionally disturbed patients request it. An influential report in the *Journal of the American Medical Association* rejected the distinction between transsexualism on the one hand and transvestism and homosexuality on the other, and argued strongly against sex-change surgery:

> Although our subjects share certain needs, wishes, and personality characteristics, it would be completely erroneous to conclude from these similarities that they represent a homogeneous group. The need for surgery that these persons share does not in itself represent a disease entity but rather a symptomatic expression of many complex and diverse factors.
>
> (Worden and Marsh, 1955: 1297)

Professional opposition to sex-change surgery and disputes over its legality (Holloway, 1974; Hastings, 1966: 599) inhibited recognition of transsexualism as a disease for several years. In 1966, however, Johns Hopkins University physicians admitted performing experimental sex-reassignment surgery and claimed to be able to diagnose true Benjaminian transsexuals (Johns Hopkins University, 1969). A 1965 survey showed that only 3 per cent of US surgeons would take seriously a request for sex-change surgery, yet by the early 1970s such operations were becoming commonplace (Green, Stoller and MacAndrew, 1966). In 1966 Benjamin (1966: 105) complained that the subject was 'still largely unknown (except in the tabloids) and [was] still an almost unexplored field in medicine'; yet by 1970, the director of the gender identity clinic at the University of California at Los Angeles announced: 'For me, at this time, the critical question is no longer whether sex-reassignment for adults should be performed, but rather for whom' (Green, 1970: 270). As recognition of transsexualism as illness increased, physicians' perception of its incidence heightened. In 1953, Swedish physicians had described Christine Jorgensen's case as an 'exceedingly rare syndrome' (Hamburger, Sturup and Dahl-Iversen, 1953). Today, US medicine recognises transsexualism as a 'serious and not uncommon gender disorder of humans' (Edgerton, 1973b: 74).[3] The thousands of operations performed in the United States to date attest that medicine is indeed 'oriented to seeking out and finding illness, which is to say that it seeks to create social meanings of illness where that meaning or interpretation was lacking before' (Freidson, 1970: 252).

Medical exemplars and professional motivations

The treatment of hermaphrodites, persons born with the sexual organs of both sexes, set several precedents for sex-reassignment of transsexuals. Surgical techniques for reconstructing genital abnormalities and standards developed to determine the direction of hermaphroditic sex assignment were both applicable to transsexualism. Some physicians who treated hermaphrodites stressed chromosomal characteristics; surgeons generally stressed the nature of the external genitalia. From their study of 105 cases of hermaphroditism, Money, Hampson and Hampson (1957) proposed that up to the age of 2½ years, the external genitalia should be the principal determinant for sex assignment; in persons older than 2½, surgery should conform to the established direction of gender-role socialisation. By reporting dramatic instances among hermaphrodites of chromosomal men who have been successfully socialised as women, and vice versa, they demonstrated the independence of biological sex and gender. Money, Hampson and Hampson (1955: 290) claimed, however, that gender 'is so well established in most children by the 2½ years that it is then too late to make a change of sex with impunity'.[4] They acknowledged that sex-reassignment could be made in later years if hermaphrodites themselves felt some error had been made in their assigned sex – a concession that proved important for the treatment of transsexuals.

Money et al.'s claim that all the hermaphroditic children in their sample were 'successfully' reassigned from one sex to another before the age of 2½ provided the only empirical support for gender-role fixity. Only five children in their sample of 105 were reassigned after this age, though four were judged by unspecified criteria as 'unsatisfactory'. Anomalies were soon reported, though these studies are rarely cited in the transsexual literature (Berg, Nixon and MacMahon, 1963). Dewhurst and Gordon (1963) reported fifteen successful cases of reassignment among seventeen hermaphroditic children up to 18 years of age. Thus, there were at least as many cases in medical literature of patients successfully altering their gender-roles as there were cases of those who did not.

Psychiatrist Ira Pauly (1968), a proponent of sex-change, acknowledged that such anomalies cast some doubt on the otherwise considerable clinical evidence for gender-role fixity – a theory crucial to the argument that psychotherapy is ineffective for transsexuals (Benjamin, 1966). Pauly claimed, however, that psychiatrist Robert Stoller had clarified the apparent contradiction. Stoller (1964a; 1964b) re-directed attention from 'gender-role' to 'core gender identity', arguing that those rare individuals who appear to change identity later in life do not really do so. Rather, he argued, they have always had a third (hermaphroditic) gender identity – 'not male or female but both (or neither)' (Stoller, 1964b: 456). Apparent cases of reversals of early socialisation were thus discounted.

Clinical experience with hermaphrodites thus established three points:

1   the refinement of surgical techniques for genital reconstruction;
2   the theory that gender-role learning is independent of physical anatomy and is fixed at an early age; and
3   the policy that, since self-identification is more important than external genitalia, 'rare requests' from adult hermaphrodites for sex-reassignment should be given 'serious evaluation' (Money, Hampson and Hampson, 1955).

Psychiatrists and plastic surgeons at Johns Hopkins University provided another precedent for sex-change operations with a series of studies of patients requesting cosmetic surgery. Here was an established field of medicine where doctors performed operations upon demand without medical justification. Yet Edgerton, Jacobson and Meyer (1960–1: 139), found that 16 per cent of their sample of patients demanding elective surgery were judged psychotic, 20 per cent neurotic and 35 per cent had personality trait disorders. Meyer et al. (1960: 194) found that of thirty patients studied, one was diagnosed psychotic, two were severely neurotic, eight had obsessive personalities and four were schizoid; fourteen others were judged as tending towards obsessional schizophrenia. Most patients rejected psychotherapy, however, as an alternative to surgery. The researchers concluded from post-operative interviews that 'psychological improvement' and patient satisfaction resulted from surgery. Even 'severely neurotic and technically psychotic patients' were judged to benefit from such operations (Edgerton, Jacobson and Meyer, 1960–1: 144).

With the publication of these findings, and those on hermaphrodites, the medical rationales for sex-change surgery were in place. Johns Hopkins

University became the most prominent centre for the surgical treatment of transsexualism in the United States in the 1970s. Psychologist John Money, psychiatrist Eugene Meyer and plastic surgeon Milton Edgerton formed the nucleus of the Johns Hopkins team.

Three factors motivated physicians to fight attempts to declare sex-change operations illegal:

1 The paramount role of the physician as healer was stressed (Benjamin, 1966: 116). Early defences stressed patients' intense anguish and the duty of physicians 'to ease the existence of these fellow-men' (Hamburger, 1953: 373).

2 The opportunity for ground-breaking research in psychiatry was recognised. Robert Stoller (1973a: 215) referred to transsexuals as 'natural experiments' offering 'a keystone for understanding the development of masculinity and femininity in all people'.[5] Surgeons, too, were interested in sharpening their skills. Several told us in interviews that they regard sex-change surgery as a technical *tour de force* which they undertook initially to prove to themselves that there was nothing they were surgically incapable of performing. Plastic surgeons, especially, found sex-change surgery strategically important for expanding their disciplinary jurisdiction.[6]

3 An over-abundance of surgeons in the United States has resulted in competition for patients and an increasing number of 'unnecessary' operations (Bunker, 1970), many of which are performed on women in the course of their sexual maturation and functioning (Corea, 1977). Although medicine is a 'market profession', it is not socially legitimised as a business enterprise (Larson, 1977). Nevertheless, sex-change surgery is profitable: reassignment operations alone cost around $10,000 in the late 1970s. Related elective surgery, consultation fees and weekly estrogen treatments push the cost even higher.[7]

Legitimising the search: etiology, diagnosis and treatment

News of Johns Hopkins University's programme touched off a renewed wave of opposition within medicine in the late 1960s.[8] Psychoanalysts in private practice led the attack. Using a variety of analytic techniques to support their position that persons demanding castration were *ipso facto* mentally ill, they labelled transsexuals as 'all border-line psychotics' (Meerloo, 1967: 263) or victims of 'paranoid schizophrenic psychosis' (Socarides, 1970: 346) or 'character neurosis' (Stinson, 1972: 246). They attacked surgery as non-therapeutic. If patients' requests represented 'a surgical acting out of psychosis' (Volkan and Bhatti, 1973: 278), then surgeons were guilty of 'collaboration with psychosis' (Meerloo, 1967: 263). The *Journal of Nervous and Mental Disease* devoted an entire issue in

1968 to the topic and concluded that the issues of etiology, diagnosis and treatment were still unresolved and that the term 'transsexualism' itself had won premature acceptance in the literature. The report concluded: 'What [transsexualism] means in contradistinction to "transvestite" or "homosexual" is not clear' (Kubie and Mackie, 1968: 431). Such criticism threatened the professional security of sex-change physicians and raised the question of whether patients could consent to such operations, since psychotics cannot legally do so.

In response, sex-change proponents legitimised surgical treatment by:

1   Constructing an etiological theory which stressed the non-psychopathic character of the illness; and
2   rationalising diagnostic and treatment strategies.

Although some physicians asserted that biological predispositions for transsexualism might yet be discovered, most stressed early socialisation in their etiological accounts. Recalling the hermaphrodite literature, Money and Gaskin (1970-1: 251) spoke of the 'virtually ineradicable' effects of ambivalent gender-role learning at an early age. Stoller (1967: 433) claimed that male transsexualism was the predictable outcome of a particular family situation involving 'too much contact with mother's body for too long and a father who is absent and so does not interrupt the process of feminisation'. The result is a son so strongly identified with his mother that he not only *wishes* to be like her, but comes to believe that he *is* like her, despite incongruous genitals. Stoller conceptualised transsexualism as an identity issue – not a neurotic perversion – resulting 'from the same kinds of forces necessary for normal development' (1973b: 216). In contrast to neurotic perversions such as transvestism, Stoller contended that transsexualism was 'not a product of neurosis, i.e., of conflict and compromise, any more than is the core masculinity in normal men or femininity in normal women' (1973b: 219).

Thus, physicians defended themselves against the charge of 'collaboration with psychosis' by claiming to resolve surgically their patients' bitter conflicts between self-image and body-image. Arguing that 'psychiatric name-calling' adds little to understanding (Baker and Green, 1970: 89), they replaced the language of perversions with a new language to describe patient demand for sex-change surgery. These demands were referred to as a 'single theme' (Hoopes, Knorr and Wolf, 1968), a 'principal theme' (Pauly, 1968), an '*idée fixe*' (Money and Gaskin, 1970–1), an 'intensive desire' (Forester and Swiller, 1972) and an 'intense conviction or fixed idea' (Sturup, 1976).[9]

Within this etiological framework, physicians were confident they could diagnose transsexualism accurately. While critics charged that 'transsexualism represents a wish, not a diagnosis' (Socarides, 1970), Baker and Green (1970: 90) asserted that 'transsexualism is a behavioural phenomenon unique unto itself. We believe that although it is related to other anomalies of psychosexual orientation and shares features in common with them, it can, nevertheless, be differentiated'. Male transsexualism, upon which attention was fixed,[10] was identified as a point on a clinical continuum along with effeminate homosexuality and transvestism. Although the boundaries 'are sometimes ill-defined' (Baker and Green, 1970: 90) and the 'transition zones are blurry' (Money and Gaskin, 1970–1: 254), Fisk (1973: 8) summarised the following behavioural guidelines for recognising the 'true transsexual':

1   A life-long sense or feeling of being a member of the 'other sex';
2   the early and persistent behaviouristic phenomenon of cross-dressing, coupled with a strong emphasis upon a total lack of erotic feelings associated with cross-dressing; and
3   a disdain or repugnance for homosexual behaviour.

Once physicians were satisfied that they were dealing with patients whose sanity was intact, and that they were not catering to perverse wishes for self-destruction, then the best indicator of transsexualism was the intensity of a patient's desire for surgery. They assumed such persistence would distinguish a male transsexual from an effeminate homosexual or a transvestite who – while behaviourally similar – none the less 'values his penis and abhors the thought of its loss' (Baker and Green, 1970: 91). The lack of erotic motivation, along with evidence of a life-long identity pattern, were taken as further proof of transsexualism. Correspondingly, ideal treatment consisted of:

1   Careful psychiatric screening to assess personality stability and the fixity of gender identity;
2   an extensive period of hormone treatment to develop secondary anatomical characteristics of the cross-sex;
3   at least one year of supervised cross-gender living to guarantee stability and commitment; and, finally,
4   surgery (Baker and Green, 1970; Edgerton, Knorr and Collison, 1970; Hastings, 1969; Knorr, Wolf and Meyer, 1969; Money, 1972).

Physicians were urged to standardise patient management policies and a number of quantitative diagnostic instruments, such as Lindgren and Pauly's (1975) 'Body Identity Scale' were developed to rationalise patient selection.[11] Scientistic accounts of transsexual treatment largely succeeded in silencing critics, for, as Habermas (1979: 184) among others has demonstrated, 'the formal conditions of [scientistic] justification themselves obtain legitimating force' in the justification of norms and actions in modern culture.

A success story: selling transsexualism

The first physicians to 'discover' and treat transsexuals were totally unprepared for the experience (Ihlenfeld, 1973b: 64). Their 'inexperience and naivete' (Fisk, 1973) was not surprising since 'there [were] no textbooks to consult, no authorities to lean on and to quote' (Benjamin, 1966: 19). Often they were required to make decisions unrelated to their professional training. By the late 1960s, sex-change proponents began publicly to extol the benefits of sex-reassignment in books, journals, newspapers, magazines and world lecture tours. Although its role is rarely acknowledged in the truncated histories of transsexual treatment presented in medical journals, the Erikson Educational Foundation of Baton Rouge, Louisiana, made three important contributions to the social movement to incorporate sex-change in medical jurisdiction:[12]

1 *Socialisation.* The Erikson Educational Foundation brought transsexualism to the attention of the public and the medical world by:
   ● annually sponsoring international medical symposia;
   ● helping to send physicians and behavioural scientists such as Leo Wolman, Ira Pauly, and John Money (a foundation board member) around the world to discuss the new 'disease';
   ● sponsoring workshops at medical schools, colleges and national meetings of professional associations;
   ● disseminating information about transsexualism through films and pamphlets to physicians, psychologists, lawyers, police, clergy, and social workers.

   Such efforts aroused public sympathy for transsexuals. In one of her daily 'Dear Abby' newspaper columns, Abigail Van Buren told a distressed wife who discovered her husband cross-dressing that he was a possible candidate for surgery who should consult the Erikson Educational Foundation. She affirmed her belief in surgical reassignment, saying: 'I believe that knowledge, skill, and talent are divinely inspired and that those scientists, physicians, and surgeons whose combined efforts have made sex-change surgery possible, do so with God's guidance' (Van Buren, 1977: C-10). Similarly, Ann Landers (1979: B-5) wrote that 'those who want the surgery should have it'.

2 *Patient advocacy and services.* The foundation created a National Transsexual Counselling Unit in conjunction with the San Francisco Police Department and issued identification papers to transsexuals otherwise subject to police harassment.[13] The foundation obtained funding for individual sex-change operations from private insurance carriers, city and state welfare agencies and vocational rehabilitation programmes. It established a national referral network for patients, which identified over 250 sympathetic, competent doctors. From 1968 to 1976 it circulated a newsletter to more than 20,000 subscribers

which cited and summarised medical and scientific reports on transsexualism.

3 *Grants.* The foundation made grants through the Harry Benjamin
Foundation to individual researchers and to several gender clinics,
including the one at Johns Hopkins University.

Physicians often complain that transsexual patients are unrealistic about
the benefits of surgery. Many 'harbor unrealistic expectations for an immediately blissful life, exciting and romance-filled' (Green, 1970). In other
contexts (e.g., arguing their patients' competence to give informed consent)
physicians defend their patients' senses of reality, but here they acknowledge that 'rarely does such a patient initiate a realistic discussion about
the obvious problems that follow surgery: legal, social, economic, and
emotional. The fact that there is pain connected with the surgery takes
some patients rather by surprise' (Hastings, 1974: 337).

Physicians fail to comprehend that medical claims themselves are one
source of such dreams and misunderstandings. Benjamin (1966) claimed
an astonishing success rate for reassignment surgery. Only one of the fifty-
one patients he examined after surgery was judged 'unsatisfactory'. He
wrote glowing accounts of these 'twice-born' patients: 'To compare the
Johnny I knew with the Joanna of today is like comparing a dreary day
of rain and mist with a beautiful spring morning, or a funeral march with
a victory song' (1966: 153). Similarly, readers of the *Erikson Education
Foundation Newsletter* (Erikson Educational Foundation, 1969: 1) learned
of anonymous transsexuals for whom 'new life is brimming over with hope
and happiness'. Physicians offered men more than just the chance to be
rid of their dreaded male insignia – they were promised the experience
of female sexuality. A representative of the University of Virginia gender
clinic told the *National Enquirer* (1979: 1) that 'following a sex-change
operation, the new female is able to function normally with the exception of having babies'. Money (1972: 204) claimed that the owner of an
'artificial vagina' from Johns Hopkins University 'enjoys sexual intercourse,
experiencing a pervasive warm glow of erotic feeling and in some instances,
a peak of climatic feeling that corresponds to the orgasm of former days'.
Human experiences such as sexual fulfilment and gender-role comfort were
thus transformed into luxury commodities available at high prices from
US physicians; victims of aberrant gender-role conditioning and other
sexual deviants were induced to seek gratification in a commodified world
of 'artificial vaginas' and fleshy, man-made penises.

Physicians now admit that '"transsexualism" was apparently made so
appealing that doctors report patients saying, "I want to be a transsexual"'
(Person and Ovesey, 1974a: 17). Early follow-up reports discouraged
patient wariness. Pauly (1968: 465) reviewed 121 post-operative cases and
concluded unequivocally that 'improved social and emotional adjustments

is at least 10 times more likely than an unsatisfactory outcome'.[14] Ihlenfeld's (1973a) evaluation of 277 post-operative patients was only three pages long; Gandy's (1973) study of seventy-four patients consisted of two pages and a table. All the reports were superficial.[15] Relying entirely on patients' self-reports that they would 'do it all again', researchers neglected the lesson of cognitive dissonance research which suggests that post-operative patients could ill afford to be critical of such a profound alteration as genital amputation.[16]

Follow-up evaluations and the discovery of 'the con'

Early follow-up studies, which minimised complications and stressed post-operative adjustment, were important for the legitimisation of sex-change operations. Gradually, however, a number of disquieting items surfaced in the medical literature, including what appears to be a 'polysurgical attitude' among post-operative transsexuals demanding repeated forms of cosmetic surgery (Pauly, 1969b: 47) and many surgical complications. In 1977, the Stanford University gender clinic, thought by many professionals to perform the finest sex-change surgery in the country, reported that their two-stage female-to-male conversion took an average of 3.5 operations and that half of their male-to-female conversions involved complications (Norburg and Laub, 1977). Post-operative complications reported in medical journals include: breast cancer in hormonally-treated males; the need for surgical reduction of bloated limbs resulting from hormones; repeated construction of vaginal openings; infections of the urinary system and rectum; haemorrhaging; loss of skin grafts; post-operative suicides and suicide attempts; persistent post-operative economic dependency; patient demands to reverse surgery; chronic post-operative depression, psychosis, and phobia; sexual dysfunctions; and pre- and post-operative prostitution, often necessitated by the high cost of treatment. Some sex-change patients threatened 'to shoot the genitals of the surgeon with a shotgun' (Laub and Fisk, 1974); others filed legal suits, euphemistically referred to by Money (1972: 208) as 'a psychopathically litigious disposition'.[17]

As the frequency and range of complications became known, physicians were shocked by a bizarre revelation: transsexuals had routinely and systematically lied. Since transsexualism is initially self-diagnosed and because there are no organic indications of the 'disease', physicians are dependent upon the accuracy and honesty of patients' statements for diagnosis as well as for their understanding of the illness. Deception became so commonplace that Stoller (1973a: 536) complained: 'Those of us faced with the task of diagnosing transsexualism have an additional burden these days, for most patients who request sex-reassignment are in complete command of the literature and know the answers before the questions are asked.' The psychiatrist's task was to judge how well patients' self-reported life histories fit the criteria for transsexualism established in the medical literature. Since the reputable clinics treated only 'textbook' cases of transsexualism, patients desiring surgery, for whatever personal reasons, had no other recourse but to meet this evaluation standard. The construction of an appropriate biography became necessary. Physicians reinforced this demand by rewarding compliance with surgery and punishing honesty with an unfavourable evaluation. The result was a social process we call 'the con'.

An elaborate and well-informed patient grapevine, indirectly facilitated by the Erikson Educational Foundation's patient services, conveyed tips on each clinic's evaluative criteria and on 'passing':

> Unlike the old medical saw that claims the last time you see a text-book case of anything is when you close the textbook, we began to see patients that appeared to be nearly identical – both from a subjec-tive and historical point of view ... Soon it became conspicuously and disturbingly apparent that far too many patients presented a pat, almost rehearsed history, and seemingly were well versed in precisely what they should or should not say or reveal. Only later did we learn that there did and does exist a very effective grape-vine.
>
> (Fisk, 1973: 8)

In many instances, the con involved outright deception. For example, a physician warned the Fifth International Gender Dysphoria Symposium in 1977 to watch out for a male-to-female post-operative transsexual posing as the mother of young, male candidates in order to corroborate their early socialisation accounts of ambivalent gender cues and over-mothering. More often, the process was less direct. Fisk (1973: 9) acknowledges 'the phenomenon of retrospectively "amending" one's subjective history. Here, the patient quite subtly alters, shades, rationalises, denies, represses, forgets, etc., in a compelling rush to embrace the diagnosis of transsexualism.' Many patients were as familiar with the medical literature as physicians were.[18]

As early as 1968, Kubie and Mackie (1968: 435) observed that patients demanding surgery 'tailor their views of themselves and their personal histories to prevailing "scientific" fashions'. Kubie and Mackie warned other physicians that such persons 'must present themselves as textbook examples of "transsexuals" if they are to persuade any team of physicians to change them'. This advice went largely unheeded until, gradually, in follow-up conversations, some model patients admitted having shaped biographical accounts to exclude discrediting information, including homo-sexual and erotic, heterosexual pasts. One patient revealed: 'When I assumed the feminine role, I really researched and studied the part, and in essence, I have *conned you and otherwise charmed you* into believing in me' (Roth, 1973: 101, emphasis added).[19]

DWIGHT B. BILLINGS AND THOMAS URBAN

Jon Meyer (1973: 35), director of Johns Hopkins University's gender clinic, complained that 'the label "transsexual" has come to cover such a "multitude of sins" '. Meyer (1974) acknowledged that among the patients who had requested and sometimes received surgery at Johns Hopkins were sadists, homosexuals, schizoids, masochists, homosexual prostitutes and psychotic depressives. Stanford University physicians, too, admitted that among the patients they had operated on were transvestites, homosexuals and psychotics – all previously viewed as distinct from transsexuals (Fisk, 1973).

The politics of re-naming

In the light of patient revelations, proponents of sex-change surgery were dangerously close to the accusations made by psychoanalytic critics – collaboration with psychosis. Fisk (1973: 8) proposed a solution. Instead of questioning the conceptual, clinical and diagnostic substructure of the 'disease', he simply replaced the term 'transsexual' with 'gender dysphoria syndrome', now a standard disease term.[20] This seemingly inconsequential shift in nomenclature had profound implications for medical practice. A wide variety of applicants for sex-change surgery, once unacceptable under Benjamin's classification, became legitimate candidates.

With transsexualism largely denuded of its diagnostic boundaries, physicians de-emphasised the technicalities of diagnostic differentiation and stressed behavioural criteria instead. As the Stanford University team put it: 'Indeed, for prognosis, it is probable that the diagnostic category is of much less importance than the patient's pre-operative performance in a one-to-three year therapeutic trial of living in the gender of his choice' (Laub and Fisk, 1974: 401). Ironically, such trials are no longer necessary, since sex-change surgery is now widely available in the United States upon demand. One physician who had performed approximately 100 sex-change operations in private practice told us that he diagnosed male-to-female transsexuals by bullying them: 'The "girls" cry; the gays get aggressive.' He also asked his female receptionist to interview candidates, since 'a woman always knows a woman', In 1978, this physician had not yet heard the term 'gender dysphoria'. Such practices have led some early advocates of surgery to decry the 'carnival-like atmosphere' in many medical settings (Stoller, 1973b). In the long run, with much of the conceptual foundation of the disease undermined, the true transsexual appears to be simply one who does not regret the surgery. At a conference we observed in 1977, Richard Green, who in 1970 had described transsexualism as 'a unique behavioural phenomenon' (Baker and Green, 1970), jokingly said: 'I guess, like love, transsexualism is never having to say, "I'm sorry" '.

Our own participant observation in a prominent gender clinic confirms that diagnosis in the post-Benjamin era remains a subtle negotiation process between patients and physicians, in which the patient's troubles are defined, legitimised and regulated as illness. The ways in which patients prove their gender and physicians' cognitive frameworks for evaluating these claims are both grounded in commonsense knowledge of how gender is ordinarily communicated in everyday life. Physicians admitted to us that they are still groping in the dark: 'We just don't know. This whole thing is experimental', said one physician. We found that admission to surgery depended less on formal, rational, or fixed criteria than on the common sense of clinicians. Physicians scrutinised patients' accounts to discover their motivations. Extensive and costly screening procedures designed to test commitment were subverted by patients schooled in withholding damning evidence, such as histories of drug abuse, arrests and inconsistent sexual behaviour. We observed patients using a special vocabulary of excuses and justifications to satisfy physicians who insisted on ritualised expressions such as 'I always played with dolls as a child'. The following dialogue illustrates the coaching we observed in interviews:

Physician: 'You said you always felt like a girl – what is that?'
Patient: [long pause] 'I don't know.'
Physician: 'Sexual attraction? Played with girls' toys?'

Despite physicians' belief that the semantic shift to 'gender dysphoria syndrome' was effective in 'allowing and encouraging our patients to be honest, open, and candid, with the result that our overall evaluations quickly became truly meaningful' (Fisk, 1973: 10), patient screening and interviewing still function as patient socialisation. Diagnosis is linked to routine everyday gender typifications (Goffman, 1977). More than anything else, physical appearance enables patients to control screening interviews; successful cross-dressing often truncates the screening process. When patients appear at a clinic convincingly cross-dressed, verbal slips or doubtful accounts are set right by covering accounts – or are simply glossed over because physical appearance confirms the gender claimed. On the other hand, discrepant appearances are taken as alarming signs. One physician told us: 'We're not taking Puerto Ricans any more; they don't look like transsexuals. They look like fags.'

Among the transsexual patients we interviewed were ministers who embraced the label 'transsexual' to avoid being labelled 'homosexual'; sexual deviants driven by criminal laws against cross-dressing, or by rejecting parents and spouses, to the shelter of the 'therapeutic state' (Kittrie, 1973); and enterprising male prostitutes cashing in on the profitable market for transsexual prostitutes which thrives in some large cities.[21] The following statement from a patient we interviewed whose lover was also a post-operative male-to-female reveals how inadequately the medical image of the stable, life-long transsexual fits some patients' experiences and motivations:

I thought I was a homosexual at one time; then I got married and had a child so I figured I was a heterosexual; then because of cross-dressing I thought I was a transvestite. Now [post-operatively] I see myself as bisexual.

IMPLICATIONS FOR CRITICAL THEORY

Forms of illness are always more than biological disease; they are also metaphors, bearing existential, moral and social meanings (Sontag, 1978). According to Taussig (1980: 3), 'the signs and symptoms of disease, as much as the technologies of healing, are not "things-in-themselves", are not only biological and physical, but are also signs of social relations disguised as natural things, concealing their roots in human reciprocity'. Even with negotiated illnesses which often lack a basis in biology, the reified disease language of natural science obscures their social origins (Holzner and Marx, 1979: 137). Disease-talk is about things, not social interaction. Patients whose subjective histories are subsumed under the unifying rhetoric of transsexualism win operations but no language adequate to express the disparate and diverse desires which lead them to body mutilation. These remain private, inchoate, unspeakable.[22]

Critical theorists describe the ideal therapy situation as a paradigm of non-distorted communication (Habermas, 1968: 214). Rather than 'treat human beings as the quasi-natural objects of description', the goal of communication is patients' self-reflection and emancipation from the reified pseudo-language of neurotic symptoms (Apel, 1977: 310).

> The real task of therapy calls for an archaeology of the implicit in such a way that the processes by which social relations are mapped into diseases are brought to light, de-reified, and in doing so liberate the potential for dealing with antagonistic contradictions and breaking the chains of oppression.
>
> (Taussig, 1980: 7)

According to this view, therapy promises either to provide patients with sufficient self-understanding to criticise society and struggle politically against the crippling effects of social institutions or to provide new fetishes and easily commodifiable solutions to personal troubles (Kovel, 1976–7).

Transsexual therapy, legitimised by the terminology of disease, pushes patients towards an alluring world of artificial vaginas and penises rather than towards self-understanding and sexual politics. Sexual fulfilment and gender-role comfort are portrayed as commodities, available through medicine. Just as mass consumer culture, whose values are illusive, offers commodities whose 'staged appearance' are removed from the mundane world of their production (Schneider, 1975: 213), surgically constructed vaginas are abstracted from the pain and trauma of operating rooms and recovery wards.

Critical theorists claim that the illusions of consumerism can be as pathological for individuals as the neuroses and psychoses symptomatic of the earlier period of capitalist industrial production (Lasch, 1978). Today, in late-capitalist consumer culture, frenzied rituals of buying contradict the puritanical self-denial characteristic of the nineteenth century. We express our identity as much by the things we buy as the work we do. Commodities promise escape from alienation, and the fulfilment of our needs. Critics compare the temporary solace of consumer spending with the transitory euphoria of a drug-induced trance (Schneider, 1975: 222). Similarly, transsexuals are in danger of becoming surgical junkies as they strive for an idealised sexuality via surgical commodities. This is what physicians refer to as a 'poly-surgical attitude' among post-operative patients (Pauly, 1969a). Male-to-female patients especially are caught up in an escalating series of cosmetic operations – including genital amputation – to more closely approximate ideal female form. They routinely demand breast implants and operations to reduce the size of the Adam's apple. Edgerton (1974) reports that 30 per cent of his patients also sought rhinoplasty (nose reconstruction); others demand injections of Teflon to modulate vocal pitch and silicon to alter the contours of face, lips, hips and thighs. Surgeons reduce the thickness of ankles and calves and shorten limbs. In their desperation to pass, male-to-female patients try to effect a commodified image of femininity seen in television advertising. In so doing, many patients are themselves transformed into commodities, resorting to prostitution to pay their medical bills.[23]

While it is difficult to assess the ultimate worth of consumer products, we can try to discern the false promises implicit in their appeal. In the absence of adequate follow-up research, it is impossible to assess the lasting value of sex-change surgery, though recent studies suggest an almost invariable erosion of the transsexual fantasy following an initial 'phase of elation' lasting two to five years after surgery (Meyer and Hoopes, 1974). Johns Hopkins University physicians stopped performing sex-change operations in 1979 on the grounds that the patients they operated on were no better off than a sample of transsexual patients who received psychotherapy but not surgery (Meyer and Reter, 1979). Other prominent clinics, however, continue to perform surgery (Hunt and Hampson, 1980).

The following excerpt from a letter written by one transsexual who underwent surgery expresses the disappointment and anguish of some patients:

> No surgery can possibly produce anything that resembles a female vagina. The operation is a theft. [The surgically remodelled tissue] is nothing but an open wound. It needs dilation to keep it open and

if dilated too much become useless for intercourse, Such an open wound lacks protective membranes and bleeds under pressure . . . A piece of phallus with an open wound below and a ring of scrotum hanging is all it is . . . Who calls that an artificial vagina is nothing but a bandit looking for ignorant and credulous people to exploit them.

(quoted in Socarides, 1975: 130)

The evidence suggests that Meyer and Hoopes were correct when they wrote that,

in a thousand subtle ways, the reassignee has the bitter experience that he is not – and never will be – a real girl but is, at best, a convincing simulated female. Such an adjustment cannot compensate for the tragedy of having lost all chance to be male and of having, in the final analysis, no way to be really female.

(Meyer and Hoopes, 1974: 450)

THE POLITICS OF SEX-REASSIGNMENT

Taussig (1980: 7) shows that 'behind every disease theory in our society lurks an organising realm of moral concerns'. In this paper we have examined both physicians' and patients' motives for sex-change surgery. We conclude that at the level of ideology, sex-change surgery not only reflects and extends late-capitalist logics of reification and commodification, but simultaneously plays an implicit role in contemporary sexual politics.

The recognition that, in this day and age, the fulfilment of human desires is less a matter of public discussion than a technical accomplishment of social administration (Habermas, 1973: 253) applies equally to sex-changes. Medicine brushes aside the politics of gender to welcome suffering patients – many fleeing harassment for sexual deviance[24] – into pseudo-tolerant gender identity clinics. Yet these clinics are implicitly political and, indirectly, intolerant.

With reproduction and sexual functioning falling under medical jurisdiction, physicians have played crucial roles in maintaining gender organisation (Ehrenreich and English, 1973). In providing a rite of passage between sexual identities, sex-change surgery implicitly reaffirms traditional male and female roles. Despite the mute testimony of confused and ambivalent patients to the range of gender experience, individuals unable or unwilling to confirm to the sex-roles ascribed to them at birth are carved up on the operating table to gain acceptance to the opposite sex-role.[25]

Critical theorists contend that, in the United States, hegemonic ideology absorbs and domesticates conflicting definitions of reality (Gitlin, 1979: 263). But rather than support contemporary movements aimed at reorganising gender and parenting roles and repudiating the either/or logic of gender development (Chodorow, 1978: 1979; Ehrensaft, 1980), sex-change proponents support sex-reassignment surgery. By substituting medical terminology for political discourse, the medical profession has indirectly tamed and transformed a potential wildcat strike at the gender factory.[26]

NOTES

1 We spent four years analysing several hundred medical journal accounts of sex-change surgery and interviewing scores of physicians and patients in a variety of clinical settings throughout the United States. In addition, Thomas Urban was a participant observer for three years (1978–80) in a sex-change clinic.

2 Pioneer sex researchers Magus Hirschfeld and Havelock Ellis described an asexual variety of transvestism in which males completely identify as females (Horton and Clarke, 1931). Benjamin (1954) only reasserted this distinction by calling attention to it with the term 'transsexual'. For doing so he is honoured as the father of 'Benjaminian transsexualism', even though Cauldwell (1949a) first used the term.

3 Freedman, Green and Spitzer (1976: 61) refer to the discovery of transsexualism as a recent major advance in the behavioural sciences. They estimate one in 40,000 men are transsexuals.

4 Subsequently, Money, Hampson and Hampson (1957) compared gender-role learning in humans to 'critical imprinting' in some animal species which, they argued, begins in the first year of life.

5 Some experiments were not so 'natural', University of Minnesota researchers, for instance, were curious about the effects of high estrogen dosage and surgery on 'profound psychopaths'. Not surprisingly, they concluded that 'if there is one follow-up conclusion that can be made with assurance at this stage, it is that estrogen and sex-reassignment surgery do not alter the sociopathic transsexual' (Hastings, 1974).

6 Such operations 'represented a unique experience and challenge to perfect techniques heretofore restricted to the treatment of congenital malformations and traditionally the province of the urologist and gynecologist, rather than the plastic surgeons' (Money and Schwartz, 1969: 255). The desire for jurisdictional expansion and prestige among lower-status medical specialties – in this case, plastic surgery and psychiatry – is especially 'conducive to the "discovery" of a particular deviant label' as Pfohl (1977: 310) shows in the case of the 'discovery' of child abuse by pediatric radiologists.

7 Physicians' fees alone – apart from hospitalisation – for 628 patients and 169 operations at Stanford University's sex-change clinic totalled $413,580.00. This figure excludes the cost of psychiatric counselling and other operations (e.g., rhinoplasty, augmentation mamoplasty and thyroid cartilage shaves) which patients usually demand. Some private practitioners have performed up to 1,000 sex-change operations. Restak (1980: 11) calls sex-change surgery a '$10 million growth industry'.

8 Other university hospitals, such as the University of Minnesota's, began surgical treatment at roughly the same time but avoided public disclosure (Hastings, 1969). In addition, a few operations were secretly performed in the 1950s at the University of California at San Francisco (Benjamin, 1966: 142). We have

learned that Cook County Hospital in Chicago was performing sex-change operations as early as 1947, predating Jorgensen's famous European surgery by five years.

9 They attempted a further semantic shift by questioning the term 'delusional', arguing that the request for sex-change surgery, given medical technology, is no more delusional than the request to go to the moon, given modern space technology (Knorr, Wolf and Meyer, 1969).

10 There was considerably less agreement on the etiology and diagnosis of female transsexualism, partly because there is no concept of female transvestism. Clinicians at the University of California at Los Angeles found female transsexuals harder to identify than male transsexuals (Stoller, 1972), while the Johns Hopkins University clinic reported the opposite (Money and Gaskin, 1970–1). An influential theory of female transsexualism was offered by Pauly (1969a).

11 The strategic political value of rationalisation/standardisation is also apparent. In 1977, at the Fifth International Gender Dysphoria Syndrome Symposium in Norfolk, Virginia, we heard a leading physician argue for a committee to prepare policy guidelines by saying: 'If we have such a committee we can hold the American Medical Association and the American College of Surgeons in abeyance.'

12 Freidson (1970: 254) has noted the contributions of such crusading lay interest groups to the professional construction of illness. These 'flamboyant moral entrepreneurs' function like advocacy organisations in movements to define social problems (Blumer, 1971; Spector and Kitsuse, 1977). They seek public support for the application of the label of illness to behaviours (such as excessive drinking) not otherwise defined as illness, e.g., alcoholism (Conrad, 1975).

13 The foundation convinced the Pennsylvania Health Department to issue authorisation permits for pre-surgical cross-dressing and it lobbied successfully throughout the United States for new birth certificates for post-operative patients.

14 Compare also Baker and Green (1970), Edgerton, Knorr and Collison (1970), Hoenig, Kenna and Youd (1971), Money and Gaskin (1970–1), and Randell (1969).

15 In the most extensive review of follow-up literature to date, Tiefer and Zitrin (1977) report that of ten unpublished and nineteen published reports, twenty-four were 'preliminary', 'anecdotal', or 'brief'. Of the five studies rated 'excellent', only two were by US physicians – with a combined sample of thirty-eight patients – despite the fact that thousands of operations have been performed in the United States.

16 Thus, one patient with a 'terrible sense of foreboding' immediately after surgery, when asked whether he had done the wrong thing, responded: 'But if I did, well, it's done and I have to find some way to adjust to it' (quoted in Money and Wolff, 1973: 248). See also Stoller and Newman (1971: 26).

17 Compare Hastings (1974), Levine, Shaiova and Mihailovic (1975), Markland (1973), Meyer and Hoopes (1974), Randell (1971) and Tiefer and Zitrin (1977) for reports on complications.

18 In addition to bibliographies and summaries of technical literature published in the Erikson Education Foundation Newsletter and Benjamin's (1966) book addressed to laymen, autobiographies of famous transsexuals are an additional resource for patient socialisation. See Jorgensen (1967), Martino (1977) and Morris (1974).

19 Physicians' efforts to be open and sympathetic to their patients, despite their need for reliable information, facilitated 'the con'. Edgerton, Knorr and

Collison (1970: 44) advised their colleagues: 'It is not difficult for the surgeon to establish a good relationship with transsexual patients – but to do so, he must deal with the patient as a member of the psychological sex chosen by the patient.'

20 Person and Ovesey (1974a; 1974b) attempted a similar renaming by referring to Benjaminian transsexualism as 'primary transsexualism'. Other patients, who lacked the non-erotic or life-long attributes, were labelled 'secondary transsexuals'.

21 See Meyer (1974) for a discussion of the diversity of sex-change aspirants seen at Johns Hopkins University.

22 See Janice Raymond (1980) for an opposing critique of sex-change as an attempt by certain men to benefit from and co-opt women's newly-won privileges which result from feminist consciousness and struggle.

23 For the correlation between financial dependency during reassignment and prostitution, see Hastings (1974), Levine, Shaiova and Mihailovic (1975), Meyer (1974) and Norburg and Laub (1977).

24 For physician reports of harassed patients, see Benjamin (1971: 77), Edgerton, Knorr and Collison (1970: 43), Meyer and Hoopes (1974: 450) and Randell (1971: 157).

25 Physicians' remarks on the prevention of transsexualism make the political implications of sex-change overt: deviations from traditional roles are potentially harmful to children. Benjamin (1971: 76) warns that male children's curiosity about female clothing 'should never be made light of by parents' and Richard Green (1969: 33) warns of 'sissy behaviour during childhood' and of 'playing "house"'. Accepting Stoller's theory of the dominating mother as the principal agent of transsexual socialisation, Green contends that 'goals of family therapy are for the husband and wife to gain some perspective on the second-class status of the husband and on the significance of their unbalanced roles in shaping their son's personality'. Similarly, Newman and Stoller (1971: 301) report success in effecting a 'therapeutically induced Oedipus complex' on a 'very feminine boy' by encouraging the child to assert his male identity by first beating a doll and then expressing aggression toward his mother and sister.

26 Said one politically aware transsexual quoted by Feinbloom (1976: 159): 'As long as society insists on requiring everyone to fit in a strict two-gender system, the whole transsexual thing will always be a game, to hide what I've been or what I want to be. If the women's movement is so into freeing up the definitions of gender, why not start with us?'

Part IV

GENDER BLENDING
AND THE MEDIA

INTRODUCTION

The large medical and psychological literature dealing with cross-dressing and sex-changing (see Part III) is probably larger than the prevalence of these phenomena would lead one to expect (Hoenig, 1985). The coverage of these topics by the mass media is probably even greater again, and certainly reaches a wider audience than does the medical and psychological literature. Cross-dressing and sex-changing, in some form, are to be found in novels (Farrer, 1992; Hoenig, 1985), plays and poetry (Hoenig, 1985), in the theatre (Ferris, 1993), on cinema screens (Ekins, 1996), on radio and television and in the press (Ekins, 1990b; 1992a).

As one moves out from the few medical and psychological specialists in 'gender identity disorders' – through specialists in other psycho-sexual areas, psychiatrists and other medical professionals – to lay members of society, it becomes probable that 'knowledge' of cross-dressing and sex-changing is framed less and less by the medical literature and more and more by the mass media. There are grounds, then, for regarding the media as potentially having the greater influence on the conceptions of these phenomena held by the general public, the largest part of the medical profession and many of those who themselves cross-dress and sex-change.

However, as we argued in the introduction to Part III, medicine has become the culturally major lens through which gender blending is viewed in modern Western societies. So, whilst, as King argues in Chapter 10, the media do not simply reproduce medical knowledge, this perspective has had a major impact on the media treatment of gender blending. Peter Farrer in Chapter 9 shows that, from around the 1930s onwards, sex-changing in literature came to reflect the opportunities that were becoming available in the real world to change sex endocrinologically and surgically. A similar trend can be seen in the popular press discussed by King in Chapter 10.

However, behind all the various press, television and radio reports and the novels films and stage plays there is a necessary backdrop – a system

119

of two gender categories, based on sex and distinguished by 'appropriate' dress, mannerisms and many other characteristics. The 'self-evidence' of this system is what gives the media content any point at all. Only on this basis can the producer and consumer make sense of it.

There has been a spate of recent books discussing isolated aspects of cross-dressing and sex-changing in literature and on the stage (Epstein and Straub, 1991; Ferris, 1993; Garber, 1992). Earlier writings included Bullough (1976), Habegger (1982) and Hoenig (1985). Whilst being valuable in their own terms, these works serve to highlight the difficulty faced by the researcher working in this area. How is the researcher to access the vast numbers of cross-dressing and sex-changing incidents and themes in literature without satisfactory summaries and indexes? It is here that Peter Farrer's research comes into its own. Farrer (1992) provides an excellent overview of English and American novels and stories up to 1900 in which the male is petticoated either in reality or imagination. This work was followed by a provisional list of novels published between 1901 and 1950 in which mention of cross-dressing is made (Ekins, 1992b). The list includes everything, from a whole novel whose central theme is cross-dressing, to a single phrase or sentence in a novel that makes reference to it. Ekins (1992b) notes that Farrer also introduced a preliminary classification scheme with such categories as 'Fauntleroy or girlish costume – normal wear'; 'boys – complete masquerade as a girl'; 'boys in theatrical performances'; 'masquerading for fun'; 'compulsory masquerade as a woman'; 'historical'; 'eccentric or effeminate men in full or partial feminine attire'; 'female disguise for concealment or escape'; 'female disguise for some practical purposes, to outwit enemies or commit crime'; 'futurist or feminist element in the cross-dressing'; 'magical change of physical sex'; 'magical transposition of male mind into female body'; and 'change of sex by science fiction'.

In Chapter 9, Farrer continues his work of documentation and preliminary classification by providing a brief survey of male cross-dressing and sex-changing in English and American literature over the last 120 years.

Cross-dressing and sex-changing have attracted the attention of the press for some time. In 1928, Havelock Ellis wrote of what he called 'eonism' that, 'although this psychic peculiarity is so difficult both to name and define, it is, strange as that may seem, the commonest of all sexual anomalies to attain prominence in the public newspapers' (Ellis, 1928: 29). Farrer (1987) reprints extracts from newspapers and magazines dating back to the 1880s, and it was in the early 1870s that the famous Boulton and Park case received prominent press coverage. So for at least 120 years, crossing the gender line has been a topic of interest to the popular press. In Chapter 10, Dave King analyses the ways in which the (mainly British) press covers the topic and considers the possible consequences of this. In Chapter 8, Billings and Urban argued that the media played a central role in 'selling' transsexualism and sex-change. King's chapter considers their claim and the similar claims of others, concluding that – at least in the case of Britain – the evidence suggests that the situation was, and is, rather more complex.

Telephone sex lines are now big business. About 330 million calls were made to premium-rate phone lines in the United Kingdom in 1992, producing a £200 million turnover for the industry. An estimated 12 per cent of this business covered adult services (ICSTIS, 1993). A large number of these services feature aspects of gender blending. In Chapter 11, Richard Ekins focuses on the pre-recorded male femaling telephone scripts that provided a new and readily accessible source of masturbatory fantasy for male femalers in the late 1980s and early 1990s. Working within the framework developed in Chapter 3, Ekins shows how the scripts co-opt facets of 'body femaling' and 'gender femaling' in the service of 'erotic fantasy femaling' with particular reference to a hitherto unidentified type of male femaling masturbatory script, namely, that of the 'intimacy script'. In doing so, the chapter provides a valuable case study in some neglected interrelations between sex, sexuality and gender. And further, it opens up a hitherto unresearched area of enquiry.

9

120 YEARS OF MALE CROSS-DRESSING AND SEX-CHANGING IN ENGLISH AND AMERICAN LITERATURE

Peter Farrer

Towards the end of the last century there was a marked increase in the number of male characters appearing in female guise in English and American fiction. This occurred at all levels of taste and readership, from a popular novel such as *A Florida Enchantment* (1891b),[1] to erotica such as *Gynecocracy* (1893).

There were several aspects to this increase. Prominent authors – such as Mark Twain, Rudyard Kipling and Conan Doyle – seem to have been particularly drawn to the idea of cross-dressing and used it on a number of occasions. Female disguise was assumed in a wider range of fiction than previously – as well as in novels of romance, history or adventure it was to be found in books for children, in science fiction, in erotica and in the writings of confessed cross-dressers. In addition, the concept of disguise was extended to include both the bodily transformation of sex and the transposition of souls between bodies of the opposite sex. More fundamentally, it was during this period that for the first time cross-dressing was seen in the English and American short story, and that entire novels were based on the disguise of the hero as a woman.

Why should this have happened when it did? This was a time when relations between the sexes were under scrutiny in a number of contexts, particularly, of course, in the political field. What rights should women have? People were also asking how should the two sexes behave towards each other. There was a movement for dress reform, but at the same time fashionable women flaunted the most extravagant and luxurious forms of dress. Against this background men and women began to reflect with a deeper interest on what it would be like to belong to the opposite sex. It was no coincidence, perhaps, that this period also saw the emergence of sexology as a discipline. For the first time, scientific writers began to classify variations in sexual life and the identities which crystallised around them (Bullough and Bullough, 1993: 174–225; Sulloway, 1980: 277–319).

BEGINNINGS IN ALDRICH, TWAIN AND KIPLING

'Mademoiselle Olympe Zabriski' (1873), by the American writer Thomas Bailey Aldrich, is the first story in English I have located in which a man dressed as a woman plays an important part. Zabriski, an acrobat, is dressed for his performance in a woman's stage costume, giving the illusion of a female acrobat. The background to the story is that some female acrobats and circus performers at this time were actually men or boys – one such was El Nino Farini, known as 'Lulu', who performed in England in 1870 (Farrer, 1992: 209). So here we have fiction elaborating upon cross-dressing in reality. The point of the story is that a very respectable Bostonian falls in love with Zabriski, believing him to be a woman. He is no longer seen in his usual haunts because he is going to every performance. He sends 'her' a diamond bracelet and is only disillusioned when the acrobat writes a comically frank letter accepting the gift.

Aldrich does not seem to have employed the idea of cross-dressing again. Mark Twain, however, as Garber (1992: 288–91) has pointed out, had a special interest in cross-dressing and sexual ambiguity. His first attempt at representing this idea was in the short story, '1,002nd Arabian night' (1883) in which two babies, one of each sex, are transposed at birth. In *Huckleberry Finn* (1884) the hero dresses up as a girl in order to find out what is happening at home since he ran away. In *Pudd'nhead Wilson* (1894) the essential element of the plot is a switch of two male babies, one with a trace of negro blood. The latter, as Tom Driscoll, dresses up as a girl to facilitate his thieving.

The English writer Rudyard Kipling used the device of cross-dressing in a number of stories of revenge. In 'His wedded wife' (1888a), for instance, a junior subaltern, a newcomer to the mess, is teased by everyone, but particularly by the senior subaltern. Finally, 'The Worm', as he is called in the story, turns. He bets his tormentor that he will 'work a sell' on him that he will remember all his life. One evening, when the ladies had joined the men, a beautiful woman enters claiming to be the senior subaltern's wife. After making a passionate scene the lady is asked for her marriage certificate, whereupon she produces a document which claims the satisfaction of the bet. This story builds upon the contemporary passion for amateur theatricals, in which young men quite often played women's parts. Later 'The Worm' explains that he has learnt to act with his sisters at home.

In 'The honours of war' (1911c) two subalterns capture and tie up in a sack an unpopular fellow subaltern. He gets his revenge with the help of Stalky and the latter's friends. They fasten the two men up in sacks, drape them in muslin, put bonnets and feathers on their heads and take them to the officer's mess. Here, enforced cross-dressing is used as a punishing humiliation.

MALE CROSS-DRESSING STORIES IN TURN-OF-THE-CENTURY PAPERS FOR WOMEN

Between 1889 and 1900 the English society paper *Modern Society* (see Chapter 1) published a number of anonymous stories which explored the idea of the man in female attire. The paper was aimed mainly at a female readership and a brief examination of a number of the stories will indicate the sort of incidents thought likely to amuse its readers.

'A Clifton masculine maid' (1891a) elaborates the use of female disguise for crime, a not uncommon theme. As a resident maid in a wealthy area, 'Milly' is in an ideal position to execute a series of robberies. 'Her' true sex and identity are kept secret both from the reader and 'her' admirer, until the police finally catch up with 'her'.

In 'Dainty Dolly's wager' (1900a) Dolly is by nature an accomplished amateur female impersonator. No one objects to this. What his friends resent is his conceit; so when he bets them he will ride a bicycle a distance of thirty miles dressed as a woman, they decide to outwit him. At a certain point they place tacks on the road and Dolly gets a puncture. He is helped by two 'ladies' in the house nearby, but these are his friends in disguise who amuse themselves at his expense and prevent him from continuing his journey.

'The twins' (1900b) concerns boy and girl twins. The occasion is a woman's golf championship and the girl twin is expected to win. When she is injured her brother surreptitiously takes her place and wins the championship. He is about to receive the prize when his father recognises him. Interestingly, in both of these stories the cross-dressing is regarded as acceptable behaviour. What is unacceptable is the young man's boasting in the first story and the fraud on the other women in the second.

CONAN DOYLE, SHERLOCK HOLMES AND DETECTIVE FICTION

It was not only in the specialised pages of *Modern Society* that such stories appeared. In Conan Doyle's first Sherlock Holmes story *A Study in Scarlet* (1888b) an unnamed man is disguised as an old woman. In 1898 *The Strand Magazine* published his story, 'The story of the man with the watches', in which the younger of two criminals assists the other disguised as a woman. Doyle also used female disguise to good effect in 'The fall of Lord Barrymore' (1912) and, again, in the late Sherlock Holmes story, 'The adventure of Shoscombe Old Place' (1927b). Garber (1992: 186) rightly refers to cross-dressing as being a classic strategy of disappearance in detective fiction.

PRE-1914 SEX-CHANGING: MAGIC, SCIENCE FICTION AND HYPNOTISM

A new way of exploring the relationship between the sexes in fiction is to have people change sex. In the days before knowledge of hormones and sex-reassignment procedures, authors used magic and pseudo-scientific procedures to effect the change of sex. Sometimes the body remains the same but a different 'soul' inhabits it. Sometimes the body itself changes. W.S. Gilbert was amongst the first to employ this device for the purposes of sex-change in his short play, 'Happy Arcadia' first performed on 28 October 1872 for the German Reeds' *Gallery of Illustration*. In this play the four people involved change sex as well as generations.

The first major novel to employ this idea as its central theme seems to have been *A Florida Enchantment* (1891b). As in 'Happy Arcadia', both sexes are involved in the sex-changing. The change of sex involved in this novel might be classified as either science fiction or magic. A person who swallows the seed of the 'Tree of Sexual Change' changes sex. The Tree is destroyed and the last four seeds come into the possession of Miss Lillian Travers, who is engaged to Dr Frederick Cassadene. When Lillian discovers that Frederick is not true to her, she takes one of the seeds and persuades her coloured maid to do the same. Her body immediately starts to change into that of a male. In her male body she falls in love with her previous girlfriend, Bessie. At this point Miss Travers and her maid are essentially men but still dressed as women. They then go to New York to establish their male identities and return to Florida as Lawrence and Jack. In due course Lawrence woos and wins Bessie, but not before Frederick has accused him of murdering Lillian. Lawrence tells him: 'I was once Lilly Travers' and considers taking the third seed. Instead, they force Frederick to take it and he becomes a woman. It is evident that there is an element of punishment in this. He is being punished for his womanising. Before the book ends, however, Frederick is allowed to take the last seed and is restored to his male sex.

The theme of sex-changing by hypnotism was explored in a number of books in the period up to 1914. Frank Richardson's mystery thriller, *2835 Mayfair* (1907) is science fiction in that the hero, Sir Clifford, is a doctor pioneering in the application of hypnotism for medical purposes and he devises a cure for cancer. Sir Clifford's hypnotic power is developed to such an extent that he can completely possess a person and take control of his or her body. He uses this power to take control of the body of a young girl so that he can enter her body at will for a period of three days at a time. When under his control the girl, who was formerly plain and wore glasses, becomes the glamorous Miss Clive. The course of the novel reveals what is happening gradually, and the full mystery is not disclosed until the end.

Two more novels of a similar sort followed in 1911. An *Exchange of Souls* (1911a) is another attempt at science fiction. Again, a doctor (Daniel Myas) is doing research with the help of a young woman (Alice Lade). Daniel's aim is to exchange souls with Alice. This is to be achieved, not by hypnosis but by the application of a strong anaesthetic to each of them simultaneously. The experiment goes wrong and his soul is transferred to the girl but his body dies, leaving the girl's soul in limbo. After various struggles charting Daniel's attempts to assert control over Alice, Alice is killed in a motor accident, but the narrator gives evidence that the ghosts of Daniel and Alice are now united in the afterlife.

A Change of Sex (1911b) uses simple magic. If two people say or think certain words together at the same time, these are 'masterwords' and their souls exchange bodies. Kinross uses this device to explore the difference between the sexes. George and Etty are virtually engaged but Etty cannot quite bring herself to accept George. At their last meeting she quotes the lines from 'Georgy Porgy', and as they both go their different ways each says or thinks these words at the same time. Immediately they find themselves in the bodies of each other, but with their own memories and knowledge. Each in turn has to cope with the situation in which the other was placed, George warding off male suitors and Etty coping with a male fishing party and the attention of a flirt who fancies her as a man. George rescues people in a fire, while Etty falls in the river. All this is done in a most amusing way and eventually they change back by repeating the masterwords and they marry in their proper bodies.

CROSS-DRESSING IN CHILDREN'S BOOKS

Episodes of cross-dressing were seen in children's books from the late nineteenth century. In *Rob and Ralph or a Trust Fulfilled* (1882) two orphan boys dress up as girls to go to London to find their grandfather, whilst in *Punch, Judy and Toby* (1895) Toby puts on his grandmother's gown when deprived of his trousers to keep him indoors. The year 1903 saw the publication of a children's story about a boy who was obliged to dress as a girl for most of the time. This was *Boy or Girl?* by an unknown author. Evelyn, although nearly 15, still has long hair for his father to paint. A lady visiting the studio mistakes him for a girl and invites him to accompany her on her travels. For financial reasons his father agrees, and the boy has numerous adventures both in and out of girls' clothes. He falls in love with a real girl and resists the attentions of a youthful admirer. Another children's book wholly devoted to this theme is *Poor Dear Esme* (1925) in which a boy is forced to spend a term at a girls' school because of a mix-up at his birth, and the return to England of someone who believes he is a girl.

EROTICA

A feature of all the examples considered so far is that no implication of eroticism or sexual perversion is ever imputed to cross-dressing or sex-changing. This is not to say, however, that there was not a deliberately erotic literature which featured cross-dressing. A significant example of this genre is *Gynecocracy* (1893). Its authorship is still a matter of speculation. It is the story of Julian Robinson, a troublesome youth of 16, who is sent away to be educated with his three girl cousins under their governess. The action of the book is essentially the flagellation and sexual exploitation of the hero. As part of the humiliation he undergoes, Julian is dressed as a girl. There seem to be two main reasons for this. One of Julian's previous misdemeanours was to have put his hand up the skirts of a maid as she was going upstairs. As a penalty for his indecent exploration of the maid's petticoats he is made to wear petticoats himself. The punishment for male aggression is to become female. But the main reason for his female costume seems to be that it is symbolic of his general subjection to women and their sexual needs. He becomes the victim and wears the clothes of the weaker sex. In these circumstances Julian finds that there is some sexual excitement caused by wearing women's clothes, particularly his governess's underwear. This is the first time that this experience was recorded in erotic literature. The book is extremely rare and would only have reached a very small readership. Nevertheless, it is a part of the output of the late nineteenth century.

MASQUERADE IN THE 1920s AND 1930s

Prior to the period of the First World War men had adopted female disguise to carry out some special task in the course of a plot. After the First World War full-length novels were written in which the adoption of this disguise is the central element in the plot. The fact that many men had taken the parts of women in service theatricals during the war gave added plausibility to the idea of successful masquerade. The first and one of the most intriguing is *A Strange Delilah* (1921). The story is told by Charles Morton who has been a very successful female impersonator in army theatricals. He and his close friend, Jim Mason, are at a loose end just after the war, when the latter sees an advertisement in *The Times:* 'Wanted a young lady as companion to a girl of 17 – highest references given and required, apply Sir Simon Waite, Balastair Castle'. It so happens that Waite has done some grave personal injury to Mason before the war and Mason wishes to recover money and exact vengeance for reasons not fully explained until the end of the book. However, we are now launched into a mystery thriller. Naturally, Charles applies for the job of companion and after some training and purchases of costume with the help of a lady friend of Jim, he enters Balastair Castle as Miss Phyllis Manners. He is amazingly successful and his disguise is not penetrated. He makes friends with the daughter, Violet, and falls in love with her. Meanwhile, Waite is fascinated by 'the strange Delilah' and is completely taken in, and Charles is obliged to resist his advances. Charles reports the results of his investigations to Mason and eventually Mason is secretly admitted to the castle. Waite is finally exposed as a German agent and his nefarious activities are brought to a violent end. Violet is not too happy about Phyllis's masquerade, but is pacified by the end of the book.

In *Miss Torrabin's Experiment* (1927a) another youth masquerades as a girl in a Scottish castle, but this time on his own initiative. Jim Torrabin has left school just after the war and his Aunt Marcia wants him to decide on a career. After a successful evening of theatricals playing a girl's part with his cousins he decides that he would like to go on the stage; his aunt is not so sure. At this point Aunt Marcia receives an invitation from a relative, Jane Faick, for Pat, Jim's sister, aged 18, to come to stay for a fortnight at Castle Faick. Aunt Marcia mentions this to Jim and Jim bets her that he will go to Castle Faick as Pat and survive detection for the fortnight. If he succeeds, he will have proved that he can act. If he fails, he will give up the idea of going on the stage. Aunt Marcia accepts the bet because she wants Jim to learn something of women from their point of view. It is arranged that Jim will go to Scotland as Pat, with Pat as his maid. Aunt Marcia will go with them to see the fun. In Scotland only Jane Faick will be privy to the secret. Jim, as Pat, is pursued by various men and receives a proposal. To his aunt's surprise he eludes detection to the very end, when one of the young men sees him bathing in a pool and he is finally forced to apply manly strength in capturing a cat burglar.

THE CONTEMPORARY TURN: CROSS-DRESSING FOR PLEASURE, SEX-CHANGING FOR 'REAL'

In the course of the twentieth century two aspects of cross-dressing and sex-changing became increasingly explored. On the one hand, more books dealt with the pleasures of cross-dressing; on the other hand, as sex-reassignment became possible, with real rather than fictional alterations of the body, so such treatments came to be incorporated into novels. I conclude with a number of examples of each new development.

It is noticeable that in the work considered so far, erotica apart, no sense is given of the pleasures of cross-dressing. It was the 'pin-up' magazine *Photo Bits* (see Chapter 1) that pioneered this aspect of cross-dressing. 'Velvet, female impersonator' (1909) marks the turn to eroticism in popular fiction. In this short story great stress is laid on the exquisite femininity of the actor, who, it is implied, revels in his glamorous costumes. The story struck a chord. The paper came under pressure to print more such stories and eventually it launched a series entitled '*Amber the Actor*' by Derk Fortescue, which ran for thirty instalments from November 1910 to June 1911. The hero is a good-looking young man, who, under the patronage of Peggy, now Countess of Tanchester, becomes a glamorous female impersonator. It is made clear in every episode that Amber, although entirely masculine, gets enormous pleasure out of wearing skirts.

The path had been cleared for further explorations that take an increasingly erotic turn. Leopold Bloom in James Joyce's *Ulysses* (1922) is a particularly well-known example of a fictional character who had a passion for women's clothes, particularly underwear. As the book proceeds, Bloom's interest in these matters is gradually revealed. In a shop window in Grafton Street he sees 'gleaming silk petticoats on slim brass rails' (p. 157). In a bookshop he turns the pages of 'Sweets of Sin' and finds this: 'All the dollar bills her husband gave her were spent in the stores on wondrous gowns and costliest frillies. For him! For Raoul!' (p. 223). When I first read this passage I thought that Raoul was going to wear the gowns and frillies himself! Then Bloom watches Gertie MacDowell exposing her underwear as she sits on the beach: 'And he could see her other things too, nainsook knickers, the fabric that caresses the skin' (p. 349). Finally, in the fantasy of the brothel scene his inner feelings are expressed when Bella/Bello says to him:

> No more blow hot and cold. What you longed for has come to pass. Henceforth you are unmanned and mine in earnest, a thing under the yoke. Now for your punishment frock. You will shed your male garments, you understand, Ruby Cohen? and don the shot silk luxuriously rustling over head and shoulders and quickly too.
>
> (p. 507)

Joyce here brilliantly conveys in a few words the erotic ecstasy felt by those who enjoy being compelled by a woman to wear her luxurious clothes.

After the Second World War two books gave particularly perceptive insights of the attraction of women's clothes to the cross-dresser. In *A Ball in Venice* (1953) an older woman seduces the hero into dressing up in her clothes. His girlfriend is puzzled by the fact that he likes it, but there is no criticism or accusation of perversion. Later he goes to the 'Ball in Venice' in a rococo gown supplied by the other woman. *Cards of Identity* (1955) included 'A Case of Multiple Sexual Misidentity', which gave an amusing picture of the life of a man with an interest in wearing women's clothes and his dealings with the medical profession. There is a vivid description of him opening the doors of a woman's wardrobe. He gasps when he sees the rows of gorgeous dresses and shoes. It is too much for him. He tears off his own clothes and tries on a ravishing evening gown.

We have already considered pre-1914 sex-changing in terms of magic, science fiction and hypnotism. This theme continued in stories and novels into the 1930s. In both *Turnabout* (1931) and *Indian Tea* (1936a), for example, changes of sex are effected through magical means as each member of the couple enters the body of the other.

With the dissemination of knowledge about sex hormones and surgical intervention, writers increasingly drew on these themes and dispensed with magic. I give three such examples which illustrate the shift from pseudo-science through to the use of hormones to full contemporary sex-reassignment. They provide a fitting conclusion to this brief survey. Reality has finally caught up with fantasy.

In *Colonel to Princess* (1936b) a princess is dying, but it is diplomatically important that she should survive. A British colonel is operated upon so that part of his brain is inserted into the brain of the dead girl. The operation is successful and the colonel becomes the princess, the crisis being averted. He enjoys the change of sex and finds it delightful to be a woman.

In *Poppy Mandragora and the New Sex* (1966) Colin Spencer uses a drug derived from a Tibetan plant to intensify the effect of female hormones and thus produce hermaphrodites with male genitals and female breasts. The candidates for this are released criminals, who in their glamorous female form are then married to prominent people, who fancy a union of this sort.

Finally, in *Myra Breckinridge* (1968) full-scale sex-reassignment is featured and elaborated upon. Myra says that she is the widow of Myron, but we begin to suspect that she was formerly Myron herself, as turns out to have been the case. She becomes a teacher in a school for acting. Her chief interest is the male student, Jake and his girlfriend, Jane. She rapes Jake with a dildo as a revenge on the male sex and falls for Jane. Jane leaves Jake who becomes a homosexual, while Myra changes partially back into a man in order to marry Jane.

CONCLUSION

In this chapter I have sought to identify, classify and describe an arena of study rather than make critical or explanatory comment. I have made no attempt to be comprehensive. Nevertheless, a number of observations do spring to mind. We have seen that many works have explored cross-dressing and sex-changing in the period under review. As might be expected, they are in part a product of their times, in terms both of theme explored and degree of sexual explicitness considered appropriate to mainstream fiction. Adventures in skirts portrayed boys and men in a variety of situations where they had to cope as girls and women, thus providing a narrative device within which to explore the relationships between the sexes. Fantasies of sex-changing enabled this theme to be explored still further. Themes previously limited to underground erotica slowly started to appear in mainstream fiction in the period under review. More recently, modern surgical techniques and advances in endocrinology enabled writers to dispense with magical transpositions of sex if they so chose. This branch of literature has been popular right up to the present day and no doubt will continue to be as public awareness of cross-dressing and sex-changing spreads.

NOTE

1 For a chronological listing of short stories and novels referred to in this chapter, see Appendix 1.

10

CROSS-DRESSING, SEX-CHANGING AND THE PRESS*

Dave King

INTRODUCTION

This chapter contains an analysis of a sample from my ongoing collection of newspaper and magazine cuttings. This began in the late 1970s and initially material came simply from the press consumption of myself and friends. Over time this has been supplemented from other sources; subcultural publications which often reproduce press reports; *Archive News* published by the Trans-Gender Archive; the private collections of individuals encountered in the course of my research; the Gay Monitoring and Archive Project. The publication of extracts from the press cuttings collected by George Ives (Sieveking, 1981) provided a small amount of material covering the years 1904–43. Some material from the 1950s and 1960s, particularly relating to the famous cases of this period, was gathered during searches at the British Newspaper Library.

I can, obviously, make no claim that this collection is statistically representative of all press coverage of gender blending. All I can do is make observations based on the material available to me. This seems an improvement though, on previous writings about the media and gender blending, such as Raymond (1980) and Sagarin (1978), which appear to be based on very little material at all.

MASQUERADE, DRAG AND SEX-CHANGE

The terrain covered by press reports is not the same as that covered by medical practice. There is some overlap but press interest does not begin or end with the medical categories of transvestism or transsexualism. Transgressing the boundaries between the categories of male and female, in whatever way, seems potentially to be always of interest to the press, embracing not only the activities of those who would probably clinically be described as transvestites and transsexuals but also those of amateur

* An earlier version of this chapter first appeared as part of Chapter 4 in *The Transvestite and the Transsexual: Public Categories and Private Identities*, Aldershot: Avebury, 1993.

or professional entertainers, disguised policemen and burglars and the once only cross-dresser at a party or church fete as well as many others. Not surprisingly, therefore, the press has its own terminology.

Most prominent is the term 'sex-change'. This term is also used in the professional literature but only with reluctance and safely enclosed within quotation marks. In the press, however, 'sex-change' is used freely and without apology in verb, noun and adjective forms. It was in use before the Second World War and a *Daily Mirror* story of 1936 (7/8/36) under the headline, 'NINE POUND CHILD BORN TO EX-SOLDIER A YEAR AFTER "HE" CHANGED "HIS" SEX', stated that, 'this is believed to be the first time in history that a person who has changed his sex has given birth to a child' suggesting that cases of sex-change were not unknown to its readers.

Early in 1952 the *Sunday Pictorial* serialised the exclusive story of 'the GI who changed his sex'. In 1962, the *Sunday Pictorial's* main headline (29/4/62) proclaimed 'A PEER'S SON LOVES A SEX-CHANGE GIRL'. Nearly ten years later the *People* announced 'SEX-CHANGE PAT TO MARRY A WELDER' (14/3/71). The *Sun* (14/6/82) reported on a 'sex-change shock' concerning a 'mother of six . . . awaiting a series of three sex-change operations on the National Health'. Another decade or so on and we have, 'SEX-CHANGE WORKER GOT HIGHER PAY' (*Guardian*, 23/10/92). Over the years the press has introduced its readership to (amongst others) the sex-change cop, the sex-change bride, the sex-change sailor, the sex-change prisoner, the sex-change burglar, the sex-change vicar, sex-change surgeons, sex-change conferences, sex-change tennis and has proclaimed London as, 'a sex-change capital of the world' (*News of the World*, 12/10/80).

The general term 'sex-change' covers several phenomena which might be distinguished by the medical literature. Although the details given are usually sparse, it seems to be used to cover various forms of physical intersexuality as well as transsexualism. And although it covers cases where surgical and hormonal intervention has taken place, it also covers those where it has apparently not. The *Sun* (14/10/82), for instance, reported that a teacher had, 'stunned students by changing sex for a second time'; the college principal said, 'last term he dressed as a woman . . . now he and his medical advisors feel he should become a man again'.

Twisting the reader's tongue, a variation is the use of 'sex swap (or swop)' as in 'SEX SWAP SHOCK OF A CHURCH ORGANIST' (*Sun* 24/7/82), 'SEX SWAP WORKER REINSTATED' (*Guardian*, 3/6/82) or 'BETTY GETS A SEX-SWAP . . . SO SHE CAN BE DADDY TO THE SON OF HER GAY GIRLFRIEND (*People*, 10/4/94).

In the press reports available before 1950, another common term was 'masquerade': 'THE MASQUERADER: FAMILIAR FIGURE IN SKIRTS PROVES TO BE A MAN' (*Evening News*, 10/4/15). The same mode of interpretation was conveyed in a number of similar terms – 'pose', 'impersonate', 'hoax', 'disguise' – but the most commonly used was 'masquerade'. This theme also appears in the medical and popular literature of the period. Impersonation has persisted in reports on entertainment but, that apart, the terminology and imagery of masquerade is now rare and, in contrast to the earlier period before 1950 is confined to reports in which a 'rational' motive is imputed, as in the *Guardian* story, 'DRESSED FOR A "KILLING"' (4/11/82) which reported how a boy dressed as his sister, 'in a masquerade intended to dupe a court official out of £931'.

Although the term has been available since 1850 (Baker, 1968: 18), 'drag' only seems to have entered the press vocabulary in the 1960s. It is used to cover a range of behaviours and persons from those also described as transvestites and homosexual 'queens' through cross-dressing in entertainment to 'fancy-dress'. It seems, by the 1970s, to have become the preferred term when there is no possibility of using that of 'sex-change'. 'BLESS MY SOUL, IT'S THE VICAR IN DRAG', exclaimed the *Sunday Mirror* (11/8/74) when a cleric appeared in fancy-dress at the church fete. In 1982, the *Sun* (27/7/82) proclaimed 'ANGER OVER LEGACY FOR A DOC IN DRAG' over an article which began 'Transvestite doctor . . .'. And it's a term which lends itself to the headline writer's love of puns and other such devices; 'DRAG ADDICTS' (*Guardian*, 18/5/90; *Sunday Mirror*, 22/8/93); 'SOMETIMES IT'S A DRAG TO BE A WOMAN' (*Guardian*, 17/6/93).

'Sex-change', 'masquerade' and 'drag', then, have been or are the primary labels which the press in particular apply to the range of cross-dressing which they report. The first two terms appear to be used for both male and female gender blending. 'Drag', though, is only rarely used in the case of female subjects. It does not appear to have been used in headlines concerning female gender blending but it occasionally crops up in the body of articles on aspects of entertainment. So the *Sunday People* told us how in a film, 'Bubbling Brooke Shields . . . forsakes her thigh-high sexy image to become a bit of a drag by dressing up as a man . . .' (6/3/83), and in the film *Victor/Victoria*, the *Guardian* informed us that 'Julie Andrews is in drag' (1/4/82).

The medical terminology and conceptions of transvestites and transsexuals and their respective '-isms' have in the main only been used by the media as secondary terms, that is, when journalists or other commentators are outlining medical thinking for their audience although they have had some primary usage.

Until the late 1960s, cross-dressing and sex-changing were topics mainly confined to the popular press. There were some exceptions such as the piece in the *Manchester Guardian* (19/3/54) headlined, 'WHAT IS A MAN? PARLIAMENT MAY HAVE TO DECIDE', which arose out of the controversy surrounding the case of Roberta Cowell, or the *Times*, review of the television programme 'Horizon' ('BBC TAKES A CANDID VIEW OF SEX-CHANGE', 22/11/66). But by the early 1970s the topic had became more fully established as a legitimate and serious one with a corresponding increase in the display of expert terminology and opinion. A number of factors contributed to and constituted this change. In July 1969 the first International Symposium on Gender Identity was held in London. Most press reports were short and concentrated on the figures which were given of the number of sex-changes ('BRITAIN'S SEX-CHANGE TOLL' – *Kent Evening Post*, 28/7/69). Even the more detailed accounts in the serious press stressed the numbers aspect ('1,000 SEX-CHANGES IN 20 YEARS' – *The Times*, 28/7/69; '41 HAD CHANGE OF SEX' – *Guardian*, 28/7/69), but the terms transsexual and transvestite and their medical usage appeared fairly widely. Then, the Ashley–Corbett case and the discussion of transsexual marriages in Parliament during the debate on the Nullity of Marriage Bill in 1971 were widely reported and raised an 'issue' on which the press could focus. In April 1974 Jan Morris's autobiography was published and a series of four extracts in the *Sunday Times* together with many book reviews and background articles brought the topic firmly within the purview of the 'serious' press. The early 1970s also saw the growth of formalised associations among transvestites and transsexuals with national conferences organised in 1974 and 1975. By the early 1970s also the identities of some of the doctors treating transsexual patients had become known and possibly the numbers of doctors so involved had increased. The effect of this was that the media had easier access to experts, both doctors and patients, who they could approach for material and who (less so in the case of the doctors) may even have been eager to 'educate' the general public.

Nevertheless, transvestite and transsexual remained secondary terms; usually appearing where doctors were being quoted or medical knowledge was being explained. Their use in headings remains rare and their use in the body of press articles occasional and unsystematic.

Such usage can be confusing to those familiar with the medical literature where transvestism and transsexualism are usually depicted as discrete clinical entities with only the latter concerned with sex-change: 'TRANSVESTITE TURNED TO CRIME FOR SEX-CHANGE' proclaimed the *Newcastle upon Tyne Journal* in a bold headline (11/3/80) and on 2 November 1980, the *Observer* printed a story about Brazilian transvestite prostitutes having sex-change operations. And the *Star* on 15 August 1987 under the headline, 'SEX-SWOP MR BOOTE GETS BOOT', said 'transvestite Alan, 36, who hopes to have a sex-change operation.'

The term 'transvestite', though, has been used with a greater variety of referents than that of 'transsexual'. The latter when it is used has some reference to changing sex. 'Transvestite' is also used to refer to this and to almost any form of cross-dressing except where this occurs within acceptable limits (see below).

Except where it is used to refer to changing sex, there have appeared no 'issues' in press reports on transvestism comparable to those raised over transsexuals, such as marriage, birth certificates, employment or participation in sports. Nor have there emerged any non-sex-change 'celebrities' except in the case of professional female impersonators, who are not referred to as 'transvestites'.

These then are the ways in which the press categorise cross-dressing and sex-changing. The terms used are primarily the media's own although as we have seen medical terminology has played a part. Now we turn to look in more detail at the reports themselves.

TYPES OF REPORT

Some reports have a specific focus. There are two main types of these. Firstly, there are reports which are person-focused. These tell the life story of a person and/or focus on their lifestyle and personality. The obvious example is the sex-change story. The stories of all of the 'sex-change celebrities' of the past forty years or so, such as Christine Jorgensen, Roberta Cowell, April Ashley and Jan Morris, have been told in the press, often serialised over several weeks. Many single stories have been told about others, most quickly forgotten. The stories of women who have changed, or who wish to change, sex are also told. These appear to be rarer although more common recently. 'PAUL HEWITT HAS ONLY ONE WISH ... TO HAVE HIS BREASTS AND HIS WOMB REMOVED' was the rather wordy headline for a recent example (*People*, 16/1/94). In this type of report there is little reference to general aspects of changing sex or to the issues involved; it is told as a personal story.

Secondly, there are those which are event-focused. These items report events or happenings with less concern for the persons involved or for the wider context or implications. They may concern a fancy-dress occasion ('DRESSED UP FOR CHARITY', *Birkenhead News*, 31/1/78); a suicide ('BOY WHO DIED LIKE HIS IDOL MARILYN', *News of the World*, 1/6/80); a court case ('YOUTH WITH SEX PROBLEM IS JAILED FOR 6 MONTHS', *Lancashire Evening Telegraph*, 21/6/80); a marriage ('BRIDE FINDS OUT HER GUY IS A GIRL', *News of the World*, 6/12/81); losing a job ('SEX-OP LANDS PILOT THE SACK', *News of the World*, 16/8/81); or facing eviction ('TRANSVESTITES FACING EVICTION THREAT', *Sheffield Star*, 10/4/72).

Other reports have a much wider focus. Again, there are two main types. The phenomenon report outlines the nature of the condition, its prevalence, causes, and so on, in a general way. On the same day in which the final part of Jan Morris's serialised autobiography appeared in the *Sunday Times*, the *Observer* published such an article headlined simply 'TRANSSEXUALS' (28/4/74). These reports may rely on professional sources, as in the *Observer* article just mentioned, or they may present it from the point of view of the transvestites or transsexuals themselves ('A MAN IN WOMAN'S CLOTHES', *Yorkshire Post*, 14/5/72) or their wives ('WHEN WIVES FIND OUT HE WANTS TO BE A WOMAN'; *Sunday People*, 7/4/74). More recently, some have focused on women who cross-dress ('GIRLS WILL BE BOYS', *Guardian*, 24/9/91).

Finally, there are the issue reports which focus on an issue or controversy. Legal issues have been a common source of stories ('WHAT IS A MAN? PARLIAMENT MAY HAVE TO DECIDE', *Manchester Guardian*, 19/3/54; 'COMMON'S DEBATE ON MARRIAGE AFTER SEX-CHANGE', *The Times*, 2/4/71; 'THE MAN WHO NEVER WILL BE', *Guardian*, 18/11/86). Other reports have focused on the right to cross-dress at work or college ('STUDENT IN A SKIRT COLLEGE ROW', *Manchester Evening News*, 7/11/80); the treatment of a transsexual prisoner ('A BLOND LOCKED UP WITH 15,000 MEN IN THE SCRUBS', *Guardian*, 30/1/80); or the merits of sex-change operations ('ANGER OVER SEX SWAPS ON NHS', *People*, 4/7/93).

Many reports combine two or more of these foci, although one is usually dominant. At times different items in the same or another publication or medium may display different foci on the same 'story'.

Some reports embody other elements in addition to cross-dressing or sex-changing; elements which may be seen as supplementing the news value of the particular item (see Hall et al., 1978: 72). Among these other elements are the following;

1 The involvement of elite persons or celebrities:
   'A PEER'S SON LOVES A SEX-CHANGE GIRL' (*Sunday Pictorial*, 29/4/62);
   'IT'S GOLDEN GAL TOMMY' (*Sunday Pictorial*, 10/7/60). (Picture of Tommy Steele in a dress and a wig taking part in a show with Alma Cogan);
   'YARD IN VIP SEX PROBE' (*Sunday Mirror*, 20/3/83) (Revelations by a 'transvestite prostitute').

2 The presence of a controversy, dispute or conflict:
   The first British television programme (BBC2's *Horizon*, 21/11/66) on sex-changes was linked to the dispute over the sex of Russian women athletes.
   'SEX-CHANGE VICAR HAS TO RESIGN' (*News of the World*, 28/5/78);
   'SEX OP MAN SHOCKS LADIES' (*Daily Mirror*, 28/6/79).

3   A linkage with crime, vice or other forms of deviance:
    'CAMBRIDGE RAPIST PLEADS TO BE A WOMAN' (*People*, 8/10/78);
    'IT'S THE MOST EVIL STREET ON EARTH' (*People*, 27/4/69).
4   Female glamour:
    'HER SECRET IS OUT: THE EXTRAORDINARY CASE OF TOP MODEL APRIL ASHLEY' (*The People*, 19/11/61);
    'JAMES BOND'S GIRL WAS A BOY' (*News of the World*, 6/9/81);
    'MISS TURNED OUT TO BE A MR' (*News of the World*, 8/11/81) (part of a series on 'Miss World scandals').
5   Novelty, the bizarre, humour:
    'SEX OP BID TO BE DORIS'S DOUBLE' (*People*, 14/1/79) (an article about a man who planned to have not only a sex-change operation but also to have plastic surgery to become a replica of Doris Day);
    'BIRTHDAY SEX-CHANGE AT 77' (*Yorkshire Post*, 13/12/80) (concerned a grandfather who hoped to change sex before his 78th birthday).

I would hypothesise that the greater the degree to which these elements are present or seem to be so, the greater will be the chances of a potential item actually appearing. Other factors which would seem to influence the chances of an item appearing are the production of similar items by rival newspapers, channels or media.

Just as these elements may be said to add value to a report on cross-dressing or sex-changing, so too can the latter be elements in a report on another topic to which they likewise add value. Thus the *Justice of the Peace* commented in 1938 that in the press appeared, 'offences which in themselves would attract little attention at the hands of the reporter, but, from the fact of dressing up, gain some romantic flavour' (*Justice of the Peace*, 1938: 135). An example of this would seem to be a *News of the World* report ('THE BLONDE BURGLAR IS UNMASKED', 5/10/75) in which the news value of a story about a case of burglary was enhanced by the discovery that the burglar was a woman disguised as a man.

ACCOUNTING

When something is perceived to be strange or unexpected an account (Harré, 1979; Marshall, 1981; Tully, 1992) is looked for. As Harre (1979: 169) defines it: 'accounting is speech which precedes, accompanies and follows action. Actors give accounts to ensure the twin goals of intelligibility and warrantability, that is the meaningfulness and propriety of their actions'. Explicitly explaining cross-dressing and changing sex is not a central focus of most media reports; nevertheless a variety of explanatory accounts are implied or made explicit. These are usually reported as given by transvestites or transsexuals themselves, by 'experts' commenting on the case or on the phenomenon in general, or are gleaned by journalists from the professional or other literature.

Across the whole range of reports the vast majority of accounts make reference to individual factors. The main exceptions are those which are concerned with androgynous fashions in pop music and youth culture (see, for example, *Guardian*, 3/6/83). Here, the image of a social movement is paramount and accounts are offered in terms of the nature of adolescence and the nature of society.

The other accounts fall into two main types. The first invites classification of the act, actor or phenomenon as normal: the second implies deviance.

The dividing line between normality and deviance is sometimes hard to draw, especially when there is no overt hostility. Nevertheless, there are many reports where the account implicitly or explicitly offered has the effect of retaining the act or actor within the bounds of normality, without detracting from its news value. Thus, an act of cross-dressing may be explained by simply mentioning certain contexts – fancy-dress party, church fete, carnival – and the actor is thereby absolved from any implications of deviance.

A variety of other normalising motives may be invoked which, although other forms of deviance or crime might be involved, serve to make the cross-dressing appear understandable: a soldier avoiding capture by the enemy impersonates a woman's dead daughter (*Daily News*, 11/12/18); a boy impersonates his sister in a fraudulent attempt to gain money (*Guardian*, 4/11/82); and a crane driver who dresses as a woman so that his 15 year old girlfriend, 'would think him slightly odd and deranged and would have nothing more to do with him' (*News of the World*, 27/9/81).

Garber (1992), discussing the case of Billy Tipton, a married jazz musician discovered after his death to have been a woman, focuses on the way in which his 'transvestism' was 'normalised' by 'interpreting it in the register of socio-economic necessity . . . s/he did this in order to a) get a job, b) find a place in a man's world, and c) realise or fulfil some deep but acceptable need in terms of personal destiny, in this case by becoming a jazz musician' (Garber, 1992: 69). Garber notes that this interpretation is common in many cross-dressing stories and argues that, 'the ideological implications of this pattern are clear: cross-dressing can be "fun" or "functional" so long as it occupies a limited space and a temporary time period; after this carnivalisation . . . the cross-dresser is expected to resume life as he or she was' (Garber, 1992: 70).

The second type of account categorises the act and the actor as deviant. They are also deterministic, seeing the actor as a special kind of person who has no choice but to act as he does. With regard to sex-change, the favourite determinant of the press is biology, often only vaguely specified. Sometimes biology is depicted as beginning a process of sex-change which is then completed by surgery. The Press Association Statement on Roberta Cowell stated how Cowell became:

> conscious of changes in his physical condition and mental outlook. Consultations with eminent doctors followed and he was told by a Harley Street sexologist that his body showed prominent feminine sex characteristics which were developing at an unusually advanced age. He accepted the fact that his life would have to alter completely and irrevocably.
>
> (*News Chronicle*, 6/3/54)

Cowell's change was depicted as the result of sudden, but vague, physical and mental changes. The story of April Ashley which appeared in the *News of the World* in May and June 1962, was, by contrast, not one of sudden change but of unhappiness and tragedy dating back to childhood. Biological changes (the growth of breasts, widening of the hips) were also mentioned as factors which eventually 'drove' her to change sex.

Twenty years later, the *Daily Star* (8/3/83) asserted that Tula, a model, 'by some freak combination of genes was born Barry Cossey, and for the rest of her life wanted nothing else than to be female'. 'The fact that she was born a boy must have been a mistake', it said.

Accounts which stress psychological influences are rarer and, although some of the possibilities are sometimes repeated in 'phenomena' focused articles on transsexualism, they are most often found in relation to transvestism. Here too may be found occasional references to a broader sociological 'cause', i.e., the demands of the male role (*London Evening Mail*, 25/8/71).

Most reports imply or explicitly invoke the notion of a long-standing condition or orientation which explains or makes understandable the specific acts of cross-dressing or changing sex. The biological or psychological factors, if mentioned, are then offered as explanation of the condition from which the actor is often said to 'suffer' or of which he is a 'victim'. It is rare to find an article which suggests that transvestism or transsexualism may be a temporary 'illness' brought about by a specific 'cause'. One such report is to be found in the *Woking News* (19/8/71) which declared that, 'depression turned a young man into a transvestite'. The subject, a man charged with stealing women's underwear, said, 'it all started when I was in the RAF when I was depressed. I turned into a transvestite to help me get over it.' As stated above, accounting is not usually a central focus of press reports. There are, however, a small number of reports in which the apparent motive is the main focus because of its unusual or bizarre nature. The 'SEX-OP BID TO BE DORIS'S DOUBLE' story mentioned above said the subject was seeking a sex-change operation and plastic surgery to, 'turn himself into another Doris Day' (*Sunday People*, 14/1/79). 'HUSBAND CHANGES SEX TO KEEP LESBIAN WIFE WHO FELL FOR A NANNY' announced the *News of the World* (10/9/78), although the article under this headline recounted a story which suggested that the desire to change sex was only tenuously related to these circumstances.

CONSEQUENCES

This section is intended to be speculative and suggestive. There is no available research on the consequences of the press portrayal of cross-dressing and sex-changing. Nevertheless, several writers have suggested some possibilities which I shall discuss alongside some others.

I will first of all focus on the consequences for the subjects of press or other media reports. Most obviously, I am thinking of the individual trans-vestite or transsexual, whose status as such becomes known through media reports, and their families and friends. It doesn't require much imagina-tion to think of some of the likely negative consequences in, for example, the areas of personal relationships or employment. On the other hand, there can also be some positive consequences at least for the transvestite or transsexual: the need for secrecy is removed and for some individuals the publicity may further new careers. Christine Jorgensen, for example, complained in her autobiography of the invasion of her privacy and that of her family by the press. But she also recognised that the publicity she received had furthered her career as a night-club performer. Thus, she concluded that, 'like Janus, the press has presented two faces; one detri-mental and one advantageous' (Jorgensen, 1967: 331). I suspect, though, that for most people who do not attain such celebrity status, the conse-quences for them and their families and friends of media exposure are on the whole likely to be unwelcome. Transsexual 'celebrities' are also likely to find that they receive letters from people in similar circumstances requesting help and information and they may find themselves being placed in the role of spokesperson or expert on the topic.

We may also consider the consequences of exposure for those members of the medical profession who achieve fame through the press. Like most transvestites and transsexuals, most members of the medical profession practising in this area try to avoid publicity. In the past some surgeons feared criminal charges; more recently there is still a fear of negative reac-tions from colleagues, damage to a career or simply the trivialisation and perhaps the jeopardising of their work. Certainly, articles such as that which appeared in the *News of the World* on 12 October 1980 claiming that two named London doctors had turned the city into the 'sex-change capital of the world' are hardly likely to encourage medical practitioners to speak to the press.

Another consequence of publicity for the medical profession is possibly an increase in the number of patients referred. Consider this piece by Norman Haire:

From time to time one reads sensational reports in the newspapers of persons who are alleged to have had their sex-changed, usually by operation. And, whenever this occurs, well-known sexologists usually receive a spate of letters from persons who have read the newspaper reports and who write asking for the operation to be carried out on themselves.

(Haire, 1950: 200)

Nearly three years later the case of Christine Jorgensen received world-wide press coverage. Hamburger, the endocrinologist involved in the case, wrote an article based on an analysis of the many letters he received from people around the world who learned of his existence through the press reports and who were seeking similar treatment to Jorgensen (Hamburger, 1953). The involvement of Charing Cross Hospital with transsexuals apparently began in the 1930s when work with physically intersex persons by Broster (see Broster et al., 1938) was reported in the press in terms of sex-change (WERE ONCE SISTERS, *News of the World*, 2/8/43; TWO SISTERS TURN INTO BROTHERS, *The Star*, 25/8/39).

Media reports can have other consequences for the medical profession. Media interest may stimulate the codification of medical knowledge. Benjamin's first article on the topic (Benjamin, 1953) began, 'this article is the result of the wide publicity given to the case of Christine Jorgensen'. The report by the Danish team involved (Hamburger, Sturup and Dahl-Iverson, 1953) also resulted from the same publicity (Jorgensen, 1967: 209–10). Sorensen and Hertoft, having examined the medical records and interviewed Sturup, the psychiatrist involved, concluded that the medical team dealing with Jorgensen, 'were not aware of any independent noso-logical unity' (Sorensen and Hertoft, 1980: 62). They, 'regarded Chris Jorgensen as a homosexual man suffering from his homosexuality and since he himself asked for castration, they would not deny him this oper-ation' (Hertoft and Sorensen, 1979: 168). So castration and hormone treatment were originally employed, not with a view to changing the patient's sex but in order to treat homosexuality, and the legal permission necessary for the castration was obtained with this argument. 'Not until afterwards, when the press published the case, did the team behind the procedure accept it as a sex-change' (Hertoft and Sorensen, 1979: 168; see also Chapter 8 in this volume).

So these are some of the possible effects of the media on those who become their subjects. I now turn to the effects on the receivers – the audience or readership.

Firstly, we can consider the influence of the press or the media as a whole on the knowledge which the audience has about cross-dressing and sex-changing and also the attitudes which are common towards these phenomena. No one has so far discussed this issue in relation to transvestism but some writers have argued (complained?) that the American media, pushed by a greedy medical profession and self-interested transsexual groups, have presented a glowing picture of transsexualism and sex-reassignment to the public.

Sagarin (1978) sees the media, along with part of the medical profession, as presenting transsexualism and sex-changes in such a way that these phenomena are seen as legitimate and in such a way as to encourage people to bestow and accept the label 'transsexual' gladly. He complains that the media place unwarranted emphasis on the 'happy transsexual'. 'The media', he writes, 'in the freedom to choose the material for presentation, seize upon the sensational, and a successfully transformed man into woman is more newsworthy than the lonely, forlorn, psychotic or suicide prone eunuch' (Sagarin, 1978: 258).

Billings and Urban (1982) and Raymond (1980), whose work I have discussed elsewhere (King, 1987; 1993), have also asserted that the media have been partly or largely responsible for promoting the idea of transsexualism as a genuine condition for which sex-reassignment is an appropriate response. Among Raymond's (1980) suggestions for dealing with 'The Transsexual Empire' is a call for more media attention to be given to what she calls, 'different perspectives on the issue of transsexualism' meaning anti 'sex-change' perspectives. She would like to hear more from those who have overcome 'their gender identity crises without resorting to the medical technical solution', those professionals not in favour of surgery and those, 'such as feminists and homosexual men who have experienced sex-role oppression but ultimately did not become transsexuals' (Raymond, 1980: 184).

Some medical writers too have been critical of the media for glamorising sex-changing and for encouraging unrealistic expectations in patients (Roth and Ball, 1964: 424–5; Stoller, 1982). Criticism of the media is also often expressed by transsexuals and transvestites themselves for neglecting serious (medical) perspectives on these phenomena, for focusing on the atypical and the distasteful and for generally spreading confusion and misunderstanding.

Pearce (1981: 309) commenting on the British press is the only one of all the authors cited here to produce any evidence supporting his comments. His main focus is on the press coverage of homosexuality but he also notes briefly the sympathetic portrayal of the transsexual compared to that of the homosexual. This is so, he argues, because the transsexual resolves the anomaly of a mismatch between sex, gender and sexuality.

It is possible, without much searching, to find in the popular press, the kind of reports which Raymond and Sagarin seemingly have in mind. In these, often autobiographically presented, stories a tale is told of a person tragically miscast. Facing many problems and encountering many difficulties, the hero/heroine eventually finds fulfilment. Changing sex is the final solution; in individual terms, the person finds him/herself, is made whole, past problems are explained and transcended; in cultural terms, the categorisation of gender is vindicated as the misfit finally fits. Silverstone's exhaustive analysis (Silverstone, 1982) of the BBC 2 trilogy 'A Change of Sex' (October 1980) documents the mythical structure to be found therein. He finds the theme of the hero/heroine faced with a task, hindered and helped along the way but finally triumphant in the story of a relatively brief period in the life of a transsexual and specifically in relation to the task of satisfying the demands of an NHS psychiatrist. A similarly rigorous analysis would probably reveal a similar structure in the serialised life story of April Ashley (*News of the World*, May/June 1962) imposed on a longer life period and in relation to the more general task of 'finding oneself', as well as in the stories of others which have appeared over the years in the press and in popular autobiographies.

Pearce's explanation would seem to fit this type of report well. The press are most comfortable with the story of the man who not only changes sex but who also appears to embody to a high degree the cultural attributes of femininity. The attractive model on the arm of a wealthy man is the press's ideal ending to a sex-change story (see, for example, the *Daily Star* 8/3/83). Conformity to the cultural ideal of gender legitimises sex-change for the press (or at least the popular press) as it has done for some parts of the medical profession (see Chapters 7 and 8).

The arguments of Billings and Urban (1982), Sagarin (1978) and Raymond (1980) concerning the media promotion of transsexualism may or may not be true for the USA since none of these authors provides any empirical evidence to support their claims (I suspect, though, that it is actually more complicated than they suggest). In Britain, however, there are plenty of reports which present a less favourable picture of transvestism and transsexualism.

In some instances, press reports bristle with indignation and disgust. On 20 and 27 April, 1969 The *People* printed two articles on 'she-men' prostitutes in Singapore who it said were, 'leading our servicemen into shame and degradation'. They 'preyed' on our servicemen who, 'fell into their clutches'. The second article, with the headline 'IT'S THE MOST EVIL STREET ON EARTH', told of the 'she-men' in bars who, 'minced around pestering their audience for drinks'. In collecting the 'sordid evidence' on these 'creatures' the reporter witnessed, 'as disgusting a display of public homosexuality as I have ever seen'. Not only sex but drugs were involved in this 'unwholesome' business. Expressions of disgust are found in articles concerning other forms of gender blending. One example is the report on a 'kinky copper' (*News of the World*, 11/10/81) said to have a 'sinister side' and also described as 'creepy' and 'mincing'. His 'insatiable fetish' for women's underwear was said to be behind the burglaries for which he received a suspended prison sentence. The report reassured us that, 'he is now receiving psychiatric treatment'. The *Sunday People* would, no doubt, have liked to have been able to give us the same reassurance concerning Roberta Cowell who, contrary to the picture painted in the remainder of the press, they portrayed as an 'unhappy freak' and a 'horror' with an 'abnormal craving' (*Sunday People*, 11/4/54; 18/4/54). Finally, clearly considered to be beyond the pale are the American 'Sisters of Perpetual Indulgence', described by the *Sunday People* (13/12/81) as, 'a bunch of homosexual weirdos whose only mission in life is to shock'. The *News of the World* (15/7/84) managed a piece which linked them with Christian fundamentalists, animal rights protesters, prostitutes and the All Species Group (who dress as vegetables) when they reported that, 'riot police fought running battles with thousands of punks, gays and transvestites dressed as nuns in San Francisco'.

Another category of press reports contain accounts of violent criminals who are said to be transvestites or to dress in women's clothes. The crimes are the main focus. The cross-dressing emerges as part of the press portrait of the criminal.

During the lengthy coverage of the case of David Martin, who was jailed for shooting a policeman, the point that he was a transvestite was often made (see for example *News of the World*, 16/1/83; *Sunday People*, 16/10/83; *Daily Star*, 15/3/84). 'Sex beast', Ian Bealey, was described more enigmatically as a 'former transvestite' (*News of the World*, 3/7/83).

A man described as a 'brute' who murdered and mutilated three teenage girls was said to be a 'sexual deviant and transvestite' (*Manchester Daily Express*, 3/5/77). 'GUN LOVING TRANSVESTITE KILLER' was the title given by the *Cardiff Western Mail* (31/3/76) to one man charged with murder.

Similarly descriptions of the crimes of the 'Cambridge Rapist' reported him dressing in women's clothes (*News of the World*, 5/10/75) and later, the *Sunday People* told us 'CAMBRIDGE RAPIST PLEADS TO BE A WOMAN' (8/10/78) claiming that he has, 'asked for a sex-change'. Five years later he was still asking, according to the *News of the World* (11/9/83).

Then there is a group of reports about transvestites or transsexuals who are reported as being 'conmen' or generally untrustworthy. The publicity concerning 'transvestite prostitute' Vikki de Lambray (see for example the *Sunday Times*, 27/3/83) is one example. Another example is an *Observer* magazine (9/11/75) feature concerning a Mrs Elizabeth

Carmichael, a transsexual on trial in America for nineteen charges of grand theft.

Arson (*News of the World*, 24/1/82), mugging (*Sunday People*, 23/9/79), armed robbery (*Journal,* Newcastle-upon-Tyne, 11/3/80), behaviour likely to cause a breach of the peace (*Kidderminster Times*, 3/12/71), theft and burglary (*Daily Express*, 13/2/76), grievous bodily harm (*Daily Mirror*, 26/8/78) and assaulting a police officer (*Yorkshire Post*, 4/11/80) are among other reported offences involving persons described as 'transsexual' or 'transvestites'.

There are also press reports which, whilst not condemnatory, present a picture of sex-changing as anything but glamorous. There are reports of cases of transsexuals who have regretted surgery; 'THE TRAGIC CASE OF THE WOMAN WHO WAS ONCE CALLED DONALD' (*People*, 5/11/67); 'I WANT TO BE A MAN AGAIN' (*Sunday Mirror*, 1/5/83); 'SEX SWAP GIRL WANTS TO BE A GUY AGAIN' (*News of the World*, 7/3/93). The cautions of experts have also been reported; 'SEX-CHANGE NOT ALWAYS THE CURE' (*Kilburn Times*, 14/6/68); 'SEX OPS THAT END IN MISERY' (*Daily Mirror*, 31/5/79); 'WHEN SEX-CHANGE IS A MISTAKE' (*Independant on Sunday*, 24/10/93).

In addition to reports such as these there are also many which, although they do not present sex-changes as 'failures', focus on the problems faced by some transsexuals. 'MY SHATTERED DREAM' (*Daily Star*, 14/3/81) focused on the fate of one well-publicised transsexual facing eviction, financially insecure, her marriage hopes 'dashed' and with an operation that had not been totally successful. Other reports have emphasised loneliness, legal entanglements, long waits for operations, suicides and 'botched' operations, summed up by the *News of the World* as the 'PRICE OF NEW LIFE IN SEX-CHANGE CITY' (12/10/80). Such reports, whilst often sympathetic to the plight of the transsexual, are clearly expressing a scepticism about the presumed benefits of changing sex.

The fact that these items have appeared at all and the usual readiness of the media to report on any scandal or controversy suggests that there is unlikely to be an aversion for whatever reason to reporting the negative side of sex-change surgery. In a time when changing sex in itself has probably less news value than it had, scandals or controversy will increase the value of a story.

It is clear, then, that the press presents a more complex picture of changing sex and cross-dressing than Raymond and the other critical authors allow. But this is all about the content of media reports and we cannot assume that the messages found there are passively received. Where people have no alternative sources of information it is reasonable to assume that the media will be most influential, although this influence will be limited by pre-existing attitudes towards, in this case, such things as gender and sexuality.

147

In addition to encouraging positive attitudes towards transsexualism and changing sex, Billings and Urban (1982), Birrell and Cole (1990) and Raymond (1980) argue that one of the wider consequences of the media dissemination of current conceptions of and responses to gender dysphoria is, by affirming the link between sex and gender, a reinforcement of an oppressive gender system. In a similar vein, Garber (1992) argues, with regard to the discussion of the motives of Billy Tipton (discussed above), that 'such normalisation reinstates the binary' (male/female) and 'recuperates social and sexual norms' (Garber, 1992: 69). A discussion of the ideological role of the media is beyond the scope of this chapter (but see Thompson, 1988). However, it is clear that the topic of gender dysphoria is only a fraction of media content which could be said to reinforce gender relations.

Finally, I want to move on now to consider the effects of media material on a particular section of the audience, that is, those readers viewers and listeners who are, or might be considered transvestites or transsexuals themselves.

In the stories of transsexuals in particular, encounters with media reports occur frequently and are accorded some significance. Here is an example from the early 1950s:

> By 1951 I knew for certain that I wanted to be a woman ... Much as I tried I could find none who would help me. I waited and hoped ... Two long years later Christine Jorgensen achieved that which I had almost grown to accept as the impossible. She had changed sex. My pitiful little life became no longer liveable in the knowledge that it was possible. Dr. Hamburger, to whom I had immediately written, recommended that I should consult Dr ...
>
> (letter written in 1954)

In Chapter 2 Mark Rees describes the impact a newspaper article had on him:

> In 1969, four years after my WRNS' discharge, I chanced to see an article in the *Times* of London which described the condition of transsexualism. It was a moment of enlightment; at last it all fitted into place. I was transsexual.

These writers, then, credit such media reports with having a profound effect on their understanding of themselves. In the reports they found clarification of puzzling thoughts, feelings and behaviour; they found the suggestion of a possible solution to their problems; and the first writer even found enough practical information to begin to reach that solution.

This is not a state of affairs which is welcomed by some writers. Newman and Stoller, for example, wrote in 1974 that:

The press, television and the movies have so popularised the idea of sex-change that the patient may come to the psychiatrist already sure of his diagnosis and treatment.

(Newman and Stoller, 1974: 438)

Steiner, in a similar vein, has commented:

Today's public media is responsible for giving the lay person considerable information regarding transsexualism and other disorders of gender identity . . . Yet this increased information, and at times, misinformation, has made the diagnosis of transsexualism more difficult for the practising physician.

(Steiner, 1985: 325)

Critics from outside the medical profession such as Raymond (1980), Sagarin (1978) and Billings and Urban (1982) have, as discussed earlier, argued that sections of the medical profession and the media have created a climate of opinion which is too accepting of the idea of transsexualism and sex-change. Sagarin (1978: 252), for example, asserts that the 'glorification' of transsexualism and sex-changing in the media and the professional literature has induced 'impressionable and susceptible' people to 'flock to the gender identity clinics'.

Of course all media reports do not have such a dramatic impact on all transvestites and transsexuals. By itself, the latest sex-change sensation is not going to send people scurrying off to the nearest gender identity clinic. Some people fight against their wish to change sex and are disturbed by reports that suggest it is possible. Nevertheless, it is clear that media reports are used in various ways by people who are struggling to reach an understanding of their own feelings and experiences. They can also suggest possible courses of action and provide information which is sometimes used. This is not something which is peculiar to the area of transsexualism but is likely to occur in any situation where people perceive, via the media, an answer to their problems.

There does not seem to be so much concern about the effects of the media on those who identify themselves as transvestites but presumably, here again, media reports can influence self-identification and understanding and provide practical information.

CONCLUSION

In our culture as Annie Woodhouse (1989) has said, sex, gender and gender appearance form a kind of 'holy trinity'; we presume and expect that they will fit together in some natural way. The topics of sex-changing and cross-dressing are startling because they question this natural 'fit'. This may explain why they receive so much press attention.

This attention, though, is a double-edged sword for transvestites and transsexuals. Individual transvestites and transsexuals may be damaged by the exposure they receive; but other transvestite and transsexual viewers or readers may be inspired, educated or entertained by it. The general public may be misled or misinformed but it may also be educated and enlightened.

The media of mass communication are a central component of modern culture. The development of printing, the growth of literacy and then the spread of films, radio and television have brought about new forms of cultural transmission and information diffusion. Many people, probably the vast majority, will never, knowingly, meet a transvestite or a transsexual in their lifetime. But mass communication makes them available to everybody. To understand the meanings which transvestism and transsexualism have in our culture, then, we have to look at how media products in these areas are put together and how they are received.

11

MALE FEMALING, TELEPHONE SEX AND THE CASE OF INTIMACY SCRIPTS

Richard Ekins

INTRODUCTION

The 1980s saw the inception, development and establishment of a new commercial configuration of sexual deviancy (Bryant, 1977) – that of the widely and immediately accessible telephone sex line. In previous decades the term 'telephone sex' popularly evoked images of unwanted obscene phone calls, or of consenting lovers arousing each other with erotic talk over the telephone. Occasionally, more specialist uses were noted. Brockopp and Lester, for instance, highlighted the telephone masturbation that accompanied the advent of open-line therapy agencies. Here, the male caller is sexually aroused by the sound of the female therapist's voice. No obscenities are uttered (Brockopp and Lester, 1969; Lester, 1973). Today, however, it is the array of small advertisements widely featured in the tabloid press which are more likely to be evoked in most people's minds when the subject turns to telephone sex. Callers are promised instant untold sexual delights by pressing a few buttons on a telephone:[1] 'If you've got a phone you've got a friend! Dial us and get stuck in!' *(Sunday Sport,* 7/1/94).

Those who dial the advertised numbers soon learn that the fare is multifarious, indeed. The more forthcoming may choose to interact with live 'performers' ('Call me 1 to 1 we'll talk'; 'Telephone Threesomes'). Specialist preferences are commonly indicated ('Domination – Strict Mistress will phone you back', *Sunday Sport,* 7/1/94). For the less forthcoming, eavesdropping on the 'live chat' of others may be a more preferable option. The more reticent have a vast range of non-interactive or variously interactive pre-recorded audio tapes from which to make their selection. Non-interactive tapes run from start to finish, without the caller doing more than keeping the telephone off the hook after dialling. Interactive tapes demand, at the very least, a sound from the caller to trigger the script. In their more complicated variations, different responses call forth different scripts. Again, gaps may be provided in the tape

151

recorded scripts to enable a simulated live conversation. The caller is invited to respond to alternative sets of pre-recorded scripts designed to cater for the variations in the caller's preferred fantasies.

It is these pre-recorded scripts which provide a particularly rich and readily available resource for the researcher interested in the minutiae of sexual fantasy. Prior to their inception, the researcher had to look to his own fantasies; to those of peculiarly frank informants; and to the reports of those with a professional expertise in the sexual fantasies of others – most notably, to those of prostitutes, pornographers, sexologists and psychoanalysts. Now, however, telephone sex lines give the researcher instant access to an ever-increasing array of diverse scripts previously only available to the most doggedly determined seeker of these things.

TELEPHONE SEX AND MALE CROSS-DRESSING AND SEX-CHANGING

Soon after establishing the Trans-Gender Archive at the University of Ulster, in 1986,[2] I began to receive information relating to telephone sex lines which featured aspects of male cross-dressing and sex-changing. Initially, this material was difficult both to access and acquire. Whilst a so-called 'Transvestite Trevor' purported to be at the end of a line widely advertised in the back pages of the popular press, for instance, I never did manage to locate him. In those early days, there was frequently no particular match between what you saw advertised and what you heard should you actually phone. The casual caller was likely to be disappointed.

By the end of the 1980s, however, a number of specialist lines, catering for particular interests, were establishing themselves as a reliable source of script. These lines frequently featured well-crafted scripts made by specialists for specialists. One informant, for instance, explained to me how he would draw on his own masturbatory fantasies and day-dreams to concoct his scripts. His intention was to provide the maximum erotic stimulation for 'transvestite' callers, over the maximum possible time span. In essence, this entailed so crafting his story that the caller's curiosity about the outcome would lead him to hold on until the end of the tape. He tried to so structure the story that sexual arousal would be maintained in waves of ever-increasing pleasurable foreplay until the climax. He attempted to conclude the tape by providing an aesthetically and sexually satisfying climax for the caller's ejaculation. Callers were, then, invited to dial the same number in subsequent weeks to hear a continuation of the story. Soon, he had a number of different stories available on different lines. He was pleasantly surprised by the number of callers who responded to his very modest four-line advertisement in a national newspaper.

Increasingly, more sophisticated operations were launched. By the early 1990s it became common practice for a phone line operator to engage a number of specialist writers and script readers. The writers, often drawing upon their own favourite fantasies and those of their associates, would submit scripts which would become increasingly fine-tuned in response to user comment and popularity. Halcyon, for instance, runs *Apron Strings*, for 'forced to feminise fans', *Apron*, for 'transvestites' and *Pinafore Pages*, for 'male maids'. These privately circulated magazines feature scores of phone lines in each issue and invite suggestions for future lines: 'If you want any particular type of line write . . . with all the sexy details. A free pair of knickers for the best suggestions'. By 1993, Halcyon had so perfected its specialist lines for cross-dressed submissives that it was receiving over 1,000 calls a day to its several hundred lines (Berry, 1993). Callers frequently report an increasing addiction to the lines. As one user put it: 'I used to ring cheap rate times and be thinking "God! How much is this costing?" Now, I think, "What the hell and ring whenever I'm feeling randy".'

MALE FEMALING, MASTURBATORY SCRIPTS AND TELEPHONE SEX

In this chapter I focus upon these pre-recorded scripts as a resource for accessing masturbatory fantasy. I assume that the scripts are, indeed, masturbatory scripts. In particular, I place the emphasis upon what the scripts tell us about the complex interrelations between sex, sexuality and gender, and between self, identity and world – a research domain which I introduced in Ekins (1993) (see also Chapter 3 in this volume) in the context of the basic social process of 'male femaling'.

The report should be set in the context of over ten years of qualitative sociological research in the United Kingdom with 'male femalers': males who wish to 'female' in various contexts, at various times and with varying consequences. It draws, primarily, however, on a grounded theory (Ekins, 1993) analysis of over 200 'male femaling' telephone sex line scripts collected between 1988 and 1994. The analysis of the scripts was supplemented with information obtained from unstructured interviews and correspondence with over thirty telephone sex line producers and consumers. The two scripts I have selected as illustrative of 'intimacy scripts', were provided by two separate informants. These informants discussed with me their responses to the scripts and are in broad agreement with my account.

In the terms which I introduced in Ekins (1993), users of TV/TS ('transvestite/'transsexual') telephone sex lines, who employ the scripts for masturbation, are 'male femalers' who are engaged in 'erotic fantasy femaling'. 'Male femaling' takes place in three major modes: body femaling, erotic femaling and gender femaling (Ekins, 1993). These are broadly comparable with facets of sex, sexuality and gender, respectively, where 'sex' refers to the biological and physiological aspects of the division of humans into male and female; where 'sexuality' refers to 'those matters pertaining to the potential arousability and engorgement of the genitals' (Plummer, 1979: 53); and where 'gender' refers to the socio-cultural correlates of the division of the sexes (see Chapter 3).

In the process of telephone sex, the caller variously enlists the aid of the masturbatory script to 'fantasy body female' and 'fantasy gender female' in the service of 'fantasy erotic femaling'. The progression of the scripts traces shifting interrelations between the different modes of femaling. Different objects, events and actions are variously co-opted in the process. Furthermore, different persons (bodies, selves and identities) are variously utilised, and the male femaler's own person (body, self and identity) undergoes various alterations in the service of orgasm. It is the purpose of this chapter to explicate this complex process.

THE PARADOX OF EROTIC FANTASY FEMALING

It is the being, or becoming, female that provides the core of the erotic fantasy in all male femaling masturbatory scripts. What that being, or becoming, female is seen to entail – how the transition is effected, and how far; and what takes place when it is – constitutes the variations in the scripts.

For the male erotic fantasy femaler, the fantasy of being or becoming female is erotic in itself. He has, to a greater or lesser extent, substituted the pleasures of identification with women for those of securing a female object choice. Whereas the conventional heterosexual male desires a female, the male femaler in varying degrees wishes to become one or feels that he is one. Having become female, he may experience desire for an object, but the desire is female desire whether 'heterosexual' or 'lesbian'.

Erotic fantasy femaling rests on a paradox. Fantasy femaling for masturbatory purposes presupposes an erotic focus on the penis, which will become erect and be a central source of pleasure, particularly as the channel of ejaculation. It might be supposed that this male source of pleasure would inhibit the identification with the female. However, this is not so, and it is the function of the masturbatory script to see that it is not. Fantasy femaling scripts frequently feature 'she males' – 'females' with a penis. They may be the source of both identification and object choice. 'She males' are, or have become, phallic *women*, however. They are not men. In other scripts 'she males' never feature, enabling the male femaler to 'disavow' his maleness entirely, including his genitalia. Either it is 'as if' he has no genitalia or his male genitalia becomes fantasied as female genitalia.

TEMPTRESS SCRIPTS, SADO-MASOCHISTIC SCRIPTS AND INTIMACY SCRIPTS

Male femaling masturbatory scripts fall into three major types. These I term 'temptress scripts', 'sado-masochistic' scripts and 'intimacy scripts'. All scripts within each subtype feature female narrators. Overtly homosexual male femaling scripts which feature male narrators are not the subject of this chapter, nor are those scripts which feature male narrators seducing females with whom male femalers might be identifying.

The temptress scripts, whilst being widespread in conventional heterosexual scripts, are relatively rare in male femaling scripts. In these scripts the narrator affects the sexy, husky tones of the stereotypical, enticing seducer – the irresistible whore. In 'TV wedding belles' (Crimson, 1993), for example, the caller is met with a 'Hello, my darling! Are you ready for your big day? I hope so, because there's no backing out now, you know. Today I am going to make you my wife. My gorgeous blushing bride dressed in silk panties . . .' Throughout the script the narrator maintains the sort of excitable, heavy tones most frequently associated with erotic scripts of a conventional heterosexual sort. Locations are not referred to. The caller and narrator remain encapsulated in the private space of a bedroom. The script ends with the caller kneeling on the bed, 'her' wedding dress thrown up over 'her' buttocks, 'her' silk panties pulled down, submitting to the narrator as man, as 'her' husband, enveloped in a torrent of sighs, squeals and the other accompaniments of sexual orgasm.

Temptress scripts are based on a limited role reversal in a stereotypically erotic situation. The narrator assumes certain facets of the male role, in order to feminise the caller. She is active in 'his' feminisation. She does, however, remain the stereotype of the alluring seductress, even as she may don a dildo to finalise the caller's feminisation.

Very much more common are the sado-masochistic scripts. These follow the basic patterns detailed in previous accounts of 'transvestite fiction' (Beigel and Feldman, 1963), and 'transvestite pornography' (Stoller, 1970). Buhrich and McConaghy (1976) give the flavour:

> The innocent male is coerced into wearing female clothes. The change is 'fantastically successful' . . . the protagonist decides to live permanently as a woman. Real women in the stories are 'feared and hated', often subjugating the transvestite to their every whim and even at times castrating him.

Accordingly, the tones adopted by the narrators of these scripts are dominant and bullying until the protagonist is feminised. At that point, the tones may become loving and protecting, although the subjugation must continue and the submissiveness be maintained. Frequently, third parties are involved. Thus, in 'Maid for the dildo' (Halcyon, 1993b), for example,

Peter is prepared by Joan for her mistress Olga. After numerous attempts at feminisation to become the 'perfect' woman for Olga, Peter finally becomes Alice. Having been so prepared, he is left on a bed to be raped by Olga. The script leaves him heading towards the kitchen to spend the rest of his life as an obedient housewife.

Male femaling sado-masochistic scripts tend to overlap with sado-masochistic scripts more generally. In 'Transvestite spanking!' (Halcyon, 1993c) Peter is forcibly cross-dressed. He is then 'spanked and humiliated by his own wife, in front of his mother-in-law, and maid (sic) to kneel and serve dominant women'. In 'Husband enslaved' (Halcyon, 1993a) 'a fat, ugly bullying wife dominates a she-male husband'. The bizarre tends to take precedence over subtleties of femininity in these sado-masochistic scripts.

In intimacy scripts the emphasis is upon close familiarity with women and upon participation as an equal in a shared women's world. The narrator's tones are sweet, friendly and confiding. Females are initiated into various biological, psychological and socio-cultural worlds from which males are excluded – worlds of menstruation, worlds of make-up and beauty routines, worlds of women's magazines, and so forth. Intimacy scripts favour these matters in their content. In 'So you want to be a girl – like me?' (Eazee Come, 1993b), for instance, Dave is dressed as Joanne, when the doorbell rings. 'She' goes to the door as a woman and is met by Kate, who is a representative for a firm selling fashion clothes and accessories. The time flies by as they 'chat away, woman to woman', discussing the various items in the catalogue. In 'Girls must work' (Eazee Come, 1993a), Suzanne (the male femaler) takes a job as a waitress. Jenny helps 'her' in the selection of 'her' uniform. Later, Suzanne is able to repay the friendship, by taking over the cash till, temporarily, whilst Jenny visits the Ladies, with the onset of her period. An intimate glance from Jenny is all that Suzanne needs to fully understand the situation and substitute for 'her' new-found friend.

Intimacy scripts celebrate what is seen by fantasy femalers to be part and parcel of the everyday world of everyday (principally, young) women. In these scripts, the male femalers become these women and variously feel and act like them.

THE CASE OF INTIMACY SCRIPTS

Male femaling intimacy scripts have been hitherto unexplored as a major source of masturbatory script. They are, however, particularly instructive in illustrating neglected subtleties in the interrelations between sex, sexuality and gender and their interrelations with body, identity and world. In the first place, they entail a disavowal of the male body in its entirety and the adoption of a fantasy female body, which is then sexualised. In the second place, they illustrate the importance of gender in the process of sexualisation. Finally, the scripts variously depict the role of identity changes in the service of the erotic.

There are two major variants of intimacy script. In the first, the script details the male femaler's progressive initiation into a female world, from which there is no exit. These I term 'initiation identity scripts'. In the second, the oscillations between the male and female identities of the male femaler are detailed. These I term 'oscillating identity scripts'.

'TV DREAM LINE': AN INITIATION IDENTITY SCRIPT

In 'TV dream line' (CIC, 1993b) the caller is speedily introduced into the all-female world of the beauty salon. The caller's female identity is progressively reasserted and confirmed until, 'there is nothing more you can do about it. It's too late. You are a girl.' The callers' male identity is extinguished in the process of fantasy femaling leading to orgasm. There are various uses made of body femaling and gender femaling to procure this erotic femaling finale.

The emphasis upon erotic fantasy male femaling is made explicit at the outset, as the tape begins: 'Our TV wet dream line will guide you into *your* fantasy through the erotic feminine scenes that we've created for *you*. Femininity as you've not experienced it before, because you'll become part of each encounter.' That an intimacy script is to follow is also made clear. The caller will be taken 'into a massage salon with other beautiful young girls'. 'Your beautician is there waiting to probe your feminine body into sexual submission'.

'I'm Sarah, there now, don't be shy', begins the script.

You're only with other young girls, and I'm here to relax you into femininity, working my hands into every inch of your body. You'll be in a room with other girls and you can keep your bra and panties on if you like. You might like to talk feminine talk with them while I gently rub over your body. And as I do that, either Ann or Joanne will be waxing your legs to get them nice and smooth right up to your bikini line. Feel the soft delicate skin of my hands, rub inside . . . your legs. Right up to your crutch. Feel the motion of my body urging into every movement.

The 'bra and panties' are emphasised repeatedly throughout the script. As garments covering the female *body* – breasts and genitalia – they are associated, particularly, with body femaling. In the case of the male femaling intimacy script, their function is to simultaneously hide the male body and aid in the transition to, and maintenance of, the fantasy female body. As intimate and feminine undergarments, moreover, they are associated with both the erotic and the gendered. They, therefore, serve as a male femaling leitmotif which can utilise both body and gender femaling in the service of sexual arousal.

> When I move up to your breasts and gently work the oils into your cups, close your eyes as you think of being and feeling feminine . . . your breasts . . . your panties. They'll feel so silky soft and smooth to the touch. Permanently feminine. Isn't that what women like? Like yours . . . shapely, in your bra and little white panties.

The movement up the body continues. 'I move into your neckline and caress your shoulders, with my firm arms forcing my feminine motion into every fibre of your body.'

Then, the other girls are introduced. Our caller is not, merely, one girl being treated by one other. He is placed firmly as a girl amongst many others in an exclusively female environment.

> Hear the sounds of the other girls around you talking, and laughing and chatting, in their soft, high, feminine voices. Be aware of their presence, here, with you. Girls, here, around you. Girls' talk . . . Sweet and feminine. And you feel the femaleness in you, as my body heaves into forcing you into feminine relaxation. Forcing you into our female way of life . . . the bra the panties . . . just give in. There's nothing more you can do about it. It's too late. You are a girl. Relax into that thought and just . . . submit . . . Our female way of life . . . The bra . . . the panties . . . submit.

It is as if the repetition is lulling our caller into a female world from which he is quite unable to escape.

Now the emphasis shifts from Sarah's hands and voice to her own body. 'Now be aware of my femininity. Open your eyes. See my breasts, perfectly formed. And hanging idly over your face, in the cups of my bra.'

No shift is intended, however, to Sarah as a heterosexual object choice. Her body is being made available to our caller as a mirror image of his own.

Female bodies are accentuated by female clothes, the wearing of which reaffirms the femininity of the wearer. Body femaling, gender femaling and erotic femaling coalesce as the script continues:

> Imagine yourself . . . with girls . . . like you . . . wearing little gathered skirts tight at the waist and falling gently over the hips. The soft, delicate, feminine material wafting round their thighs, in the breeze . . . to reveal long, shapely, smooth legs. You know . . . the sort of thing you enjoy wearing when you want to go out and feel good.

The presence of onlookers further confirms the female identity. Furthermore, that identity is made retrospective:

I bet you've accidentally bent over and people have caught a glimpse of your delicate panties. We've all done it, haven't we? How embarrassing. And how your bottom sticks to the seat, on those hot days. Just like when you were a schoolgirl.

'Are you coming?' signifies the pending intended end point of the script. The caller is now a 'woman', and able to indulge in the sort of fantasy gender femaling which appeals to many male femalers. 'Are you thinking of all those feminine things? That only you ... as a girl ... could experience ... The bra ... the panties ... little short, flared mini-skirts.'

Once again, the fact that the caller is a girl like the narrator is reiterated:

As you look down the length of my body, you become aware of my panties ... tight, on my hips ... Just like yours ... Don't you want to be like that? The wonderful clothes . . The pretty underwear ... Come on. Feel my hands probing your panties, as you submit to these feminine thoughts.

Climax is reached: 'Climax, with my fingers in your panties.'
As the waves of pleasure increase to orgasm:

Now ... Our female way of life ... The bra ... the panties ... your breasts. Just give in. There's nothing more you can do about it. It's too late. You are ... a girl. Our female way of life. There's nothing more you can do about it. It's too late. You are a girl. Relax into that thought. And just ... submit.

COMMENT

'TV dream line' is an erotic fantasy femaling script which is designed to have the caller enter as female, and remain so until orgasm. Erotic fantasy femalers who have consolidated (Ekins, 1993) their male femaling around this mode of femaling will return to their male selves with the incident of fantasy femaling over.

Graham, for instance, after a period of cross-dressing in public ('doing femaling'), settled down with a girlfriend. He did not want to lose her, was frightened to tell her of his interest in male femaling and stopped his cross-dressing. However, as Graham's sexual relationship with his partner deteriorated, he turned, increasingly, to telephone sex lines as the focus for his sexual life. He began to consolidate his male femaling around the erotic fantasy femaling that his telephone sex enabled him to enjoy.

He told me how he could 'scarcely believe (his) ears' when he first heard 'TV dream line' – so uncannily did it fit his own 'perfect' masturbatory fantasy. In the past he had visited beauty salons dressed as a woman and had received various beauty treatments. He did not experience these expeditions as erotic, at the time. He disavowed his male body. He did not have erections in his penis. Rather, he considered that he experienced the treatments in the same way as a woman might – as enjoyable, as relaxing, as pleasurably sensual. With the reality of the trip over, however, he would find himself incorporating incidents that had occurred in the salon into his masturbatory scripts. He would recall the time, for instance, when the beautician unexpectedly slipped his bra straps over his shoulders, in order to make space for the unimpeded movement of her hands, as she cleansed and toned his face and neck. He would recall the conversations about boyfriends, Christmas presents, and so on, he had shared with the 'other girls' in the salon. 'TV dream line' revived his own experiences and provided embellishments upon them. He incorporated the script into his most preferred masturbatory routine, telephoned the line regularly and eventually made a tape recording of it.

'GIRLS' CHANGING ROOM': AN OSCILLATING IDENTITY SCRIPT

Oscillation between male and female identities is well illustrated by 'Girls' changing room' (CIC, 1993a).

In 'Girls' changing room' the female identity, 'Amy', takes over from the male identity 'David', and it is Amy who goes shopping. Amy finds 'herself' in a communal girls' changing room confronted by a near-naked 'attractive' girl. As sexual attraction emerges in David, Amy disappears and David begins to return. The script provides an excellent example of the inverse relationship between heterosexual object choice and identification that is frequently reported by male femalers.

The script starts with an involuntary identity transition:

> Yes, something inside was pushing him into changing. The transition, transformation, call it what you like, it made no difference. Amy, beautiful Amy, was about to appear as a fully fledged attractive female, and there was nothing Dave could do about it. Nothing got in Amy's way. Soon, Dave would be gone. And Amy would take over completely.

Soon Amy is admiring herself in the mirror (reinforcement of the identity shift), her body 'filled with feminine warmth and charm' (body femaling emphasis).

The gender femaling that follows is emphasised both to reaffirm the identity transition and to provide erotic focus. Amy has momentarily forgotten her earrings. 'Oh! she muttered, forgotten your earrings, again. Darling, this will never do.'

'But soon, Amy had flittered out of the house with breezy air, to joint the rest of her society, in her rightful place (as a woman).' The caller is left with the suggestion that the script is going to be an 'all girls together' intimacy script. 'Of course, to Amy that meant shopping, as it does to most girls.' Further gender femaling is then elaborated. Amy enters a 'lovely' boutique. Great emphasis is placed on the 'glamorous and gorgeous outfits' inside, on the feminine materials – the chiffons and the satins – , and so on. Amy's natural place is seen to be within this gendered female world.

Just as 'TV dream line' introduces the beautician to reaffirm the caller's female identity, so in 'Girls' changing room' a boutique assistant is introduced to serve the same function.

'Goodness me! Yes!' says the assistant, 'That's just you.' 'It's not too short, do you think?' enquires Amy. ' Oh, no Madam! It's got verve and life in it. And the little short flared skirt will simply swish around your thighs, causing the greatest attention to your legs' (continued emphasis upon fantasy gender femaling, to accentuate fantasy body femaling).

Amy makes her way towards the communal changing room. As she enters it, she is in her element. She can now become part of an intimate female world, try on clothes to her heart's content, exhibit herself in front of the mirror, and so on. The fantasy male femaling caller will be identifying with Amy in these various confirmations of her identity. It is the identification with Amy that is erotic for him.

As a 'woman', the caller will not find the other women in the changing room potentially sexually desirable, as a heterosexual man, he might. It is this dilemma which the oscillating identity script exploits. Appropriately, a transitional passage follows which introduces TVs (transvestites) in order to presage the female-to-male identity shift which is to follow.

The sight that beheld Amy's eyes could have started any TV's (transvestite's) eyes streaming. There were boobs, and buttocks, distributed all over the changing room. With panties and tights ... bras ... strewn in all manner of haphazard ways on the floor.

Initially, Amy maintains a distance from all this.

Amy was Amy. She loved the attention. The feminine atmosphere. The feeling of being female. Amy was high. Drugged to the eyeballs with her own infatuation of simply being a woman. And now she was. She was here. Bare bottoms and breasts. Femininity, females. She was here.

However, a girl (Estelle) next to Amy smiles at her. She is 'wearing only panties'. As she steps into her skirt, 'her breasts idly swing down in movement to her hips'. This is all too much for the heterosexual Dave. Dave's identity begins to reassert itself.

The script 'explains':

161

But I suppose that's what started it. You know. That deep down urge that something is no longer right. The drug was waning. The heart was not so much pumping in anticipation as in fear of what she was really doing here. With all these near naked women around her, close to her, Amy should have been as high as a kite. She had made it. She had passed, successfully. But something else was beginning to happen. Dave was beginning to make himself apparent. What the hell was he going to do now? By now (Estelle) was standing in front of Dave, wearing only a skirt. He became aware ... of her breasts ... idly hanging down ... forming a perfect cleavage. Her hand gracefully rested on her hip. And she was looking straight at him. Girl to girl. Dave swallowed. Err ... err ... erm ... my name is – Amy, she croaked in his best feminine voice. The girl relaxed. The atmosphere, so tense, up to now, calmed a little.

Will Amy vanish without trace? If she does, how will Dave escape his predicament? Or will Amy return?

Amy's eventual reappearance is enabled by what the script refers to as 'an unusual show of high feminine behaviour'. Exclaiming that the dress is 'quite awful', she adds that Dave wouldn't like it, either. She is now free to leave the changing room with her new-found friend. They look through the racks of clothes and eventually make their purchases as 'girls together'. With the intimacy of the 'girl-to-girl' interactions, a female order is reimposed. Intimate gender femaling reaffirms and maintains Amy's identity.

The 'girls' chat. Amy shows Estelle a particular dress she likes and they both make their way to the cashier to pay for the items they have chosen. 'After you!' said Estelle. 'Oh thank you, darling' (intimacy affirmed, again). 'Amy placed the dress on the counter, and the young cashier totted up the bill on the computer.'

So relaxed is Amy in her identity, now, that she can joke with the female cashier (more girls together): 'How would Madam like to pay for all this? She asked. Not at all, replied Amy, whimsically. She took out a credit card and passed it to the cashier.' However, from that moment disaster struck, for the cashier calls the manageress to check the discrepancy between the male name on the credit card and the female Amy before her.

Confronted with an abrupt questioning of her identity, Amy's fragility is revealed, and Dave returns. Just as he is wishing he wasn't there, his wish is granted. The entire sequence is now revealed to have been a dream.

Amy has gone and it is now Dave who awakes in a sweat. He clasps his hands over his face. He gets out of bed and looks around for reassurance. He sinks down in relief. 'Dreams', he sighs, 'Goodness! If I ever try that one ... I'll be absolutely mad. Fantasising's fine but that was murder. And as for Amy ... I think he'd got a point. Don't you?'

COMMENT

It does, perhaps, stretch the limits of credibility to suppose that a male femaler would enact such a fantasy and use a credit card with a male name. Maybe the device was used simply to secure the ending of the script or to provide a particular twist to the story line. Many male femalers, however, do acquire credit cards in their female identities. This strategy frequently enables a more satisfactory outcome for the male femaler.

Jeremy, for instance, used his credit card in his female identity at every available opportunity when he was out shopping as a female. Indeed, his favourite male femaling activity was to shop in women's boutiques and pay for the goods he would buy using the credit card made out in this way. Like David/Amy, in the script, he took particular enjoyment in being a woman in a woman's world. He savoured the moments as he would go through the racks of women's clothes. Like David/Amy he was never bold enough to try on a dress in a communal changing room – 'that would have been too risky'. Rather, he tried skirts. As he put it: 'With my handbag over one arm and a selection of skirts over the other, I feel exactly like all the other girls as I approach the changing room.'

Jeremy would feel a mounting sense of excitement as he entered the changing room. What would happen if his male identity was detected? He was never quite sure he would not be detected, but, as yet, he had never been knowingly suspected. In particular, he would recall the tremendous feeling of well-being he experienced on his arrival home with his purchases. As he reflected upon the various male femaling activities of the day, his thoughts would ponder the 'highlights'. Invariably, it was what he took to be the affirmations of being a woman that provided him with most pleasure: the waiting in the queue of girls and women making their purchases whilst some of their boyfriends and husbands waited for them, at a distance, at the side of the queue; the appraisal of himself and his clothes in the mirror, and the like. Paying for his purchases with his credit card made out in his female name was very important to him. It added the final icing on the cake. Here was a (preferably) female cashier accepting him as another female, as he made his female purchases for his female self in his female name.

Just as with Graham's visits to the beauty salon, Jeremy did not find his shopping trips sexually arousing, at the time ('That would not be ladylike!'). It was only when they were over that their erotic potential arose. Alone, at home, as he thought about his exploits, he would find himself becoming sexually aroused and wanting to masturbate. As he masturbated his thoughts would oscillate. For the most part he would be thinking of himself as female in the all-female world of the boutique and changing room. In these thoughts he was just one woman amongst others. But then, and most usually involuntarily, he would find himself thinking of the glimpses of the women he had observed trying on their own potential purchases. While it was sexually arousing to *be* one of the women, he also lingered on the thoughts of the women in the changing room as they looked at themselves in the mirror, unaware of his gaze. As with David/Amy, it was at these moments that Jeremy's male identity re-emerged. Little wonder, then, that 'Girls' changing room' was one of Jeremy's favourite masturbatory scripts. For him, the oscillating identities featured in the script enabled him to enjoy the best of all possible worlds. They reminded him of his own experiences. Furthermore, he could enjoy the pleasures of identification with both David and Amy as he revelled in the oscillations of identity and their various concomitants.

CONCLUSIONS AND IMPLICATIONS

This chapter has been concerned to explore erotic fantasy femaling masturbatory scripts from the standpoint of the interrelations between body femaling, gender femaling and erotic femaling, and identity, self and world. It has highlighted some of the neglected interrelations between facets which have previously been conflated, with particular reference to an unidentified major subtype of male femaling masturbatory script – the intimacy script.

Telephone sex lines are an underresearched area. Inevitably, therefore, the chapter raises a host of issues that would profit from further work. Principal amongst these are the following:

1   Random sampling of telephone sex lines suggests that every conceivable erotic fantasy will be available in principle. The social process/grounded theory approach adopted in this study might be extended to the full range of scripts, and would order a mass of 'intimate detail', hitherto unresearched. Content analysis of the major themes is needed.
2   The meanings of telephone sex lines will be different to different users, as will the use made of such scripts. This warrants comprehensive investigation, both inside and outside the specific area of male femaling.
3   The scripts themselves provide a ready resource for ideological analysis and studies in the sociology of knowledge. What, for instance, do they tell us about sexual life in a technological age? Are they telling us anything new, or are they presenting old themes via a new media? What do they tell us about the present arrangement between the sexes? In particular, what do they tell us about erotic fantasy femalers' perceptions of the present arrangement between the sexes?

NOTES

1   From July 1994 callers from the United Kingdom could only access the majority of telephone sex lines either by obtaining a security personal identification number or by using a credit card (ICSTIS, 1993). 'Information lines' were exempt from the new regulations and, as a result, many lines for cross-dressers and sex-changers were rephrased in terms of their providing information – as, for instance, in 'True TV experiences' (TIC, 1994).

2   The Trans-Gender Archive contains a comprehensive collection of material on cross-dressing and sex-changing – the first public collection of its type in the world (Ekins, 1988; 1990a).

Part V

GENDER BLENDING AND GENDER POLITICS

INTRODUCTION

Until the late 1960s, to write of the political aspects of gender blending would have made little sense. However, with the second wave of feminism and a new focus on the myriad dimensions of gender, it became possible to conceive of ways in which the apparently private practices of cross-dressing and sex-changing could have political significance.

In the era of the Gay Liberation Front in the early 1970s, 'it seemed to many homosexuals that a new day was dawning, ushering in an era of spontaneity, openness and liberation' (Weeks, 1977: 185). In retrospect, it seems that what became known as the transvestite/transsexual community emerged too late to benefit greatly from the period of 'liberation'. By 1974, the end of the gay liberation period, cross-dressers and sex-changers were only just struggling to reach the position from which their gay counterparts had begun. Whilst there were some small groupings which showed a willingness to engage with the issues being raised by the gay and women's movements, the importance of these radical groupings, like those of the more conservative ones, probably lay in their provision of a means whereby gender blenders could come together and forge identities as transvestites and transsexuals.

In the mid-1970s, the largest and most influential organisations for transvestites and transsexuals were the American Foundation for Full Personality Expression (FPE) and its many offshoots, such as the British Beaumont Society (King, 1993) or the Australian Seahorse Club (see Chapter 5), all of which were criticised by sections of the gay and women's movements as well as by other transvestites and transsexuals (Brake, 1976; Weeks 1977: 224–5). These organisations were attacked for their failure to engage openly in sexual politics; for their low-profile 'closed closet' form; for their support for conventional norms and structures such as marriage and the family as well as traditional sexual stereotypes exemplified in the image of women portrayed by members and in their publications; and for their attempt to normalise transvestism by excluding from or denying the presence within their membership of, for example, transsexuals, homosexuals or fetishists.

Such criticism could probably be summarised as a call for transvestites to come 'out of the closet' and join the struggle for sexual and gender liberation. Brake, in an article originally given as a conference paper in 1974, noted that transsexuals and transvestites could be perceived as, 'revolutionaries who publicly challenge the notion of ascribed gender' (Brake, 1976: 188), although he clearly noted their ambiguous relationship to the issues of sexual politics and the charge of sexism that could be levelled at some aspects of their behaviour:

> Transvestites and transsexuals polarize the problems of gay activism. At one level they are accused of sexism because of their concern with traditional femininity, but it must be remembered that the masters are not supposed to dress as slaves, and men who dress as women are giving up their power as men. Their oppression is similar to that experienced by gay men and all women.
>
> (Brake, 1976: 187)

Brake sees establishment medicine as a source of oppression and is critical of the obstacles placed in the way of transsexuals seeking surgery. He sees the medical profession as responsible for inducing stereotypical femininity in male transsexuals, 'the transsexual is coerced into passing as a programmed woman, with the dignity befitting a lady' (Brake, 1976: 191). He argues that :

> The only way that the tyrranous dictates of ascribed gender can be challenged is for the women's movement and Gay Liberation to recruit and demystify their oppressed transvestite and transsexual brothers and sisters, whilst developing sensitivity to each other's problems.
>
> (Brake, 1976: 191)

The idea that transvestites and transsexuals share the oppression of lesbians, gay men and all women and that the political way forward lay in unity is also to be found in the pages of *Come Together*, published during the early years of the gay liberation movement (Walter, 1980).

Raymond (1980), however, saw transvestites and (particularly) transsexuals as servants of the enemy. At the heart of her position is the denial of the legitimacy of the transsexual's 'chosen' gender. How much acceptance Raymond's thesis has had is difficult to tell, but it has clearly been widely read and discussed. Stone (1991: 283) writes of Raymond's book that, 'here in 1991, on the twelfth anniversary of its publication, it is still the definitive statement on transsexualism by a genetic female academic'. Janice Raymond's *The Transsexual Empire* is summarised and criticised by Carol Riddell in Chapter 12.

These are not merely 'academic' arguments. As Riddell wrote to us (personal communication, 1994):

> At the time this pamphlet was written, a small but very active section of the feminist movement, the 'Revolutionary Feminists', were taking over some positions in the radical subcultures of extreme feminism. They owed a little intellectually to Mary Daly and her ex-student Janice Raymond, from whose doctoral thesis *The Transsexual Empire* was written. There were reports of threats to transsexuals in London, and I myself was threatened with violence when I attended a Bisexuality conference there. *Divided Sisterhood* was an attempt to portray a different kind of feminism, a different kind of consciousness, lived in the heady days of the British Women's Movement of the middle 70s.

Many groups who are, or consider themselves to be, oppressed or discriminated against have sought redress through the legal system. Others, adversely affected by their impaired legal status, have sought law reform (as personally described by Mark Rees in Chapter 2).

In Chapter 13, the radical transsexual activist Terri Webb, formerly known as Rachael Webb, outlines her present position as to the sorts of activities transsexuals should be pursuing in relation to equal opportunity policies and rights issues. For many years, Terri (as Rachael) was a housing officer with the London Borough of Southwark and a councillor in Lambeth, where she worked with groups promoting equal opportunities (Hodgkinson, 1987). She is now a continental truck driver. She remains as committed as ever to socialist and radical feminist politics, but considers that to argue that she is other than a man who has received reassignment surgery is to live a lie. She does not regret her operation – for her, there was no 'choice' in the matter – but she does advocate a serious consideration of whether reassignment procedures should continue.

Gender blending is not a static phenomenon which remains unchanged as we look at it from different perspectives. At times, the perspectives we use can have a major impact on its nature, as many writers have argued the medical gaze has had. However, as a social and cultural practice, it changes as a result of other dynamics. Over the past ten to fifteen years, gender blending has become more complex and diverse. It has also been subjected to some reassessments and new interpretations of its political significance. For some, the issue of transsexualism has been largely superseded by debates over transgenderism or what has been called 'sexuality's newest cutting edge' (Raymond, 1994: xxv). In particular, gender blending has achieved a position of prominence in a number of recent contributions to cultural studies and in what has come to be known as 'queer theory'. Stephen Whittle examines these approaches in Chapter 14. In the final chapter, Janice Raymond, in an extract from the introduction to the new edition of *The Transsexual Empire* (Raymond, 1994), gives her assessment of what has come to be known as 'transgender politics'.

12

DIVIDED SISTERHOOD

A critical review of Janice Raymond's
*The Transsexual Empire**

Carol Riddell

AN OUTLINE OF THE MAIN ARGUMENTS OF *THE TRANSSEXUAL EMPIRE*

Who are transsexuals?[1]

Ms Raymond makes her position absolutely clear. Transsexual women 'are not women. They are *deviant males*' (Raymond, 1980: 183). Transsexual men are not men, but women. The first, basic, underlying cause of transsexualism is the sex stereotyping system in a patriarchy: 'a patriarchal society and its social currents of masculinity and femininity is the *First Cause* of transsexualism' (p. xviii; italics in original). Thus, transsexuals exhibit one form of response to the same problems that women face in a patriarchal society:

> Like transsexuals, many women have felt hatred of their bodies and its functions [sic]; and have found themselves in a psychically disjointed state because they could not accept their role ... feminists have become social critics and have organised, as feminists around issues of sexism and sex-role oppression.
>
> (pp. 175–6)

The major secondary cause of transsexualism, she argues, is the medical speciality which has grown up around the performance of transsexual operations. This is the Transsexual Empire. Not only surgeons, but psychiatrists, psychologists, counsellors, deportment instructors, speech therapists, electrologists and the like have formed powerful teams, sometimes using national funds, which enable the fulfilment of the wish. Transsexualism is, apart from scattered historical myths, a new phenomenon, dating from

---

* An earlier version of this chapter first appeared as Parts 2, 3, and 5 of 'Divided sisterhood: a critical review of Janice Raymond's *The Transsexual Empire*', Liverpool: News from Nowhere, 1980.

the growth of the transsexual operators in the 1950s. These medical specialists, since they cannot create real women, attempt to create pastiches,
which are trained to be models of the kind of women men would like to
see. The gender identity clinics therefore act as reinforcers of patriarchally
defined stereotypes. They are already beginning to 'treat' children in some
places, attempting to cure them of 'incipient' transsexual leanings, i.e., to
get them to conform to existing, prescribed ways of behaviour. The clinics
may develop to become 'gender enforcers' for the readjustment of those
who deviate, quite apart from transsexuals. The apparent existence of
transsexual *men* is, in fact, a subterfuge, for the real purpose is to subor-
dinate women. Transsexual men are 'the tokens that save face for the
transsexual empire' (p. 27). They make it appear that a universal problem
is involved, when there is actually a problem of control. Furthermore,
transsexually operated men could potentially have been woman-identified
women, and are thus lost to feminism. 'Woman-identified women' are
women who are committed to women in every way.

Janice Raymond's view is that biologically, the basic indicator of sex is
the chromosomal pattern, XX (female), XY (male). Since this cannot be
changed, no person can change sex in reality. All that can be done is
various procedures to simulate a biological state that is chromosomally
denied. If there were no stereotypical behaviours prescribed by patriarchy
for either sex, transsexuals could behave as they liked – subject to some
general morality, of course – and would not have to have operations. Thus,
a moral problem is created within our society, and transformed by the
gender identity clinics into a medical one, one of 'adjustment', in this case
physical as well as social. These medical procedures are used for patriarchy as a means of social control of gender stereotypes, which act in the
interests of men.

Causes

Ms Raymond outlines the various theories that have been put forward
by the sex researchers to account for transsexualism. They fall into two
categories:

- *Antenatal.* Inadequate hormonal stimulation of the foetus has led to
  the brain being 'predisposed' towards female or male behaviour in
  opposition to male or female biology;
- *Postnatal.* These argue that abnormal features of early socialisation are
  responsible. Typically, the responsibility for creating both male and
  female transsexuals is laid on the shoulders of the mother.

The sex researchers always phrase the problem in terms of the transsexual's need. They assert that gender identity is immutably fixed by the
age of eighteen months. They then argue that it is therefore right to accept

a person's belief as to their gender identity. In Ms Raymond's view, what such arguments actually allow is the legitimisation of medical experimentation to produce 'synthetic females', geared to male conceptions of 'proper' femaleness. By adding to this the possibility of extra-natal conception, Ms Raymond has a nightmarish vision of a future in which biological women might become redundant.

In the present time, the people 'created' by what Ms Raymond calls a process of 'male mothering' are unfortunate hybrids, neither female nor male, dependent on the male medical establishment for their existence. Ms Raymond talked with thirteen transsexual women and refers to a book by Thomas Kando, who interviewed seventeen others (Kando, 1973). They presented highly stereotypical notions of female behaviour, nor did those interviewed appear to experience the role-strain of normal women. This indicates that they are not really women, but propagandists for male-defined images of women, not only in their words but in their very existence. Transsexual women writers demonstrate this as well, particularly Jan Morris, whose 'female self' is a mirror image of a stereotypical male (Morris, 1974).

Transsexuals and the feminist movement

Some few transsexual women have attempted to escape this stereotyping by becoming involved, as lesbian-feminists, in the women's movement. In Ms Raymond's view their position is even worse than that of other transsexuals. No transsexual woman has had the full experience of socialisation as a woman, which other women have. She is chromosomally XY. There can be no question of her being accepted as a woman and allowed access to feminist spaces. Transsexual lesbian-feminists can only 'play the part' (p. 103). But the transsexual woman in the women's movement has an even more sinister role:

As the [transsexual woman] exhibits the attempt to possess women in a bodily sense while acting out the images into which men have moulded women, the [transsexual woman] who claims to be a lesbian-feminist attempts to possess women at a deeper level, this time under the guise of challenging rather than conforming to the role and behaviour of stereotyped femininity'.

(p. 99)

Although the transsexual woman has no penis, in the feminist movement 'her whole presence becomes a "member" invading women's presence and dividing us once more from each other' (p. 104).

When real men decide that the real women's movement needs containing, they will be able to use these pseudo-women as their agents (p. 106). Thus, it is a matter of important principle that transsexual women are excluded from feminist spaces. Women who don't accept this, for instance, the collective of Olivia, the women's record company, who had a transsexual woman among them, are exhibiting some or all of the following confusions. Liberalism, in not wanting to be intolerant; gratitude, that one of the ruling sex has renounced privileges; naïvety, in not realising what is going on as Ms Raymond sees it; retaining elements of male identification, by being fearful of being called man-haters and since they are still subject to the attraction of the male persona (pp. 112–13). Not only does the transsexual feminist 'perform total rape' (p. 112), but 'lesbian-feminists who accept transsexually constructed lesbian-feminists as other selves are mutilating their own reality' (p. 119).

Philosophical problems of transsexualism

By allowing transsexuals to resolve their problems by medical means, the sex researchers are denying them the right to challenge the patriarchal stereotyping system which ultimately creates them. Transsexual surgery is a form of behaviour modification and control which is allowed conditionally, if transsexuals accept and learn to present themselves in terms of patriarchally approved stereotypes. It follows typical male patterns in that it fetishises forms, artificial vaginas, removed organs. The transsexual is inherently masochistic, and the 'rebirth' experience reported by some transsexuals after operation is equivalent to total orgasm and irresistibly tempting when offered (pp. 139, 144). Reports of greater happiness by 90 per cent of transsexuals after operation are quite superficial and cannot be set against the drug dependency, stereotyped personality and physical health risks involved. The practice of transsexual surgery, in its blindness to the wider human ethics of the transsexual problem, has parallels to the Nazi experiments in concentration camps, which Ms Raymond describes at some length, where people were subjected to barbaric tortures in the name of 'medical science'. She does, at one point, note that the practices are not equivalent.

Finally, the problem is presented by Ms Raymond in more philosophical terms. The transsexual state after operation is an inadequate mode of being. It substitutes a superficial integration for a total human integrity, which would accept the mind–body unity and alter the conditions giving rise to conflict, rather than mutilating the body. Transsexualism operates at best on a principle of *androgyny*. This merely adds up qualities thought to be masculine and feminine. Transsexuals therefore combine bits and pieces of social qualities that maleness and femaleness are supposed to have in patriarchy. The ways they do this in no way transcend the problem of dissatisfaction with one's gender but make transsexuals unsatisfactory pastiches, even if they feel themselves to be satisfied with the result. Ms Raymond lists seven rhetorical questions to give the essence of these arguments.

1   Is the price of individual satisfaction individual role conformity and the enforcement of social role stereotypes?
2   Is transsexuals' capacity for social protest and criticism restricted by their operations and other treatment?
3   Are false opposites integrated to create a sense of transsexual well-being?
4   Are larger possibilities of being restricted by defining well-being in terms of bodily features?
5   Are transsexuals violating their bodily eco-systems so that they damage themselves physically, e.g., by being liable to cancers?
6   Is transsexual surgery creating medically dependent people?
7   Is transsexual surgery a male conception of happiness, an attempt by men to bypass the creative energies of women by artificial means?

Ms Raymond would like us to answer, yes, to all these questions. Their answer is, in fact, no. I have explained why this is so in the next sections without dealing with each question individually.

In spite of her arguments, Ms Raymond does not feel that transsexual operations should automatically be legislated out of existence. The first thing is to legislate against sex-role stereotyping, the real cause of trans-sexualism. The proliferation of gender identity clinics should be stopped. Counselling and consciousness-raising techniques, which focus upon the restrictive aspects of transsexualism for true integrity in human person-hood, should be used. Ms Raymond, perhaps ironically, considering her attitudes, does not wish to be regarded as treating the 'anguish and existential plight' of transsexuals unsympathetically.[2]

A CRITIQUE OF *THE TRANSSEXUAL EMPIRE*

As I read Ms Raymond's book, I felt angry, irritated and very bitter. I scribbled pages of critical notes. In one respect the book doesn't hurt me personally, because it is all so far removed from who I am and what I'm about in this world. But I know that its publication has made my personal space in the women's movement more problematic, makes it less easy for me to trust women who don't know me well, and vice versa. It also makes things harder for pre-operative and post-operative transsexuals in general. It is this knowledge that causes my bitterness. It is clear that, in spite of Ms Raymond's claims of sympathy to the 'existential plight' of transsex-uals and her use of the conventional mode of formal scholarship, which enables her to disguise her emotions, she actually experiences hatred and fear when thinking about transsexuals. These feelings surface when she writes about the minuscule number of transsexuals who are involved in the women's movement.

Faulty arguments

Innumerable points of disagreement spin in my head. It's best to start by considering the method that Janice Raymond uses. Her proposition that the first cause of transsexualism is the patriarchal gender system, stated again and again throughout the book, is an assumption. The possibility that transsexualism might have any other background causes is absolutely unacceptable to her, and unconsidered. The method of the book is thus dogmatic, theological in the worst sense. When one believes firmly, without the possibility of doubt, that something is explained in a particular way, then what we, as other human beings, actually experience as happening, can not challenge that explanation. Actual experience is denied, distorted or ignored in order to fit in with the theory. Since she starts with a dogmatic assumption, it is easy to present arguments that seem to follow logically from the first. Given the primary assumption, each of them is equally unchallengeable. For Ms Raymond, the patriarchal gender-role system is responsible for her oppression as a woman, she extends that argument to cover transsexualism as well. In my view the *structure* of patriarchy is the crucial factor in women's oppression, i.e., the sexual division of labour which centres women's primary existence around the bringing up of children and the servicing of people and men's around the production of things. The gender-role system is a consequence of this (Chodorow, 1978). The implications of this difference of view are discussed in the final section. But neither the gender-role system nor the structure of patriarchy is responsible for transsexualism.

Ms Raymond goes on to define transsexualism as a creation of the sexist medical establishment. In order to establish or refute this, it would be necessary to look at:

- the history of transsexualism prior to the 1950s, and its cultural extent, which Ms Raymond *defines* out of existence;
- something of the background of the development of the gender identity clinics themselves, which Ms Raymond ignores, and
- the significance of transsexual *men* whose existence she denies, for it refutes her assertion that transsexualism is a creation of man, for 'men'.

In a gender-role-free society, Janice Raymond argues, transsexualism would not exist, because anybody's behavioural desires could be expressed in whatever way they wanted, so 'changing' sex would not matter. Transsexualism is not, however, a behavioural desire alone. The explanations of women's oppression do not fit transsexualism.

Ms Raymond's assumptions make criticism impossible, except on matters of detail. Since, by her definition, transsexual women are not women, and transsexual men are not men, our arguments, which are based on our experiences as women or men, are invalidated from the start. Sex researchers who disagree are trying to uphold patriarchy, so their arguments are worthless. Women who have lived with, and experienced transsexual women as the women they are, she sees as merely deluded. Since I, writing this, am not myself but someone defined away as a male excrescence, raping the women's movement with the purpose of sowing dissent, no arguments I present need be considered (cf., p. 112). This is naive, axiomatic, dogmatic thinking. Its implications as a mode of thought for the women's movement as a whole are, frankly, disastrous. They are discussed in the final section.

Secondly, although Ms Raymond attacks the particular aims of the sex researchers, she herself adopts general propositions of patriarchal scientific ideology. For her, who we can be is rigidly defined either by biological criteria of body and cell structure or by learned behaviour derived from social interaction. In other words, we are only what patriarchal science tells us that we may be. Yet women as a whole have never accepted that rational male scientism, ideological product of eighteenth and nineteenth century capitalist development, told the whole truth about existence. We are now rediscovering and developing a wider view which, in the West, was destroyed in large part by the witch-hunts (Ehrenreich and English, 1974). Even male writers from within science are challenging the assumptions of their disciplines, which are now seen as restricting enquiry. They argue that subtle energy forces exist which are at levels behind biology (Capra, 1976; Watson, 1974). Ms Raymond attacks the sex researchers for assuming that biology and socialisation are destiny (her Chapter 2), but she assumes just that herself: 'It is biologically impossible to change chromosomal sex, and *thus* the transsexual is not really trans-sexed' (p. 126).

> Women take on the self-definition of feminist and/or lesbian because that definition truly proceeds from not only the chromosomal fact of being born XX, but also from the whole history of what being born with those chromosomes means in this society'
>
> (p. 116)

In other words, biology plus socialisation equals destiny. If we abandon biological-sociological determinism, other causes of transsexualism become feasible. Further, although transsexuals have a unique life experience which differs from that of other men and women, other feminists, at least as responsible and aware as Ms Raymond, have not found this a bar to accepting transsexual women.

A third problem of Ms Raymond's method is that she uncritically accepts the patriarchal academic establishment's separation of personal feelings from factual presentation. I do not believe that people's feelings can or ought to be ignored in understanding the things they write about. At the least, they influence the manner in which things are presented. One can easily divine from the text that Janice Raymond feels deeply threatened

177

and scared by the idea of transsexualism. This is most clear in her chapter on transsexual women in the women's movement, who are trashed in the bitterest terms as 'rapists' and 'energy stealers', male agents who sow dissension among women. In fact, the very tiny number of transsexual women in the women's movement are quite well integrated into their women's groups, sharing energy with other sisters and being accused of nothing by the women who associate with them. We only become visible as a result of attacks from women who do not know us. They see trans-sexualism as an abstract problem which they can, abstractly, regard as an extension of patriarchy. The opposition to Sandy Stone, a transsexual woman in the Olivia women's record collective, did not come from the women who worked with her, lived with her, knew her and loved her, but from women who did not know her at all. I want to know where Janice Raymond is *coming from* about transsexuals. She does not admit to any feelings on the matter, an attitude which just follows the false male division between reason and emotion. If Ms Raymond sorted out her projections about transsexuals it might lead her to want to write in a different way.

The Transsexual Empire sets out to prove something which it has already assumed, allows only the definitions of patriarchal science for its deter-mination of gender identity and tries to deny us the right to know what the author is really feeling beneath her 'scientific veneer'.

Are gender identity clinics the real threat?

Janice Raymond attacks the sex researchers as the evil-intentioned instru-ments of patriarchal sex-role coercion. While her criticisms of their views are sound, she gives them too much importance. From personal experi-ence of the London gender identity clinic, I cannot regard her idea that the clinics are experimenting towards a new, artificial replacement of biological women (cf., p. 168) as being anything more than a paranoid fantasy. The fact of the matter is that the gender identity clinics are not regarded with favour by most of the medical patriarchy. They were estab-lished and exist in spite of the opposition of the most respectable elements of the medical profession, men who regard transsexualism as an even more disgusting aberration than does Janice Raymond, if that is possible. Their reasons, however, are diametrically opposite to Ms Raymond's, since for them transsexualism seems to threaten the 'natural order' of things, while she believes it reinforces that order. The clinics developed under the intense and unremitting pressure of transsexuals who would go to any length to obtain an operation and for whom no treatment, other than operation, was satisfactory. The clinics thus came into existence *in spite of* the medical patriarchy, but, like all marginal institutions, they strove to justify themselves by their conformity. Hence, all the ghastly gender-amendment training which transsexuals have to suffer. In Britain, a few years ago, there were at least three centres doing operations under the National Health Service. Now there is only one. In the United States, they form a tiny part of the medical establishment. However horrific their gender conformity programmes may be to transsexuals, the clinics are quite insignificant when compared to the thousands of gynaecologists, with equally sexist opinions, who are mutilating women with breast inserts by the hundreds of thousands, unnecessary hysterectomies, caesarian sections (50 per cent of all births in some Californian hospitals) and other atrocities on women's personhood. Further, what about the psychiatric patriarchs who, after pumping patients full of drugs and excoriating them with electric shocks, wheel round the make-up trays, encouraging women to that conformity to male-defined conceptions of female 'nature' that were responsible for most of them arriving in the hospitals in the first place (Chesler, 1973; Ehrenreich and English, 1979). The real 'empire' is the whole patriarchal medical establishment. To call the transsexual medics an 'empire', is ludicrously to inflate their significance.

Transsexuals do have both history and valid experience

Janice Raymond denies a significant history for transsexualism before the 1950s since that is what her theory demands. In order to do this she has to ignore the evidence from a book to which she refers, *The Transsexual Phenomenon* (Benjamin, 1966). This demonstrates clearly enough that transsexuals of both sexes have existed in all historical periods and in cultures from all continents. The phenomenon does not date from the 1950s and it is not exclusive to biological males.

Transsexual men are fewer in numbers than transsexual women, but they exist, they are equally determined about themselves and they are not the token creation of the patriarchy's representatives in gender identity clinics. To deny these facts is to deny transsexual men any humanness, any sense of personal identity at all, and to turn them into the passive agents of sexual manipulators. A transsexual man I knew used to be in the women's movement and talked about his situation there. He received tremendous encouragement to go on living as a woman and was offered every opportunity to adopt non-sex-stereotyped behaviour within the limits of his biological sex. He has now come out as the man he always knew himself to be and is active in the men's movement. On Janice Raymond's terms he has no right to be there. The fact that there appear to be smaller numbers of transsexual men than transsexual women is not really relevant, since they are not simply tokens of the male medical establishment, as Ms Raymond assumes. But there are many possible reasons for the discrepancy in numbers, some of which have been pointed out by Karen Hagberg (Hagberg, 1979). The female state is genetically primary, so

179

possibly more anomalies occur in the differentiation to maleness. The operation is more costly and complex and less satisfactory. In addition, aspects of the socialisation of women involve learning acceptance. Transsexual men have been conditioned as women. This makes it that much more difficult to take the active steps necessary to realize their true identity (cf., Raymond, p. 26).

Nowhere in her book does Ms Raymond give any accounts of transsexual life experience. She interviewed fifteen transsexuals, two of them men, the rest women. The only place she gives any information about these individuals is in the section which shows that transsexual women conform to sexual stereotypes. None of them emerges as a real person with a biography. No sensitive or caring account of the life experience of transsexuals, either pre-operative or post-operative, is presented. Instead, the most damning quotations possible are put together. Not only this, but sometimes totally irrelevant information is presented as if it made a point. In order to 'demonstrate' that transsexuals in the women's movement commit total mind-body rape, Ms Raymond quotes at length from an obviously cynical and meant-to-be-funny story by a man in, of all places, *Penthouse* magazine. That is dishonest scholarship. Her individualised attacks on transsexual women in the women's movement are morally indefensible.[3]

It is little wonder that the picture of the transsexual that emerges is a static caricature. There is no suggestion that people's attitudes might change over time. Many pre- and immediately post-operative transsexuals show highly stereotyped attitudes about how they, as women or men, ought to be. For example, transsexual women were, because of our biology, usually brought up as male children, forced to live as men in order to survive and therefore developed ideas of what the actuality of women's existence is through the blinkers of male identity. This distorted view was reinforced in many cases by obligatory sexist counselling and demands that we conform in order to get an operation. No wonder a lot of disturbed people emerge at the end. Pre- and immediately post-operative transsexuals are sometimes very confused and not easy to get on with.

But women's oppression is not merely the consequence of a set of historical experiences. *It is an existential condition, an oppression that is re-created from day to day by the lives that women have to lead, the opportunities open to us, the attitudes presented to us.* This is as true for transsexual women as for any others. Excited from the achievement of something that has involved a lifetime's struggle, unaware of the male stereotypes that have formed their idea of femaleness, reinforced in those stereotypes by crudely patriarchal gender identity clinics, it is hardly to be expected that transsexual women who have just come out will present a challenge to male sexist ideology about women's existence. Ms Raymond cites extensively from Thomas Kando's study (Kando, 1973). None of the transsexual women interviewed there were operated more than two years previously. Jan Morris's embarrassing book, *Conundrum* (Morris, 1974), was published within two years of her operation (she was operated on at the same time as me, in the same clinic). At least *Conundrum* demonstrates that lack of success in the state of maleness has nothing to do with transsexualism. Jan was almost classically successful in her presentation as male before she came out.

The important thing for transsexuals is ongoing experience. Every woman's history of oppression is re-created in her day-to-day life. In having the same experience, the transsexual woman gives real meaning to her suppressed past. I'd predict that after several years of public female existence, transsexual women would show, on average, just as much uneasiness about social expectations of women's identity as other women round them – no more, no less. But it is not only immediate post-operative transsexuals who seem satisfied with a tinsel notion of women's existence – many born women publicly and vociferously urge these roles upon us, through the media, books and the innumerable pages of women's magazines. We are *all* our own keepers. To single out the small number of transsexual women as being particularly significant in the struggle against cripplingly deforming sex-role stereotypes deflects energy from real causes – the patriarchal system and its agents who peddle conformity through the media.

Sex differences are not absolute

Behind Ms Raymond's arguments that sexual difference – biology apart – is exclusively a product of the male-defined values of a patriarchy, lies an absolutist view of sex difference. This expresses itself most clearly in the horror and revulsion at the thought of the lesbian-feminist transsexual. She asserts that transsexuals in the women's movement have 'renounced femininity, but not masculinity and masculinist behaviour' (p. 101). Since such transsexual women behave characteristically like other lesbian feminists, this is equivalent to saying that lesbian-feminist behaviour is masculine. We all carry a baggage of maleness, expressed in attitudes, modes of thought and behaviour, attitudes which Ms Raymond shows in her work that she shares in full measure. But lesbian-feminist behaviour is not masculine. It searches for a cultural identity which transcends the stereotypes of gender with which we are all conditioned in this society. The transsexual feminist's search is exactly the same and not a demonstration of masculinity, as other feminists can verify. Ms Raymond simply denies it and refuses to admit any evidence to the contrary. In our behaviour and attitudes we are *all*, not just transsexuals, conditioned by existence in a patriarchy. In trying to develop the condition of female humanness, *all* of us have to renounce much powerful cultural learning we have been subjected to, and have internalised. Its content varies widely from woman to woman. For any of us to be successful, other human beings have to be involved in the same personal struggle; transsexual women's experiences have a validity as well. The separation from men adopted by some women is the result of the degree of sexual oppression, intentional and unintentional, shown by men in our societies. But transsexual women's transformation, despite different backgrounds, is not incompatible with that of other women, since they, as separatists, are able to accept and work with transsexual feminists. For example, I was accepted and integrated into an ongoing consciousness-raising group which met weekly for nearly a year. According to Ms Raymond's paranoid definition of a feminist transsexual as personalised phallus, rapist, and agent of patriarchal oppression, this would hardly have been expected to be the case. In order to cope with the fact that transsexual women can be, and are, integrated into women's spaces, Ms Raymond denies the experiences of the other women involved as well, thus setting herself up as a judge of their feminist credentials. This self-elevation to arbitrate feminist consciousness is discussed further below.

Philosophical sophistry

Finally, the philosophical language of the book cloaks bad argument, distortion and suppression of fact in academic respectability. The philosophical sections are mystification, playing with words in a way that obscures Ms Raymond's ethical absolutism. She sets as her standard of measurement, the term 'integrity'. At the other extreme, 'androgyny' represents an adding up of qualities which derive from an immorality – the patriarchal definition of sexual identity. It is necessary to transcend such a summation, to pass from 'integration', the aim of the transsexers, to the higher 'integrity' of the human spirit, where mutilation is not involved. In a general sense, one can accept the concept of integrity as a legitimate aim of human endeavour, though I'm uneasy about it because it is seen only in terms of individual goals. People may feel it necessary to deny the 'integrity' of their own existence for some wider goal of benefit to humanity. What is the content of 'integrity'? How do we determine whether an act contributes to our 'integrity'? Has anyone else the right to determine it for us: if so, to what degree, and in what respects? All these questions are at the heart of ethics. Most of us in our lives are faced with contradictory alternatives for action. The choice of one alternative, which may contribute to our perceived 'integrity', may reduce it in another respect. It is often argued that the withdrawal of women from men practised by separatist feminists is a denial of an existent human reality. One could say it denies 'integrity' in the interests of 'integration' of certain aspects of human experience. But we may reply that the terms of interaction demanded of us by men are so harsh that only through with-drawal from such an experience can we begin to realise an 'integrity' that provides a model for all human behaviour. Ms Raymond's conception of integrity involves biological naturalism. Thus, the transsexual woman violates the integrity of her male biology: and the transsexual man vice versa by submitting to hormones and operations. But the alteration of the body is not an issue of absolutes. Do we deny the limbless artificial limbs? Is all transplant surgery unethical? Should a woman whose uterus has developed an incurable infection be denied the possibility of an opera-tion for hysterectomy? If there is really no other course, her bodily 'integrity' is violated for the continuation and development of her total integrity potential as a woman. As a result of a hysterectomy, incidentally, she also becomes dependent on external hormonal medication in order to be able to realize her 'integrity'. Or perhaps the person denied the use of artificial supports is really realising their true 'integrity' as a human person by their death or disablement?

Who is the judge of such questions? Who dares to set themselves up as such an absolute arbiter of human experience? Janice Raymond does, with regard to transsexuals at least. We violate our chromosomal identity by having operations. But is this identity to be the criterion on which to judge our actions? It is perfectly legitimate to argue the contrary, since the evidence of its violation is positive. Ninety per cent of post-operative transsexuals experience their operations as having positive results, a very high figure for medical intervention. Ms Raymond says that this positivity is superficial. Who is she to say so? Even to begin to talk about it would involve investigations of before – and after – living patterns, with follow-ups. Even though transsexuals do not become biologically identical with other women or men as a result of operations, enough can be done to allow the development of 'integrity', so deeply denied before, when so much of our energy was taken up trying to comprehend a fundamental fault in our identity construction. Are we dependent on medication for our survival? Yes, but no more so than many others. My father had, for many years, to take pills to control his blood pressure. Without them he would have died. Taking such pills did not make him inadequate, a slavish dependant of the medical establishment, but enabled him to develop his 'integrity' in his later years, i.e., to stay alive. I also need to take some pills, twenty-two days out of twenty-eight, but otherwise I am not depen-dent on patriarchal medicine. An endocrinologist assures me I run no greater risk of cancer than other periodless women on hormonal treat-ment, but even if I were at risk, the risk would be insignificant compared to the value for me of what I have done.

Ms Raymond also says that 'integrity' is denied by the creation of crea-tures who are satisfied to exist within the limits of the current sexual stereotypes. These stereotypes damage all of us all the time, but most women do not *consciously* challenge them to any fundamental extent. Why should transsexual women be singled out and *forced* to experience ongoing hell in order supposedly to make them revolutionaries in the sexual struggle. Not only would it not have such an effect but it would deny us any element of autonomy, thus violating another aspect of our 'integrity'. Is a person who just does what she is told really changing anything? It sounds to me like an ideological press gang for 'revolution'. Sexual stereotypes do not cause transsexualism, they confuse transsexuals as well as the rest of us. We have to find our own way out, through our own judgement of arguments and our own experiences of living, not by the forcible imposition of another person's view of who we 'really' are.

Thus, there is no prima facie case for arguing that the transsexual situation is one that denies 'integrity' for the transsexual, either on humanistic or medical grounds. Transsexuals, like all of us, are caught in a net of oppressive gender expectations, which we have to sort out as best we can in situations where the social agencies to which we may refer only make our problem worse. But it is not transsexualism which is the problem, rather it is the way we are pressured to live in the world. Another attack on our potential for 'integrity' comes from individuals such as Ms Raymond, projecting their own hatred and fear in spurious philosophical arguments. I cannot find any section of Ms Raymond's book which does not bristle with half-truth, distortion, suppressed information, all passed over with a sugar coat of scientific veneer. Above all, and uniquely for the feminist movement, Ms Raymond has written a book concerning a group of people, human beings, without the slightest insight into any of our life histories, the problems of our existence as we see it, our own perceptions of the world. Transsexuals are given no validity as humans with wills of our own; no picture of the transsexual experience as a human condition emerges from her pages. We are presented merely as the manipulated tools of the patriarchal establishment, monstrosities or tokens, hollow shells to be arranged in this or that parody. One might expect that a person writing about a group of human beings would present them to us as human beings, but perhaps that is just an example of the naive liberalism that Ms Raymond accuses women who have come to accept transsexuals of having. One way of dealing with oppression is to pass it on to even more vulnerable groups. Ms Raymond has chosen that method, and her book is therefore of no value to women or to transsexuals, of either sex.

DIVIDED SISTERHOOD: *THE TRANSSEXUAL EMPIRE* AND FEMINISM

The Transsexual Empire is a dangerous book. It is dangerous to transsexuals because it does not treat us as human beings at all, merely as the tools of a theory. Its arguments may make things more difficult for trans-sexual women and men as they strive to come out. It seeks to create hostility towards us among women who have no actual experience of trans-sexual people, who find the subject disturbing and want some simple, straightforward answer that allays their unease. I think transsexualism is frightening to many because, in an unstable, insecure world, basic sexual identity, male or female, is one of the few fairly firm constructs we have. However much we wish to modify our behaviour, our sense of our sex is very deep, and transsexuals seem to bring it into question. Yet we do not seek to change sex, but to modify a biological anomaly so that genuine human existence as the women or men we are already is possible.

I think that *The Transsexual Empire* has relevance to a wider group than transsexuals. I see its negativity as threefold. Firstly, I mistrust its attitude to feminist culture. Secondly, its emphases deflect attention from the more important problems and tend to lead to scapegoating. Thirdly, its ideological dogmatism and anti-experiential viewpoint lead right back into the methods of patriarchy. Such methods have emerged in the feminist movement in other areas too. In conclusion I will address these three points.

Is feminist culture produced by vanguard groups?

Ms Raymond believes that every transsexual man is a potential woman-identified woman. Although this is not true, as I read, I began to ask myself, in what way does Ms Raymond look at feminism? The book does not give a clear answer. The main argument is that male and female cultures are the creation of a male-defined sex-role system. Overthrowing this system would enable human beings of integrity to behave in all the morally legitimate ways available to humans to behave, irrespective of sex. Sexual differences would be merely biological – the ability of women to give birth, chromosomal difference, physical differences in anatomy. However, at another point, Ms Raymond talks of the 'multi-dimensional female creative power, bearing culture, harmony and true inventiveness' that transsexual women are supposed to covet (p. 107). Where do these characteristics come from? They cannot be biological in origin, because she rules out this kind of explanation in attacking John Money's theory that hormones feminise or masculinise foetal brains (pp. 48–9). There are two other possible alternatives. Perhaps there is some 'woman-spirit', or 'woman-energy', underlying biology, which has the above characteristics. But, if so, then transsexual women may have it, though they have a male biology, and all Ms Raymond's arguments fall. Alternatively, these characteristics are social in origin. But if sexual differences are defined by the *negative*, patriarchally imposed sex stereo-typing system, where do these *positive* characteristics come from? No clear answer is given, but the text of the chapter on transsexuals in the women's movement places a lot of emphasis on the lesbian feminist. She is the most significant challenger, not only of male dominance in society, but also of female compliance in it. Ms Raymond follows the arguments in the famous article by the Radicalesbians, the 'Woman-Identified Woman' (Radicalesbians, 1971).

It is possible to look at things in a different way. Suppose we don't focus on sex stereotyping, but on the *position* of women in the structure of patriarchy. From this perspective, women's position in patriarchal structure gives rise to a female culture which is potentially and partly in continual conflict with male culture. Women's position means that we ensure the continuance of the human race and develop personal qualities in keeping with this task, while men threaten it in conflicts over authority, production and allocation of human resources (Burris, 1971; Starrett, 1976). Men not only try to contain this conflict between female life energy and male death energy by imposing notions of the feminine, they also control intellectual systems and thought processes and educate us to internalise them. The separatist lesbian feminist who does not challenge herself about such internal processes, may retain important elements of male identification, in spite of her separatism. Once these elements are brought into the women's movement they can undermine it from within.

The female culture of resistance emphasises caring, respect for others' identity, the ability to share and grow from the experience of a common and allied oppression, the essential acceptance of another as equal, the integration of intellect and feeling and an experiential attitude to knowledge, which men sometimes contemptuously refer to as 'being closer to nature'. Men, on the other hand, exist in a world of *exclusion*, each group is seen as exclusive of others, and each individual feels himself in a potential competition with his fellows in every aspect of his behaviour. It has long been so. To adopt this kind of exclusiveness *within* the women's movement, however physically separate a woman keeps herself from men, however much she professes to hate them, actually encourages the same kinds of destructive divisions that men use. If, on the other hand, we have a certainty of the *positiveness* of female culture, in spite of its distortion and deformation by patriarchal attempts to control it, the *inclusion* of marginals is not a threat. Karen Hagberg makes a similar point: 'It does not seem prudent for feminists to perpetuate a strict male/female dichotomy in a patriarchal atmosphere which both fears and loathes sexual ambiguity of any kind'. Janice Raymond's book is an example of hatred and exclusion. An academic intellectual, she has been infested by another aspect of the patriarchal culture she professes to attack.[4]

Scapegoating

The tactic of *deflection*, attempting to deflect attention from the source of a problem to a relatively innocent and defenceless party onto whom resentment can be channelled is a very basic tactic of patriarchal divisiveness. Find a scapegoat, and patriarchal power is safe. Witches were not responsible for the social evils of the medieval form of patriarchy; they attempted to alleviate them. But because wise women seemed a little different it was possible to single them out and whip up a campaign against them, leaving the main cause untouched. Nazism used the same method, projecting blame on to Jews and homosexuals. McCarthyism channelled social discontent against those who were attempting to find the causes of social unease by labelling them 'communist', and manipulating public opinion against them. Women have experienced this method all too often to our detriment. Janice Raymond's book has the same effect in two respects:

- She gives a much more central role to the gender identity clinics than they deserve. As I have shown, they are really the 'poor relations' of patriarchal medicine, to whose sexist, exploitative structure and organization they kow tow. It is like trying to destroy a monster by focusing on his little toe.
- She encourages the deflection of energy and anger which needs to go outwards, against the male system, inwards, against a small group of vulnerable women, by labelling them rapists, personifications of male organs, and such nonsense. This is not merely incitement to hate, but totally destructive. Such energies, when directed inwards, will soon find new groups to attack as witch-hunts proliferate. Ms Raymond encourages this too: 'lesbian-feminists who accept trans-sexually constructed lesbian-feminists as other selves are mutilating their own reality' (p. 119). Recently in internal women's movement newsletters women with male children have become another target. These methods of approaching problems are those of our enemies. We take them up ourselves at our peril.

Ideology versus experience

A major weapon which men have used against women is the power to define our situation by their ideology. Central to the women's movement is the challenge to the ideological definition of reality. By accepting male definitions presented in abstract terms, our own feelings, experiences and personal understanding of reality can be denied. I remember when I was associated with a left group, the women's almost constant dissatisfaction with what was going on was never allowed any validity, since it did not seem to fit in with Marxist-Leninist method or theory. But it also happens every time a man exclaims, for instance, that 'women are so emotional'. The whole consciousness-raising practice, fundamental to the women's movement, has been our oppositional culture's basic alternative to such methods. It is based upon respecting another woman's understanding of her situation, giving validity to her experience, not judging her inadequate if she did not see her situation in the same way as you, not defining the answers to problems beforehand. It recognises that we all have something to learn from each other, we all have valid experiences of the struggle that comes from belonging to an oppositional culture so we can share and develop collectively. I believe that it has been this refusal to 'define and demean' that has enabled woman strength to be so powerfully developed in the women's movement. Anything which threatens this openness in the name of some ideological purity is an imported threat which can undermine us, turn us against ourselves. Janice Raymond's book is the most explicit example of such an ideological, dogmatic approach that I remember reading. She thinks she has the answer to transsexualism. Transsexual experience is invalid by definition. Any woman who dares to assert her own experience to the contrary is guilty of self-mutilation, of 'liberalism', of 'naïvety', of 'gratitude', of 'fear of being labelled as a 'man-hater', of 'attraction to masculine presence' (pp. 113, 119).

The women of the Olivia records collective, lesbians and feminists who had struggled to develop the world's first all-woman feminist recording company, wrote, in relation to the transsexual woman who was a member of their collective; 'day to day interaction with Sandy Stone has convinced us that she is a woman we can relate to with comfort and trust'. According to Ms Raymond, if they had been more honest, they'd have said they 'needed a man around' (p. 103). The same, presumably, applies to the women who accept and relate to the few other transsexuals in the women's movement, including myself. She believes they are deluded. This is what Elizabeth Rose is talking about when she writes, in 'Chrysalis', of another article by Janice Raymond,

> I am upset that a magazine of 'women's culture' . . . is basically encouraging the elitist/separatist attitude that self-definition [is] . . . subject to the scrutiny and judgements of those who, in the name of political purity, claim the power to define who is allowed entry into the feminist community . . . and now, who is, or is not female.
>
> (Rose, 1978: 6)

What is an alternative method which recognises women's experience and does not invalidate it? Janice Raymond could have gone and talked to the women of Olivia and to Sandy. She could have gone and talked to Christy Barsky (another feminist transsexual she identifies) and her friends. She could have shared experience with them and reported what they said, communicating the different experiences, to give women who have no access to transsexuals some means of making provisional judgement. Instead, she argues that all women who have such experience are inadequately feminist. We have heard that kind of ideological divisiveness before, from men, and at the date of writing are hearing it again in the British women's movement from small numbers of women who arrogate to themselves the right to be the custodians of feminist purity. Taking Janice Raymond and her methods as their mentor, they extend their attitudes to heterosexual women and lesbians with male children. Patriarchal invasion is insidious. The denial of female experience in the name of ideological purity is neither a product of nor a contribution to feminist culture. As transsexual women we must claim the integrity of our own life experience; and other women who know us are also asserting that their right to their own experience is fundamental. When we have to assert this right against other feminists, for whatever reason, confusion reigns and patriarchy gains. And following the dogmatists come the enforcers of the 'law'.

My living space is threatened by this book. Although I have had to challenge its attacks on transsexual women, its dogmatic approach and its denial that female experience is our basic starting point are a danger signal of trends emerging in the whole women's movement.

NOTES

1 In this chapter, I have used the correct gender references to transsexual people. Transsexual women are women born with a male biology and mistakenly socialised as males, who have to undergo physical conversion operations (and years of re-learning) to realise their sexual identity. Transsexual men are men born with a female biology and mistakenly socialised as females. In quotations from Ms Raymond's book, I have either used her terms, which are oppressive and insulting to transsexuals, in inverted commas, or I have inserted correct terms in brackets.

2 Many persecutors feel that they act in their victims' own interests. Cf., Dr Acker, in Piercy, 1979.

3 She also uses this method in her discussion of the behaviour of eunuchs in history (pp. 105–6) and of Nazi medical experiments (pp. 148–53).

4 This is not to say that the only ways that women can be oppressive are by internalising male ways of thinking. I don't think classism and racism, etc. can be reduced to this, though the ultimate 'first cause' of such oppressions may be a patriarchal system.

13

AUTOBIOGRAPHICAL FRAGMENTS FROM A TRANSSEXUAL ACTIVIST

Terri Webb

As a Marxist and activist in the trades union and labour movement I have campaigned for over ten years for transsexual rights, ever since I took those first life-altering steps of receiving hormones as a prelude to electrolysis and surgery. Even as I have done so I have had a fundamental feeling of personal inauthenticity, which I attribute to a basic awareness of alienation in an existentialist sense.[1]

In the early 1980s, I, with so many other transsexuals, advocated legal reform to secure equal rights. I sought, for instance, the 'right' for transsexuals to change their birth certificates in order to achieve legal recognition in their reassigned sex. Over the years, as a result of a combination of 'common sense' and the force of the arguments put to me by feminist friends and feminist theorists, I have been forced to drop my demands one by one. Now, I only have one demand – the right to have our personal agony over socially defined gender roles taken seriously. It may be that this demand will go the way of the others.

My doubts even about this last demand arise over my inner knowledge that I am other than I pretend to be. I believe this is not a matter peculiar to me. I am convinced that it applies to each and every male-to-female transsexual that I have ever met, read about or seen on television. We pretend to be other than we are. Many transsexuals claim to be women when we are in fact men. Whereas a couple of years ago I could only speak for myself when stating this view, now I feel able to speak for all male-to-female transsexuals when I say that without any doubt we are men, albeit men with a desperate need to be women. Whatever our need, however, it does not alter the fact of what and who we are.

I do not doubt the very desperate need. I remember, some years ago, when I was contemplating taking steps to alter my body so that I could 'become a woman', thinking to myself that I would sell my soul to the Devil, if I could go to sleep and wake up as a woman. I would be willing to face an eternity in hell rather than experience my male body.

I feel now, however, that the desperate need is rooted in a basic envy of women's reproductive abilities. This was added to, in my case, by a childhood experience of sadistic homosexual abuse. I believe this led me to a horror of all that is male. My mistake was to have projected this hatred onto my own body instead of having developed a social theory which challenges the sexism and gender-role stereotyping of the world around us.

In a sense, all transsexuals have taken a wrong turn at some point in their lives. We have taken a decision to internalise and project onto our own bodies the horror we feel about our maleness, by using hormones, having electrolysis and seeking the surgeon's knife. What we should have done is examined the nature of the gender-role stereotyping that led us to this point.

From this new standpoint our position on rights' issues appears very differently.

BIRTH CERTIFICATES

Birth certificates are a key to many transsexuals' demands (see Chapter 2). In the past I have advocated the 'right' to change my birth certificate to alter my name and sex. However, a birth certificate saying a person is female does not turn a man into a woman. In my view, there is no good reason why birth certificates should state anyone's gender. It is only in a society in which gender-roles are central to our existence that it is necessary to state a baby's sex when it is born. Better to advocate equal rights in this way rather than with a strategy prefaced upon the fact that we are pretending we were female babies when we were not.

MARRIAGE

We are living in a world in which it is increasingly becoming a preferred option not to legitimise a relationship by legal marriage. It is significant that it is transsexuals who are so frequently in the forefront of reaction on this issue of marriage (see Chapter 2). I have no sympathy with this 'orthodox' transsexual thinking at all. I know one doesn't have to accept a sexist definition of society in order to contemplate marriage, but in this case why get married? As far as I know all the advantages of marriage could be covered by a civil contract that any competent solicitor could draw up. It should not be impossible to make arrangements for any children that might be involved.

If there is a case for demanding equality in marriage then legislation along the Danish lines, which allows homosexual and lesbian marriage, would appear to meet transsexual demands. Interestingly, this proves not to be so when the option is pointed out to transsexuals. This strengthens my opinion that what so many transsexuals are after is the legitimisation of a fantasy rather than civil rights.

My own belief is that anything that transsexuals could legitimately demand is already covered by the legitimate demands of the lesbian and gay community – the advanced sections of which reject a lesbian and gay model of heterosexual marriage as perpetuating bourgeois property relations.

There is not one single demand made by transsexuals and our supporters which would not be better dealt with by fighting for equal rights generally and by fighting against sexism. We have the right to despair, but not the right to assume that our despair makes us unique or that we suffer uniquely.

Looking back over the last ten years of my activism I feel that I am looking at an unsuccessful attempt to get others to legitimise my fantasy. I have heard a psychiatrist give the opinion that if a man comes to him and claims to be Napoleon he does not attempt to cure him by amputation of one of his arms. The question we should now be asking ourselves is whether we have the right to pretend to be women, not what 'rights' the rest of the world should give us in order to go along with our fantasy.

My search is for a sociological or political theory which resolves the contradiction between pursuing my rights as a male transsexual and my commitment to women's rights. If such a theory exists I have never heard of it. My position is rooted in a basic acceptance of feminist arguments concerning the misogynist nature of society and in the belief that male transsexuals perpetuate misogyny when they indulge in a manipulative game of getting others to collude in their fantasy that they are women.

We will need a great deal of help to construct our theory and practice – both from amongst ourselves and from outside. Help from outside really means assistance from women who identify with the feminist movement. When we ask for this help we must understand women's reluctance to have their energy drained by men whingeing about men's sexual hangups. Women have been oppressed, excluded and marginalised by men for thousands of years and it is imperative that we understand the nature of this oppression when we ask for their aid.

On the other hand, women might have much to learn from us. When feminist women wonder why their relationships with men often go wrong, they might find some of the answers in talking to us. Male transsexuals are particularly well placed to discern unnoticed links between male violence, the oppression of women and male envy of women's bodies.

Whilst I was writing this chapter, for instance, I read a newspaper article in the English *Guardian* about Michael Buchanan, a diagnosed 'personality disorder', who on his release from psychiatric care killed someone he hardly knew. Buchanan was black, brought up in care and lived in Stonebridge Park Estate, one of the most notorious of such inner-city estates of a type I have managed as a Housing Officer and tried to deal with as a Ward Councillor. Reading on, I saw, near the end of the article that one of the 'crimes' this man had committed was to pound a shop window with his fists until it broke. He then seized a woman's dress on display, ripped off his own clothes, put on the woman's dress and ran round the shopping precinct.

I am not suggesting that Michael Buchanan's illness was 'caused' by transvestism or transsexuality. It may have been. I am not in a position to know. What I am saying is that his behaviour was inextricably linked to misogyny and oppression. In my view, all transvestism and transsexuality is linked to oppression of one sort or another – as both a symptom and a cause. Hannibal Lecter in *Silence of the Lambs* was being too kind to transsexuals when he said that 'Buffalo Bill' (the other serial killer in the film) was not really a transsexual because transsexuals tend to be passive. In my view, all male transsexuals do violence to women in their need to adopt a woman's skin.

I never cease to wonder at the number of men who express some sort of dissatisfaction with their identities and roles as men. I believe this is always connected with envy of women, particularly an envy of their ability to procreate. I think it is imperative that such feelings are brought out into the open and recognised for what they are, so that we can deal with them in a constructive rather than a destructive way. For this reason we must create an environment in which we can admit to our feelings, even if this leads us to reject sex reassignment procedures.

I think it possible that our experience as transsexuals may represent something which is common to all men. We male transsexuals want to possess the body of a woman, that is, we want to own such a body to the extent of being it ourselves. It seems to me that this is not dissimilar to the desire of 'healthy' heterosexual men to own women in a possessive and misogynist sense.

If I am right in this it follows that we male transsexuals who are gay (who relate sexually to men) have taken all that we envy and fear in women and reduced it to what we can control. We then present it to a homosexual partner and in so doing try to escape the guilt we feel at what we have done to our bodies and to women. The 'solution' does not quite work, however, and our conscience returns to haunt us. I understand Janice Raymond (1980) to be saying (see Chapters 12 and 15) that transsexuals are the plastic expression of men's desire – both our own and that of the male dominated 'transsexual empire'. In this she is right. She is wrong, however, when she attributes our desires to homophobia.

TRANSSEXUALS ANONYMOUS

I now advocate a 'transsexuals anonymous' group in order to examine the particular nature of our particular method of dealing with the horror of gender-role stereotyping. I cannot see that we will ever strike a chord with others in society if we insist that it is the world that has misunderstood us, rather than us having chosen a particular method of coming to terms with our feelings. A sexist division of society necessitates that there will be many casualties. We are amongst those casualties and we must begin our examination of our position by being honest.

Whatever the conclusions of those of us who have gone through the various transsexual 'rights of passage', one thing is certain; others coming after us will suffer the same delusions that we have. Thousands will believe that they can become women. We ourselves will continue to manipulate situations where we are accepted as women. I know from my own experience how pleased I am, and what a thrill it is, every time I am accepted as a 'lady trucker' or 'lady breaker' in my new life as a truck driver driving throughout Europe. We must understand that we perform the most amazing mental acrobatics in order to pander to our delusions. I am no exception.

I believe a future 'transsexuals anonymous' has three basic questions to discuss.

1   Should we admit that our sex reassignment was a mistake and do what we can to identify ourselves as the men we are?
2   Should we campaign for hormonal intervention and sex reassignment surgery to be terminated?
3   How can transsexual and transvestite inclination be channelled into challenging gender-role stereotyping rather than reinforcing it?

This last question is crucial.

I admit that I would be loath to give up the female status that I do have, even though I do – as we all do – suffer from the fear that some-one will say, 'You're a man, aren't you?' For me, the fear is not a great one, in spite of the fact that I have attracted a certain amount of press publicity in the past. Without claiming to be the most convincing transsexual there is, I am able to say that those who do not know my history do assume I am a woman, born as such. I still believe there is a problem with this, however. To what extent am I, and others like me, causing harm by indulging in my fantasy?

If the answer we come to is that we are reinforcing socially defined gender-roles and thus perpetuating a basically sexist society, then the next question becomes: do we have the ability to transcend our fantasy, by recognising it for what it is? I have to say I doubt it, at least not without considerably more honesty than most transsexuals have displayed so far, and not without considerably more support of the right sort from both each other and from non-transsexuals.

The nature of my experience was such that I doubt if I would ever have come to a conscious decision that I was indulging in a fantasy, not a reasonable course of action, if I had not gone ahead and done it. In order to discover myself I had to have my medical treatment which is now irreversible. This does not mean, however, that we should not tell the truth about our predicament. Nor does it mean that we should not do all we can to explore with others who are contemplating sex reassignment whether there are not alternatives that they might pursue.

I conclude by stating that I do not believe we have even begun to write a definitive book on transsexuality. My contribution to the area is essentially an attempt to provoke debate and discussion. If my chapter is successful in this regard then it will need constant revision. To this end I ask one final question: could it be that we male-to-female post-operative transsexuals are really heterosexual men who did not want to relate to women sexually but wanted to relate to men sexually in a heterosexual way and the only way we could do this was by altering our bodies? I do not know the answer to this question any more than I claim to be certain of any of the questions, let alone the answers.

NOTE

1   As Laing put it:

> Humanity is estranged from its authentic possibilities. This basic vision prevents us from taking an unequivocal view of the sanity of common sense, or of the madness of the so-called madman ... Our alienation goes to the roots. The realisation of this is the essential springboard for any serious reflection on any aspect of present inter-human life.
>
> (Laing, 1967: 11–12)

14

GENDER FUCKING OR FUCKING GENDER ?

Current cultural contributions to theories of gender blending*

Stephen Whittle

> Queer means to fuck with gender. There are straight queers, bi
> queers, tranny queers, lez queers, fag queers, SM queers, fisting queers
> in every single street in this apathetic country of ours.
>
> (street leaflet quoted in McIntosh, 1993: 31)

AN INTRODUCTORY NOTE

Observing of culture and assessing its 'contributions' provides me with all
sorts of uneasy feelings. Stuart Hall speaks of: 'the notion . . . that movements provoke theoretical moments. And historical conjectures insist on
theories: they are real moments in the evolution of theory' (Hall, 1992:
283). To be involved in cultural studies is undoubtedly a contradictory
project. In the process, which is not only one of observation but of textualising a version of the observations, one becomes a 'cultural contribution'.
Cultural studies was defined and originated as a political project; 'it holds
theoretical and political questions in an ever irresolvable but permanent
tension' (Hall, 1992: 284). To participate, to textualise, is to become a
historical conjecture. It is an active engagement in a pedagogy with the
textual producer about whom one is textualising.

I become a part of the object of my study as I produce. In studying I
politicise and theorise the culture of gender and irreversibly change it.
The truth of any 'becoming', however, is a falsity, though it maybe true
at the level of the text. In the politics of gender, sex and the body, the
existence of the body is for us all a statement of gender from the moment
of birth. No matter how hard you try to talk about somebody else, you

---

* My thanks must go to Cath Little for all her help, thoughts and wisdom which greatly
influenced the form and content of this piece of work. I must also thank my partner, Sarah
Rutherford, who has contributed (as well as tolerated) so much over the years to the formu-
lation of my ideas.

are always going to be talking about yourself. This work is, in the words of Stuart Hall, a 'moment of self-clarification'. As well as a chronicle of cultural change it is an intervention in it, and we would do well to remember that this has both overt and implicit political aims.

All of the contributors to this book will have had overt and implicit political aims, even if unacknowledged. I am acknowledging them. Each and everyone of us goes through a process of self-identification which is located in a specific history, a specific structure, a specific culture and a specific interaction with these. I will not deny my position as a transgendered activist. I also consider myself a neo-Marxist, a transsexual man, an English liberal, a legal theorist, a father without legal recognition, and so on. The list is very long, but most importantly I am gendered, not just by myself but by everybody who knows me, by all those who write of me and 'my sort', by all those who work with transgendered people and, nearly always, by transgendered people themselves.

I, like you, cannot escape the hegemony of gendering but I also have a place in the power struggle that surrounds it, and I hope to use it responsibly, as I contribute, from my privileged position, to the culture of gender blending.

THEORISING THE SEXUAL

In order to appreciate current cultural contributions to theories of gender blending, it is essential to understand the history of theory surrounding sex, sexuality and gender. The most recent manifestation of that history is queer theory, but that has its basis in the history of the pathologies and dualism that surround these areas.

Queer theory does not stand in isolation; its origins lie in the medico-legal discussions of sexual pathologies, which have been the focus of Part III of this book. It would be naive to interpret queer theory without reference to them.

As made explicit by King (see Chapter 7), transvestism and transsexuality became recognised phenomena, separate from homosexuality, through the work of the early sexologists. Moreover, as King outlines, by the 1930s, an active role was being played by psychologists, psychiatrists, endocrinologists and surgeons in the 'treatment' of transgenderists. This continues to the present day. This history of homosexual subcategorisation highlights an inconsistency in the approach of psychiatric professionals. This was exemplified by the *Diagnostic Statistical Manual* (DSM) *III* (1974), which removed homosexuality from the list of psychosexual disorders whilst at the same time it added transsexuality. For a long time, and certainly in their origins as social categories, the two were inextricably linked.

It could be argued that queer theory's first major contribution to academic theory arose from the work done in the late 1960s by homosexuals, and by homosexual psychiatrists and psychologists in particular, to gain that removal from the *DSM* ratings of homosexuality as a psychiatric disorder. However, at the time this work would not have been recognised as the start of a major theoretical movement – rather as part of the process of political activism.

This political process and corresponding theoretical development is today being mirrored in the contributions that transgendered individuals are making to current queer theory. In particular, they have contributed to the work that removed from *DSM IV* (1994) the category of transsexualism. However, this category has been replaced by what is, arguably, an indistinguishable category of 'gender dysphoria' (see Chapter 7). There is little or no change to the symptomatic requirements, and hence gender dysphoria is made a modern name for transsexuality.

To realise the power of the contributions that transgendered behaviour, lifestyle, politics and culture are making to theory, it is necessary to recognise the framework within which these are being employed and the changes to that framework which they are bringing about. Queer theory has, for transgendered people, seemed one of the obvious starting points, along with the specific disciplines of law and psychology. Those disciplines, unlike sociology, history and cultural studies, are only just beginning to feel the impact of queer theory as a school of thought, and that has probably been indirectly through the work of postmodern theorists. However, queer theory is an increasingly powerful force in many other disciplines, not just those mentioned.

THEORY'S QUEER HER/HIS/STORY

Queer theory has a very recent history but it is based upon the late twentieth century struggles for homosexual equality. The law, through case law and legislation, changed and removed some of the restrictions on individual sexual practice in the 1960s. Some impact was also made through the involvement of lesbians or 'women-identified women' in the development of women's study courses in universities in the 1970s. Therefore, lesbians and gay men were able to find some respectability and acceptance for their private lives within academic lifestyles.

Throughout the late 1970s and the 1980s these academics explored methods of bringing their own life experiences into the research objectives that they practised. This process was not without problems. Firstly, it took a tremendous effort and will to ensure that lesbians and gay men were not just objects of study but that they could also be objective 'studiers'.

Secondly, though there had been legal change and some academic acceptance, the activist campaigns that lesbians and gay men had been involved with had not disappeared. Apparent acceptance was tainted by a number of factors: the still unequal footing in law for gay male sexual practice, the lack of employment security and the liberal assumption that with the footholds that had been gained lesbians and gay men would no longer face fear and prejudices. This was not the reality: young lesbians and gay men still faced justified fears of ostracism if they came out, queer bashing had not been eliminated from the streets and individual prejudices, often embodied in the forces of the state, were still made manifest. Equality of freedom from fear had certainly not been gained by the lesbian and gay community. Jeffrey Weeks summed up the mid 1970s sense of homosexual self as:

> Guilt, evasions, a sense of inadequacy and isolation persisted amongst many homosexuals: inevitably for they had all grown up into families which, by their very nature, seemed to invalidate their experience ... There was a highly uneven integration of homosexuals into society. On the one hand, there were the achievements: the new relative openness, the expanded and more lavish subculture: on the other, there was deeply ingrained prejudice, fear of sexual freedom, religious and social norms antipathetic to homosexuality.
>
> (Weeks, 1990: 230)

The academic community was no refuge from these forces. It perhaps provided apparent inside safety, which was then lost outside, but even inside was not without its dangers, as individuals fought hard to get their work on their own community accepted as valid and objective. Many, who came out many years later, such as Laud Humphreys, the sociologist and author of the widely acclaimed *Tearoom Trade* (Humphreys, 1970), kept their own homosexuality secret in order to achieve academic acceptance.

Activism was still an essential part of the homosexual community's *raison d'être*. Members of the academy recognised that they were potentially powerful voices of their own community, and many of them adopted an activist stance within their own disciplinary fields, as witnessed by those in the field of psychiatry who fought to remove homosexuality as a psychiatric disorder. A typical example of this is the work of Jeffrey Weeks who, in books such as *Coming Out* (1977) and *Sex, Politics and Society* (1981), brought homosexual activism into the discipline of history.

The gay liberation movement had advanced the notion that, as an oppressed minority, homosexuals would be gradually absorbed into mainstream society without too much disruption. By the late 1970s and early 1980s it had become obvious that this was not to prove the case. The public face of lesbian and gay lives became much more prominent, but full legal acceptance has proved notoriously difficult to achieve. The opposition movements to this acceptance, such as the religious right in the United States and conservative family values proponents in the United

Kingdom, were to gain strong ammunition in the battle with the recognition of the AIDS crisis in the 1980s.

The spread of AIDS in the 1980s posed a great threat to homosexual activism within the academy, just as it did to homosexual activism within the community. There was a grave danger that so many people would die or face death that activism would become targeted on a single issue, that is, solely directed towards the issue of mourning/surviving. However, the lesbian and gay communities were not able to concentrate their energies in these areas because AIDS itself also provided the next shot in their armoury. The emergence of this major health crisis did indeed destroy many lives, but it provided, as Weeks said, 'a major politicization of sex' (Weeks, 1990: 237). This afforded an impetus to members of the academy, amongst others, to fight a rearguard battle against the new right (Republican) attempts to impose retrograde and repressive steps on sexual freedoms.

Many causes were fought by the gay community during the 1980s and the early 1990s. Because of separatist and internal politics within the gay liberation movement (which will be referred to later) they were often only single-issue campaigns, such as 'Stop Clause 28' campaign in Britain or the ACT UP campaign for free and comprehensive AIDS health care and treatment in the United States. These campaigns though, of necessity, looked to members within the academy to provide the theory and evidence for their arguments.

The relationship between gay activism and the academy has remained strong, as attested by the planning and organisation of the 5th and 6th North American Lesbian and Gay Studies Conferences that took place in 1991 and 1994. Both conferences included activists as well as academics on their organising committees: the appeal of the conferences was to both academics and activists and, by 1994, because of campaigning the conference title included 'Bisexual Studies'.

Queer theory has arisen from this utilitarian mix of activism and academia. As an interdisciplinary approach, with its potential proponents (queer people) in all walks of academic life, it could be said to provide one of the greatest threats to the conceptual basis of modernist thought there has ever been. Queer theorists are attempting to undermine the very foundations of modernist thought – the binary codification of our apparent existence, the divergent sex and gender categories of a one-dimensional creed: sexual duality and its resultant heterosexist centrism.

Queer theory initially arose from the need to conceptualise same-sex desire as if not a part of medical pathology nor of legal concern, in order that homosexual behaviours and lifestyles could become part of the mainstream and that homophobic behaviours could be challenged as if they were outside of the law. This has been partially achieved through a dual approach.

Gay and lesbian lifestyles and culture, the very sense of community, have been determinedly celebrated and paraded openly. One might say that there has developed a 'balloon culture's celebration of difference'. This has brought homosexual iconography into the forefront of (post)modern culturalism. From the soft slush lipstick lesbianism of Della and Binnie in *Eastenders*, the butch/femme narrative in films such as *Fried Green Tomatoes* to the homo-erotic bonding of *East 17* or *Take That* and the macho/paedophile gay body image of Marky Mark, it is no longer possible in Western culture to avoid the real possibilities of same-sex desire.

Alongside this there has been an adoption of the 'respectable'. This has come about in order to counter the contradictory self-image that many lesbians and gay men have faced because of, firstly, legal defects and social reproach and, secondly, the crisis of AIDS – which in itself projected the very image of the gay body, whether personal or of the community, as if unwholesome. Respectability, and being respectable, has become an essential aspect of lesbian and gay lifestyles. Through the adoption of 'family/couple imagery' alongside a move from the casual sexual lifestyle many gay men practised in the 1970s, to the practice of safer (serial monogamy) sex, in the 1980s, the gay movement, and in particular the activist and academic interests have moved, as Martin Dubermann (1991: 390) puts it, from 'radicalism to reformism'.

Respectability, Dubermann would argue, is typical of the change in priorities that would mark most protest movements. As he says:

> Originating in fierce anger and initially marked by broad gauged demands for social change, they rapidly evolve into well-behaved self-protective associations, and in the process abandon demands for challenging the vast inequities in our social system, substituting (at best) token liberalism . . . pressing for narrow assimilationist goals through traditional political challenges.
>
> (Dubermann, 1991: 392)

This has led to numerous problems for the queer theorist, who is faced with attempting to reconcile the many diverse representations of gay lifestyles and community thrown up by the balloon culture which celebrates same-sex desire with the needs of the middle-class liberal view of respectability. As such, queer theory is faced with several contradictory needs and issues, of which not the least is the transgendered community and the problems it apparently poses.

Many transgendered individuals have made their home in the space inhabited by the homosexual community. There are many reasons for this. Often initial experimentation or experience leads transgendered people to debate either whether they are gay or whether it would be easier to try and lead a gay lifestyle, with or without sexual involvement, rather than try to achieve the apparently impossible – gender-reassignment. Lesbians and gay men have often provided a safe and welcoming space for transgendered people, no matter what level of commitment they have had to either cross-dressing or cross-living. It may be that many transgendered people felt like the local gay bar's lucky mascot, as they provided the drag revue, but better that than being beaten up down a dark alley as they hustled their bodies for survival. Transgendered people can obtain work in the gay community whilst they are androgynous and otherwise unemployable: others work the rent scene as 'she-males' to find the money for hormone therapy and surgery, and find this to be safer in the established 'gay scenes'. Whatever the reason, many find friends and sometimes choose to stay after successful transition. However, although the two communities overlap and interact, they are not the same.

Though many transgendered people, especially those who have gone along the transsexual road of transition and assimilation into straight society, do not consider themselves to have any involvement in the gay community, many others have found a home at least on the edge of the gay community's space. After some initial involvement, one might expect them to move on. But during the 1990s many, including those who have apparently made the transition successfully and would not consider themselves to be lesbian or gay in their new gender-role, are staking a claim as actually belonging to and being a part, and an essential part at that, of the gay community.

THEORETICAL DIFFERENCE(S)

Queer theory is a theoretical attempt to deconstruct the gendered and sexed praxis of academia. Through queer theory, the hegemonic centrism of heterosexism as practised and taught throughout academic life, thought and writing, is being challenged to justify itself or to 'get out of the kitchen'.

Queer theory is about the deconstruction and the refusal of labels of personal sexual activity, and it is also concerned with the removal of pathologies of sexuality and gendered behaviour. It concerns 'gender fuck', which is a full-frontal theoretical and practical attack on the dimorphism of gender- and sex-roles.

Yet can queer theory formulate sex desire, as opposed to same-sex or heterosex desire? Queer theory attempts to be non-gender-specific, but is this possible when the very fact that it foregrounds same-sex desire, according to Sue Ellen Case (cit. in McIntosh, 1993: 30), is gender-specific?

It could be argued that because of the gay, lesbian and bisexual history of queer theory itself, it can currently do nothing more than expound and further delineate these boundaries. The crossing of them still belongs to the world of 'vogue-ing' and the destruction of them must belong to those for whom they have always been unreal because of their inherent personal incongruity within a gender-specific world.

For example, since 1972, when most women left the Gay Liberation Front in order to take up the banner of radical feminist lesbianism, one could question whether they were ever involved in 'gender fuck'. Did they, rather, uphold the idea of women as a separate/different gender and in doing so were they reinforcing these very binary divisions? They had been complaining that gay men were doing the same thing through their domination of Gay Liberation Front meetings and through drag parodies such as the Sisters of Perpetual Indulgence.

As radical feminist separatists they found it very difficult to do more than introduce, in the academy, an oppositional standpoint to patriarchal values and a reluctant acceptance of some value in ethnographic work, through the sex-role and sex-difference research they became involved in. They were locked into a process of explanation, then deconstruction, of gender differences rather than a reconstruction of theory.

This is not to say that this is the current state of feminist theory. But in the young theoretical movement that feminism was in the 1970s, sex-role theory was an essential tool in the fight to clarify and challenge the sexist stereotypes which still pervade Western social institutions. But:

> Sex-role theory fail(ed) to situate sex-roles within a structural explanation of their origin ... where social structure is missing, biological role is present. Indeed, the terms 'female role' and 'male role', hitching a biological term to a dramaturgical one, suggest what is going on. The underlying image is an invariant biological base and a malleable superstructure.
>
> (Messerschmidt, 1993: 28)

Bob Connell said that the state of the field of feminist theory and research by the mid-1980s was a paradox. The previous twenty years had produced a mass of factual research and a lively theoretical debate around work that was highly original and very penetrating. But he did not see current work on theories of gender as converging: 'the differences between the lines of thought have become more distinct, the conceptual and political differences greater' (Connell, 1987: 38).

Feminist theory is now faced with the need to address the dichotomy of biological imperativism and social structure, the differences of sex and gender, which are no longer recognised as synonymous.

Sexual difference was easily quantifiable in the modernist enlightenment view: the sex to which an individual was assigned depended upon whether the person possessed, at birth, a penis or a vagina. The knowledge of the genital was to predetermine a person's life story such that even if their genitals were to be reconstructed in another form they would not become a member of the other sex grouping. Gender was irrevocably connected to this biological construction of sex differences. An individual's gender was not mutable.

Fixed through the knowledge of the genitals, any assertion by someone that they had been assigned to the wrong gender grouping was a form of madness. For sex-role theorists, transsexuals and other members of the transgendered community were to become, at best, a surgical construction, according to Janice Raymond (1980); at worst, 'the victims of error', according to Catherine Millot (1990). To both, transsexuals did not become members of the opposite sex, but were always part of their original gender grouping; Raymond's researchee's were 'male to constructed female transsexuals' or 'female to constructed male transsexuals' and according to Millot sexual differences belong to: 'the register of the real. It constitutes an insuperable barrier, an irreducible wall against which one can bang one's head indefinitely' (Millot, 1990: 15). As such, she referred to them as male and female transsexuals, the gender designating that to which they were assigned at birth.

The transgendered community and its individual members has a large amount of personal experience of hitting the brick walls of the main foundations of this binary paradigm – the dualities of sex and gender. For many this led to a process of self-apologia and attempted explanation which caused self-identified transsexuals to adopt the stance of being a 'woman trapped inside a man's body' (or vice-versa). Cross-dressers and transvestites upheld a view that there was a feminine side to their masculinity and maleness, rather than challenge the actual construction of their gender-role. It was as if, without genital reconstruction, personal gender-roles could not be changed, and even with it, that reconstruction provided the point of change. A transformation took place, and the idea that gender was signified through the genital was repeatedly upheld.

In this way, surgical gender-reassignment treatment and the self-organisation of transsexual and transvestite groups in the 1970s and 1980s endorsed, according to Anne Bolin, 'a formula for gender constitution in which social woman is equated with genital woman' (Bolin, 1994: 460). However, the 1990s has seen a change for many in the transgendered community of their own personal praxis concerning sex and gender, and it is this change and its cultural expression which challenges and offers to expand queer theory's 'gender fuck'. Through the real-life postmodernist practice of hearing (and listening to) many voices and the acknowledgment of their individual truisms, gender, sex and sexuality are facing not just deconstruction but also reconstruction in the practices of many individuals and in the community's view of who can claim membership.

Recent contributions to cultural studies and other academic disciplines concerning transgendered behaviour have offered an oppositional standpoint to the assumed 'naturalism' of sexual dimorphism. Marjorie Garber

(1992) refers to the 'category crises' of class, race and gender; that is the failure of definitional distinctions that we face as we enter the twenty-first century. To her, transvestism 'is a space of possibility structuring and confounding culture: the disruptive element that intervenes, not just a category crisis of male and female, but a crisis of category itself'. (Garber, 1992: 17). In other words, transgendered behaviour not only challenges sexual dimorphism in that boundaries are crossed, but it provides a challenge to the boundaries ever being there. These are the boundaries that queer theory attempts to deconstruct.

The transgendered community is now facing up to this 'category crisis' in a way which has not yet been addressed in issues of race and class. Again there are several reasons for this happening at this point and in order to understand why this is the case it is important to understand something of the recent history and creation of the community.

RECENT TRANS-HER/HIS/STORY

The *transgendered* community is a concept of the 1990s. Prior to the late twentieth century;

> only a few organised groups of cross-dressers appeared in historical accounts, including the Hijiras of India, the Kabuki actors in Japan, and the Hollies of 18th century England. Despite these occasional homosexual cross-dressing groups, there is no evidence in Western culture of what might be called a transvestite consciousness.
>
> (Bullough and Bullough, 1993: 280)

Early organisation of the community started through the work of Virginia Prince, a cross-dresser and biological male who now defines herself as transgendered. She not only organised the Phi Pi Epsilon (FPE) sorority group for transvestites (see Chapter 5), but she extensively published transvestite ephemera under the 'Chevalier Publications' publishing house, and in the 1960s she became involved in a wide-reaching enterprise to educate the public about cross-dressing (Bullough and Bullough, 1993).

From these beginnings a huge network of self-help transvestite groups has come into existence throughout the world, such as the Seahorse Society of Australia (see Chapter 5), the Elizabeth Club in Japan, the Beaumont Society in the United Kingdom and the Phoenix Group in South Africa. They have not, however, always had the same points of view concerning transvestism and other aspects of cross-dressing, and the 1980s saw a burgeoning of other ephemeral publications, many of them coming from members of different factions of the network of self-help groups.

Initially generally aimed at the heterosexual cross-dressing male, these groups were often approached by self-identified transsexuals for membership, and similarly, after some time, some members would declare themselves to be transsexual, and commence hormone treatment and seek surgical reassignment.

A close network of individuals was very involved in the organisation and motivation of these groups. Ironically, certainly in the United Kingdom, they were often the self-identified transsexuals. For example, the Beaumont Society saw itself as a solely heterosexual cross-dressing male organisation, but faced great pressure from the fact that many of its organising committee and main activists were transsexual, and as transsexuals identified as heterosexual or lesbian women.

Because of some problems of diversity and incompatibility, the first organisation for transsexuals, as such, in the United Kingdom: the Self Help Association For Transsexuals (Shaft), was founded in 1979. Of those involved, certain people stand out, Alice was one of these. A lesbian-identified transsexual woman, she is still involved with the Beaumont Trust and now organises the Gender Trust (see Appendix II), which specifically caters for transsexuals. However, whilst being involved in the running of both organisations, she campaigned actively to remain in the Beaumont Society, to allow other transsexuals to be admitted including female-to-male transsexuals and, in the late 1980s, to remove the bar on homosexual transvestites from the organisation. Such campaigning was to greatly affect how the transvestite community viewed itself and to allow a huge level of diversity, increased gender acknowledgement and many issues to be brought to the fore for discussion.

World-wide many associations now exist for transgendered people from local cross-dressers' clubs to international groups such as the two Female-to-Male (FTM) Networks that now exist and boast over 800 members between them. Though primarily North American and European, these Female-to-Male Networks have members from as far afield as Alaska, New Zealand, Russia and China.

Important to the understanding of the transgendered community's current ideas and thoughts on theories of gender are the transitions that their 'organising centres' have gone through. From the self-help organising of a few transvestite networks in the 1960s and 1970s, there is now a plethora of groups catering for a significant level of diversity in cross-gendered behaviour.

However, many of the people involved in the running of these groups have been involved for over a quarter of a century. They have an immense level of respect within their own community because of their strong commitment to, and knowledge of, the community and its history. Many of them have also gone through great changes, personally and socially, both in their own self-identification and in their public lives. This has not just been to do with aspects of their cross-dressing or transgendered behaviour, though that could be seen as being pivotal, but with their ongoing fight to get public respect and academic recognition for the work they have done in this area. Their personal roads to understanding gender and what it means have informed the current theories they hold and expound.

It has been only very recently that transgendered people have felt able to participate in the theoretical discussions. In the fight to be included they have faced several serious problems. Firstly, any discussion of gender by the transgendered community has been hampered by the medical discourse surrounding transgendered behaviour, which makes them both self-interested and decidedly barmy. Secondly, they have been hampered by social and legal restrictions which have made it very difficult to come out publicly as transgendered and which adds another aspect of self-interest to any work they might do on gender issues.

Thirdly, Janice Raymond's thesis in *The Transsexual Empire, The Making of the She-Male* (1980) discredited for a long time any academic voice that they might have, in particular, with feminist theorists. As a result of her work, feminists saw transsexuals as misguided and mistaken men seeking surgery to fulfil some imaginary notion of femininity, and further-more, upholding the gendered sex-role structure inherent in the patriarchal hegemony which sought to discredit feminist work. Fourthly, trans-gendered people have not been allowed either objectivity or sexuality. Objectivity was lost because of the combination of the other three factors, also, if they questioned gender and sex-roles they were put in the invid-ious position of having to justify any sex-role change they might undertake to accommodate their gender incongruity. Sexuality was lost, as it was constructed for them in the form of repressed homosexuality being appeased through reassignment surgery or, alternatively, heterosexuality (in their new sex-role) was imposed on them by the medical profession in order to justify what was seen as a 'medical collusion with an unat-tainable fantasy (*Lancet*, 1991, cit. in Raymond, 1994: xiii).

These difficulties have not been avoided by the transgendered commu-nity, but rather they have tackled them head on. Firstly, the postmodernist acknowledgement of multiplicity of voices has been adapted to theoret-ical stances and there is an ongoing discussion as to whether the medical profession should take a diagnostic or merely enabling role for those people who actively seek reassignment treatment. Secondly, the trans-gendered community has consistently fought through the courts and the legislature for legal recognition of any new gender-role adopted, also for anti-discrimination clauses to include not only sexuality but gender-role.

Thirdly, transgenderists have tackled radical feminist separatism by continuously asking for answers to awkward questions: for example, along with male-to-female transsexuals, Leslie Feinberg; a 'female' transgen-derist and author of *Stone Butch Blues* (Feinberg, 1993), along with James Green a transsexual man, challenged the 'Womyn born Womyn' policy of the 1994 Michigan Womyn's Music Festival (Walworth, 1994: 27) by asking for their right to enter the festival. Transgenderists have also been active in addressing heterosexism and patriarchy both within and without their own community.

Fourthly, transgendered people have questioned the whole notion of objectivity; they do not try to claim it and instead they have built upon the tradition the community has of autobiographical writing to give a voice to their self-acknowledged subjectivity. As to sexuality, they have begun to reclaim it. Through the work begun by Lou Sullivan (a gay female-to-male who died of AIDS in 1991) and other gay, lesbian or bi activists (along with the help of Ira Pauly, a psychiatrist), they have come out. The argument is simple, if you can acknowledge in yourself that what makes a person is what takes place between the ears and not between the legs, then you are in a privileged position to know that sexuality is a movable and mutable force within us all.

Unfortunately, the reclamation project by lesbian and gay historians, which could have provided support for the challenge of this sex dimorphism has placed stereotyped gendered behaviour on individuals of whom we know little beyond their sexual activity, choice of sexual partners or platonic lovers. Julie Wheelwright (1989) revealed the 'hidden history of women who choose to live, work and love as men', but it does not occur to her that these 'women' might have in fact been non-gender-specific, or even, for that matter, actually men. Jason Cromwell refers to this as a process of 'default assumptions' (Cromwell, 1994: 4).

Default assumptions are (as they always have been) one of the biggest problems facing the transgendered community's contribution to any academic work or, for that matter, any issue of acceptance at all. There is the first assumption that females do not become men or males become women, they become pastiches, surgical constructions of imaginary masculinities or femininities. As Jason Cromwell says there are other related default assumptions that arise from this initial one. These take various forms depending upon the social setting, but he cites the director of the film *The Ballad of Little Jo*, Maggie Greenwald, in which she says, 'I stumbled upon some information about the real Little Jo Monihan (sic), about whom almost nothing is known except that she lived as a man and nobody had discovered the truth about her until she died' (in Cromwell, 1994: 4). Cromwell says:

> The default assumption here is that the truth is that Monaghan was female and thus really a woman. Greenwald vividly reveals her default assumptions when she concludes in the interview 'Women discover themselves – and this is so much part of feminism – that they don't have to be fake men; to be strong; to be powerful ... Jo becomes a woman not a man. She passes through a phase to survive,

208

ultimately to be a woman'. Now let me get this right: Monaghan lived as a man, no one knew otherwise until death, but 'ultimately' was a woman.

(Cromwell, 1994: 4)

The default assumption that underlies any notion of a transgendered existence is that gender is immutable, it is fixed through biological constraints and social construction merely affects any representation that the biological may take. Gender bending thus becomes a social play, a performance of the realms of the imaginary.

Performativity is a notion well known in queer theory but it has yet to tackle whether gender is just performance or whether it just 'is'. Lynne Segal has said;

> Studying how we live our sexual and gender identities as highly regulated performances does tell us something which is useful about the instabilities of both categories beginning with the impossibility of insisting, without a brutalising blindness, on their definitive connection. But we are not free to choose our performances or masquerades at will – like a type of 'improvisational theatre' ... Mostly we can only enact those behaviours which have long since become familiar and meaningful to us in expressing ourselves. This remains so however much we realise that our self-fashioning was formed through the policing norms and personal relations of a sexist heterosexual culture; indeed however fulfilling or frustrating our routine performances may prove. Challenge to our gendered 'identities' may be more than we can handle.
>
> (Segal, 1994: 208)

Queer theory sets up a stall which is apparently deconstructive of categories and subjectives – it is about getting away from binary thinking – but according to Kobena Mercer, 'binary thinking ends up with a static concept of identity rather than the more volatile concept of identification' (cit. in McIntosh 1993: 31). Transgendered activists and academics are attempting to deal with the volatile concept of identification, but it is against all odds; the rigidity of a set of default assumptions concerning sex-roles that pervades all discussion of gender; the two have an incorruptible sameness that makes them all-pervasive.

Yet gender and sex are fundamentally different to the transgendered community. They face the everyday reality of that difference in their lives, and attempts to reconcile it have led to it being challenged in unanticipated ways. Many have had to move on from seeking the biological basis for their state of being: any search for aetiology has been unsuccessful. Any aetiology that has been proposed, whether social or biological, has been torn down by the mass of exceptions. It has been accepted that seeking aetiology is a fruitless occupation as the multiplicity of possible factors increases and, even if there were possible points of interception, would the 'cure' be wanted?

Expressing the move to a theory in which gender- and sex-roles are clearly separated (at least for a large number of people) and what that means to the modernist view of gender theory is a challenge the trans-gendered community is not ignoring, nor is it prepared to come up with trite self-serving answers. Challenging their own sense of self, looking inwards to find who they are, using the process of autobiography that they know so well, is producing some very interesting answers which challenge, not only the structured world that queer theory inhabits but the very binary structure of the complacent world in which gender was invented, and by which it has become obsessed. The transgenderist did not, after all, invent gender. Gender, like God, is a concept of the imagination that belongs within and supports the foundations of a patriarchal heterosexist hegemony.

Illustrating this move towards teaching us the limits of one aspect of the imaginary, I wish to look at two 'texts' and what they re-present.

GENDER OUTLAWS ON THE RUN!

Kate Bornstein's *Gender Outlaw* (Bornstein, 1994) takes us through a life story of sex-roles and gender confusion. It uses the politics of respectability, which she has acquired through her position as a respected performance artist, to argue for a fluidity of gender politics. She uses her experience of gender boundaries and the crossing of them to question the basic assumptions: the assumptions that there are only two genders, which are invariant and bound by the genitals; that everyone must belong to one gender or another, and that this is 'natural' and independent of science or social construction; and that any transfers from one gender to another are either ceremonial or masquerades – and any exceptions to the two genders are not to be taken seriously. She argues that there are rules to gender – but rules can be broken, ambiguity does exist, it is how we provide for that ambiguity that matters. But even more than ambiguity there is fluidity.

Fluidity provides for any number of genders: 'the ability to freely and knowingly become one or many of a limitless number of genders for any length of time, at any rate of change. Gender fluidity recognises no borders or rules of gender' (Bornstein, 1994: 52). This has meaning in the real world and in the real politics of sex and gender. To be fluid in one's gender challenges the oppressive process of gender and the power processes which use gender to maintain power structures. It makes it hard for them to know who, where or what 'you' are and to set up rules and systems which control. As Bornstein points out, transgenderists are only at the very beginnings of having any sense of community, but gender outlaws exist, though there are still few groups that 'encompass the full rainbow' (Bornstein, 1994: 68). According to her, however, any community must be based on a principle of constant change to avoid the traps that the rules of gender dictate. But to her 'a fluid identity, incidentally, is one way to solve problems with boundaries. As a person's identity keeps shifting, so do individual borders and boundaries. It's hard to cross a boundary that keeps moving' (Bornstein, 1994: 52).

In her discussion of gender terrorism she points out that it is not the transgendered community who are the terrorists, rather it is gender defenders – those who defend the belief that gender is 'real' and 'natural' and use it to 'terrorize the rest of us'. She quotes Murray S. Davis, who wrote:

> Anything that undermines confidence in the scheme of classification on which people base their lives sickens them as though the very ground on which they stood precipitously dropped away ... People will regard any phenomenon that produces this disorientation as 'disgusting' or 'dirty'. To be so regarded, however, the phenomenon must threaten to destroy not only one of their fundamental cognitive categories but their whole cognitive system.
>
> (cit. in Bornstein, 1994: 72)

Bornstein argues that the transgendered person as a gender outlaw causes the destruction of the gendered system of reality on which most people base major aspects of their lives. The gender terrorists react with acts of violence which range from the physical – as in the rape and killing of Brandon Teena, a passing female-to-male in Nebraska, in early January 1994 (Jones, 1994: 3) – to the theoretical – as in the attacks on transsexuals by feminists such as Janice Raymond (1980; 1994) and Catherine Millot (1990).

Bornstein offers a view of real-life gender fluidity, a refusal to be categorised by the limited gender-roles that are imposed, a refusal to be some cute and humorous representation of the 'third sex' as court jester. Neither is she willing to be invisible, instead she proposes a play with gender partitioning to ultimately make the partitions meaningless. She is not a third sex, but she is creating a third space; a space outside of gender: 'Every transsexual I know went through a gender transformation for different reasons, and there are as many truthful experiences of gender as there are people who think they have gender (Bornstein, 1994: 8).

WANTED: GENDER OUTLAW

The second piece I wish to look at is Loren Cameron's self-portrait. It could be argued that this is a complete education in the current position

211

of gender blending in the world of queer theory. 'Gender blending' is a misnomer to the transgendered community. Gender exists as itself, that is, as an idea, an invention, a means of oppression and a means of expression. Many in the community would see themselves as existing outside of gender, of being oppressed by it but using its icons and signifiers to say who they are.

Cameron's self-portrait says who he is through a celebration of the body. He resists imposed gender representations and assumptions by his nakedness. He acknowledges that in the struggle for himself, dress as such is not the solution. It cannot direct us to a way out of gendered or sexed roles – it merely directs us further into them.

If he was dressed, in the nature of the 'true' disguise that directs us away from questioning, he would lead us further into the traps of gender; as the passing cross-dresser he would become hidden. The gender outlaw is nearly always hidden in passing and, as a result, the gender defenders are fucked, in that their rules become meaningless because they are constantly broken, and nobody knows when or where or how that is happening.

However, Cameron chooses not to pass. Normally the nature of 'not passing' means that heads aren't really fucked, because gender rules are not transgressed, they are only highlighted. Transgenderists, if they could be hidden outlaws, have to choose to tell the story themselves, to make the autobiographical statement in order to present the gender fuck. Realistically, many will not, because their outsiderness, their otherness, means they are seeking a form of sanctuary in the gender-roles they adopt. Anyhow, once we know – won't we always know, and always have known – so the gender fuck disappears.

However, if the gender outlaw who can pass, refuses to pass, then they, once again, present the gender fuck. A world in which gender is transgressed, in which representations are resisted, is a world in which the struggle is presented by subjects rather than objects. Cameron (and Bornstein for that matter) has chosen to show that, 'gender is always posthuman, always a sewing job which stitches identity into a body bag' (Halberstam, 1992: 51).

The human is first, the gender is an addition. Cameron takes his human form and imposes gender signifiers upon it through the place of the observer. We see a bodybuilder's physique. As Marcia Ian explains:

> bodybuilders plan ... (to) ... display as much tumescent muscle as possible, the skin must be well tanned and oiled, the physique rock-hard, showing striations and bulging veins ... in other words to look as much like a giant erection as possible ... a human fucking penis.
>
> (Ian, 1994: 79)

Loren Cameron's self-portrait

Cameron becomes the human fucking penis. He is what he does not apparently possess, and which by default we would assume he desires. Yet does he desire the penis? The photograph shows a man who is proud to be without, because his masculinity does not come from a penis but from himself. We see in him the female signifier of 'lack', yet in his case the meaning of 'lack' is meaningless: he chooses not to wear a phallus because that would not be him, he is without 'lack'. He has gender through himself and because of himself. He shows his fluidity of gender through the fluidity of his tattooed body. The flames signify his flame, he just 'is' and he is proud of his being. Cameron does not 'gender blend', instead he escapes gender because it can no longer be imposed by the observer as the boundaries keep moving.

What has all this to do with queer theory? As stated earlier, queer theory arose from the mix of academic respectability and street activism. Bornstein and Cameron represent the two sides of that association but they are, even then, constantly crossing and re-crossing the boundaries. They are both activists and academics in the eyes of their own small community, and they represent the forefront of that community's current political theory around gender and what it is, what it means.

However, they choose not to gender blend, they do not claim the position of a third sex (meaning gender), rather they claim to be unique in their diversity and, most importantly, themselves. This is the lesson that they offer up to queer theory:

> The identity politics of queer theory permit us, even require us, both to take seriously and experiment with ways of thinking and being which more conventional radical theory is ready to consign to its epistemological closet.
>
> (Ian, 1994: 77)

Both are seriously experimenting with ways of 'thinking identity'. Both are bringing to queer theory the challenge of diversity, not just in terms of race and sex but in terms of gender in its most complete and fullest sense. They are challenging the imaginary assumptions through their own imaginations:

> Celebrating and affirming insurgent intellectual cultural practice . . .
> (it is) an invitation to enter a space of changing thought, the open mind that is the heartbeat of cultural revolution.
>
> (hooks, 1994: 7)

15

THE POLITICS OF TRANSGENDERISM*

Janice Raymond

The opening sentence of *The Transsexual Empire* was 'Transsexualism has taken only twenty-five years to become a household word'. Things were relatively simpler then, with normatively different sexual and gender behaviour pretty much encapsulated under the headings lesbian/homosexual, transvestism and transsexualism. Today, fifteen years later, things are more complex, and a plethora of terms such as 'transgendered', 're-gendered', 'gender blending', 'gender bending', 'gender fucking' and 'transhomosexuality' have been added to the lexicon of so-called 'gender dissonant' behaviour. The film tribute to certain aspects of the transgender phenomenon is *Paris Is Burning* and, more recently, *The Crying Game*.

The issue of transsexualism has been largely superseded by debates over transgenderism or what has been called 'sexuality's newest cutting edge'. The term 'transgender' covers pre-operative and post-operative transsexuals, transvestites, drag queens, cross-dressers, gays and lesbians, bisexuals and straights who exhibit any kind of dress and/or behaviour interpreted as 'transgressing' gender-roles. It is interesting that, like transsexuals, the majority of transgenderists are men who, rather than transcending, i.e., dismantling and going beyond gender-roles, seek to combine aspects of traditional femininity with aspects of traditional masculinity.

One side of the transgender phenomenon was written about in an article entitled 'The Next Wave' in *The Advocate*. In this article, transgender was closely allied with transsexualism. Referring to a bar called the Motherlode in San Francisco, the majority of patrons were said to be 'much more evolved in their gender expressions [than cross-dressers]. Hormones, breast implants, cosmetic surgery and in some cases sexual reassignment surgery make dedication to being female more than a dress up game for these

* This chapter first appeared as part of the 'Introduction to the 1994 Edition' of *The Transsexual Empire: The Making of the She-Male*, New York: Teachers College Press, 2nd edition, 1994, pp. xi–xxxv.

women [sic]' (Greenberg, 1993: 51–2). Although lamenting that 'trans-gender' had been excluded from the title of the 1992 gay and lesbian march on Washington, and faulting 'radical feminists, the PC lesbians, and the assimilationist gay men' for not accepting transgendered individuals into the movement, the article nevertheless is a brief for the virtues of what is called Transgender Nation.

Many male transgenderists work as prostitutes in the sex industry. The article notes that 'a high percentage of transgendered women [sic], primarily in the pre-operative phase, have at one time or another engaged in sex work' (Greenberg, 1993: 52). Although prostitution is described as an economic necessity for most transgendered individuals, there is also the admission that it is 'part of the discovery process that a transgendered woman [sic] may go through. Some of it is acting out fantasies, obses-sions, or compulsions. It's a sort of coming-of-age, a part of the transition, an identitying and validation proesss' (Greenberg, 1993: 52). So we have here an idealising of sexual exploitation and prostitution in the name of transgender transformation, identity and maturity.

This tale of transgender is also a rendition of how men are 'turned on' by other men. According to *The Advocate*, the allure of gender ambiguity and the polymorphous sexuality exuded by transgenderists, the 'hyper-feminine and hypersexual', 'chick with a dick' scene, is said to be attractive to many men (Greenberg, 1993: 52). What is described as transgression of boundaries actually turns out to be conformity to sex-roles once more, with many men flocking to hormones and surgery to attract other men as artifactual, ultra-feminine women. The article's author does admit that many transgendered individuals, through surgery or hormones, try to become the image of the perfect woman, i.e., the Cindy Crawford-like model, and that disturbing 'prefeminist' notions of femininity pervade the transgendered community, pitting those who undergo surgery (true trans-genderists) against those who remain on hormones.

Another variation on the transgender theme is what was once simply called cross-dressing, transvestism, or drag.[1] When Boy George accepted a Grammy award for Best New Artist in 1985, he thanked his US audi-ence for recognising not only his music but 'a good drag queen'. Perhaps the more flamboyant US version of Boy George is African-American RuPaul, whose musical act has become a highly successful marketable commodity. Thriving on theatrical sexuality combined with pop music, RuPaul, as *The New York Times* phrased it, is 'an amalgam of two distinct sexual archetypes: gender benders and soul divas' (Keeps, 1993: H23).

In RuPaul's act, both 'archetypes' depend upon the assimilation of stereotypical femininity, in the first instance by appropriating mini skirts, blonde wigs and platform heels and, in the second, by exaggerating femininity as 'birthright'. For this conformity RuPaul is called a 'gender illusionist' and claims that what he is doing is more than men dressing in women's clothes. It's really about 'the way everybody looks. Because what really counts is inside . . . You're born naked, and the rest is drag' (Keeps, 1993: H23). *The New York Times*' article idealises RuPaul as 'a de facto social activist' who brings drag into the mature part of the twentieth century by not simply mimicking the voice and movements, say, of a Marilyn Monroe but rather by being 'his own woman' (sic). It's too bad 'his own woman' looks and acts so much like the woman of man-made femininity. As Kathy Miriam writes, 'While "transgenderism" foregrounds the reality that femininity is a male construct, it does so by *preserving* sex difference, i.e., the heterosexual institution . . . in contrast to being a strategy of *disempowering* (politically destroying) the social system which generates the category' (Miriam, 1993: 51–2, n. 116).

There have been pleas from some feminist commentators to recognise that cross-dressing, drag and transvestism are on a continuum of masculinity and to sympathise with these ways in which some men are deviating from acceptable masculine gender behaviour. And often men dressing as women is compared to women who wear pants. There is a false symmetry here. When most women put on pants, a necktie, combat boots, or a business-like blazer, they are not trying to pass as men. Nor do most of these women stage theatrical performances that call attention to their cross-dressing. They do not mimic, for profit, male behaviour. Most women who wear male clothing are not trying to be men, nor to imitate men personally or professionally, nor do they expect to be mistaken for men. And there is no significant number of women who fetishise certain articles of male clothing for sexual pleasure or gender relaxation.

The reason that women wear pants is mainly comfort and convenience. Pants are practical in all types of weather and don't make women physically vulnerable or encourage sexual harassment, as certain styles of feminine clothes do. More significantly, a woman putting on a man's clothes is, in a sense, putting on male power status, whereas a man putting on women's clothes is putting on parody. That drag queens and cross-dressers can draw hoots and howls in audiences of mostly men says more about how women were and are perceived than it does about the supposed boundary-breaking behaviour of gender-bending men who wear women's clothes.

Cross-dressers, drag queens and heterosexual transvestites – who clandestinely parade around in ultra-feminine dress while often retaining their public personas as straight, white, male conservative pillars of the community – depend upon a certain mimicry of women's persons, roles, status and dress. That some men may find gender relief, sexual pleasure and/or stardom and financial profit in this mimicry does nothing to challenge the political power of the normative, dominant, powerful class of men that the male gender bender still belongs to. Cross-dressing could be more accurately perceived as another form of male self-expression and exhibitionism. Scratching the surface of masculinity by flaunting its opposite conventions of femininity, whether in drag, cross-dressing or heterosexual transvestism, may incur the wrath of other men and expose the cross-dressers to pain and punishment. But pain and punishment do not necessarily challenge the substance of masculinity that is male dominant political power. The mostly one-way traffic of men moving down the transgender highway is not new. Males have been imitating women on the stage and in religious rituals since time immemorial, but this has done nothing to change the reality that men, including many of these men, are in power.

Going further than the one-dimensional femininity of the transvestite and cross-dresser, many transgenderists mix and match, blending as much femininity or masculinity with its opposite into new gender recipes. The recipes, however, are a repackaging of the old gender-roles. Transgenderists still adhere to many self-selected ingredients of these roles, although mixed and matched in a supposedly gender-defiant way. But transgenderist defiance equals a kind of androgynous humanism, an individualist assertion of androgynous blending, rather than a political defiance of both roles. Many transgenderists seem to see masculinity and femininity as entities in and of themselves, to be preserved and grafted onto one another. This can take the form of switching back and forth, as in transvestism, or combining both. Much depends on appearances. While transgenderists break through the semblance of masculinity, they don't break through its political reality, that is, its power. And so androgynous humanism replaces feminist politics.

THE TRANSGENDERED LESBIAN

Although transgenderism is largely a male phenomenon, there are women who claim it as their own. One of the more moving and historically rich accounts of the complexities of gender is the novel *Stone Butch Blues* (1993), by Leslie Feinberg. *Stone Butch Blues* is basically a transgender odyssey of a woman growing up in the gay bars and working-class factories of the 1950s and 1960s. Coming of age as a young 'butch' in Buffalo, Feinberg movingly describes the working-class reality of this historical butch world with a sharp consciousness of its political aspects – a more powerful testimony to class politics than any Marxist analysis – but a less astute political analysis of gender than many readers will look and hope for throughout the book. In discussing the novel's portrait of the butch–femme bar scene, one lesbian friend commented that the book takes no account of those lesbians, who like herself, inhabited the same bars but did not succumb to these fiercely defining and confining gendered roles.

Feinberg's accounts of the relationships between butches and femmes, many of whom were prostitutes, are moving and cogently described. Using the tools of eye and heart, Feinberg lifts this world of butch and femme to a humanistic level, whereas straight history has consigned such individuals to the dregs of society. Tender and protective partnerships were forged often in the crucible of police brutality where, in the constant raids on bars, butches and femmes were swept into jail and made to pay for their gender transgressions through unrelenting, deliberate, and demeaning strippings, forced oral sex, and vicious gang rapes by the police.

The novel has many insights, especially in its intial pages, into the world of gender dogmatism. Its disappointment is its failure to extend these *personal insights* into a *political analysis* of gender. A key turning point is when Jess, the butch protagonist in the novel, undergoes hormone treatment and breast surgery. Living and working as a butch has become too painful and fraught with harassment and violence, but so has the realisation that Jess feels herself to be other than a woman – a 'he–she', feeling neither like a woman or man but 'different'. 'I don't feel like a man trapped in a woman's body. I just feel trapped' (Feinberg, 1993: 158–9).

It is significant that the only woman in this novel who offers any real political challenge to the role-defined world of butch–femme is Theresa. *Stone Butch Blues* begins with a letter to Theresa and ends with the acknowledgment that she is the woman who 'I [Jess] still carry around in my heart.' In the early 1970s, it was Theresa, Jess's femme lover, who, after becoming active in feminist groups and activities at the campus where she worked, attempted to persuade Jess that, 'Anything that's good for women is good for butches' (Feinberg, 1993: 138), and that anytime Jess disparages or disidentifies with other women, she is wounding herself. And when Jess makes the final decision to begin hormone treatment, Theresa responds, 'Jess, I can't go out with you in the world and pretend that you're a man. I can't pass as a straight woman and be happy' (Feinberg, 1993: 152).

One gets a sense in these passages of the tensions between the old and the new gender-challenging worlds of two people who love each other but who have radically disparate ideas and thresholds of what it means to exist, or to reject existence, as women in a gender-defined society, and how best to take on that society. And it is surprising that most of the story takes place *not* in the pre-feminist 1940s or 1950s, but in the emerging feminist consciousness and climate of the 1960s and 1970s, when other women are rejecting these roles and many forms of body-mutilating medicine.

Some of the more insightful passages in the book illustrate Jess's understanding of the line she had crossed after taking hormones to pass as a man: the differential treatment she received as a butch in contrast to her present passing as male and the ways in which women regard men and men in turn regard women. Jess notes that women are now afraid of her on the streets, that passing as a straight man makes her an instant expert on motorcycles, and that straight women who think she's 'cute' relate to her in a flirtatious parrying, a kind of courtship fencing. Finally, Jess observes that this latter behaviour receives public encouragement and approval.

Quite swiftly, Jess comes to the realisation that not much has changed.

> At first, everything was fun. The world stopped feeling like a gauntlet I had to run through. But very quickly I discovered that passing didn't just mean slipping below the surface, it meant being buried alive. I was still me on the inside ... But I was no longer me on the outside.
>
> (Feinberg, 1993: 173)

After undergoing continuous hormone treatments, her response to this dis-ease is to proceed further with a double mastectomy, but this additional bodily alteration doesn't resolve the question of who she really is.

> I simply became a he – a man without a past. Who was I now – woman or man? That question could never be answered as long as those were the only choices; it could never be answered if it had to be asked.
>
> (Feinberg, 1993: 222)

And so, after living for several years as a man and undergoing both hormone treatment and radical breast surgery, Jess stops the hormone injections that had refigured her bodily contours and secondary sex characteristics into a more masculine appearance, thus arriving in a no-persons land.

Stone Butch Blues is a personally moving but politically disappointing book. In the final part, there is a foresaking of the political insights that marked the beginning pages of Jess's life as a butch and, initially, of her life as a hormonally and surgically constructed male. As opposed to a prior gender-consciousness – an awareness that a woman who looked like, acted like a man was subject to being brutalised by men, was attractive to women, and was disgusting to society – there is now a kind of retirement to a gender-neutral *otherness*. The hormones, the surgery, the cessation of hormone injections finally devolve into a long-suffering self-surrender to being *other* – not a woman who is a butch and not a woman who tries to pass as a man with the help of hormones and surgery, but a transgendered individual who identifies as simply 'other'. In fact, Jess's final transformation is, *from being woman-identified to being other-identified*. And Jess's most intimate and personal relationships are no longer with women, especially lesbians, but with men who are cross-dressers and who, like herself, presumably have undertaken hormones and/or surgery. Jess's ultimate identification with otherness – in essence, her disavowal of her own womanhood, not simply the disowning of a rigid femininity that society has reduced womanhood to – is at the heart of Feinberg's final version and vision of transgenderism.

GENDER BENDING

Gender bending is a more recent version and vision of transgenderism, and k.d. lang is one of its more complex proponents. 'Gender bending has always been lang's stock-in-trade ... hers is a deeply subversive presence; after you watch her for a while you realize how warped your own stereotypes are' (Bennetts, 1993: 98). The gender bending that k.d. projects is definitely not the same as most male transgenderists who depend on surgery, hormones, passing as women or mimicking women on stage. Hers is a more dimensioned, savvy and feminist self-assertion that does not reduce gender bending to the flaunting of sexuality, à la Madonna, but expands it to point out the limits imposed upon both female gender and sexuality. However, there is a mixed message in her gender-bending portrayals.

Featured in a photo spread in the August, 1993 issue of *Vanity Fair*, k.d. lang does not define herself as a transgenderist but, instead, prides herself 'on being 100 per cent woman' (Bennetts, 1993: 97). There is much in the article that any feminist can identify with: k.d.'s incredible talent and her rise up the professional ladder, defying any attempts to make her more feminine and thus palatable to audiences; the kind of physical freedom with which she moves on stage, so unlike any other female singer; the clothing she wears that doesn't objectify or exploit her body; her refusal to engage in performances featuring her as a 'heterosexual fantasy object'; her defence of animal rights and vegetarianism; her presentation of herself as her self, never hiding her lesbianism or denying lesbian rumours, culminating in her public 'coming out'. 'She takes everything a woman is not supposed to be – big, funny, fearlessly defiant, physically powerful – and makes it not only O.K. but glorious' (Bennetts, 1993: 144).

Why then capitulate to and capitalise on a role-defined and sexually objectifying cover photo that muddles this portrait of gender resistance? If gender-roles are challenged by a full-length cover spread in which a woman (k.d.) poses in masculine vest, tie, pants and boots as her face is being shaved by a scantily dressed and provocatively positioned Cindy Crawford, then aren't we back to square one? The inside photo shoot was even more gender-defined, with k.d. and Cindy somewhat stiffly acting up in what surely doesn't cut it as a realistic lesbian sex scene, with k.d. depicted as 'check(ing) out the curves on supermodel Cindy Crawford' (Bennetts, 1993: 94–5). Further, why pose for a picture that appears to depend upon some association that the viewer will make between k.d. licking a dish (?) and k.d. licking a prick, with the caption, 'I have a little bit of penis envy. They're ridiculous but they're cool' (Bennetts, 1993: 99).

This is followed by a paean to male sexuality: 'As much as I hate it, I admire the male sexual drive because it's so primal and so animalistic' (Bennetts, 1993: 144). A new version of no means yes, 'I want it, but not really', and having it both ways?

In the *Vanity Fair* portrait, we have another version of androgynous humanism in which gender bending unfortunately reduces to assimilation – transcending gender stereotyping by assimilating aspects of it, such as sexual objectification. Assimilationist behaviour cannot fulfil political goals. When k.d. lang refuses to wear clothing or perform in ways that objectify her body on stage, she is issuing a real challenge to the encouraged female role of flaunting sexuality. But when k.d. lang's gender bending relies on being photographed with a woman whose body is sexualised in a way that lang herself would not stand for, something is wrong, and the sexual objectification of women is hardly challenged.

Gender bending is gender identity condensed to the point of little or no feminist or lesbian politics. Although k. d. lang definitely does it better, she also conforms to the heterosexist script, dissipating the political message that lesbianism at its core, erodes rather than preserves hetero roles. Taking Kathy Miriam's words and putting them in another context, this kind of gender bending:

> works at eroding the *landscape of the lesbian* by assimilating it (in this case, heterosexist role playing) into itself as a factor of patriarchal realism – by *including it*, rather than *outright resisting* it. Seen through this lens, transgenderism can be viewed as 'a plot where even the "bad" girls please men'.
>
> (Miriam, 1993: 66–7)

The language of sexual conformity as sexual rebellion has come to dominate the public field. Transgenderism is the product of a historical period that circumscribes any challenge to sex-roles and gender definitions to some form of assimilating these roles and definitions. In much of the Western world, the general effect of the 1980s has been to move back the feminist gains of the 1960s and 1970s. It has encouraged a *style* rather than a *politics* of resistance, in which an expressive individualism has taken the place of collective political challenges to power. And in the process it has de-politicised gender by de-politicising feminism. The new gender outlaw is the old gender conformist, only this time we have men conforming to femininity and women conforming to masculinity. Or to be fair to another version of transgender, men and women mixing and matching but not moving beyond both. The transgenderist assumes the posture of rebellion, but only as restricted by the sex-role scene, and going only as far a melding of both roles.

The ideal of transgender is provocative. On a personal level, it allows for a continuum of gendered expression. On a political level, it never moves off this continuum to an existence in which gender is truly transcended. Its supposedly iconoclastic rebellion against traditional gender confinement is more style than substance. What good is a gender outlaw who is still abiding by the law of gender?

The claim for tolerance, based on the notion that transgenderism in all its forms is a form of gender resistance, is alluring but false. Instead, transgenderism reduces gender resistance to wardrobes, hormones, surgery and posturing – anything but real sexual equality. A real sexual politics says yes to a view and reality of transgender that transforms, instead of conforming to, gender.

NOTE

1   While I realise that much of the traditional literature distinguishes among drag queens, cross-dressers and transvestism, and that there are some significant differences among these groups, what they all have in common is that they wear women's clothes. Further, they wear the kind of hyperfeminine women's clothes that many women would never wear. Thus, I use these terms interchangeably for purposes of this chapter.

APPENDIX 1

A chronological listing of English and American short stories and novels featuring cross-dressing and sex-changing

1873. Thomas Bailey Aldrich, 'Mademoiselle Olympe Zabriski', in *The Writings of Thomas Bailey Aldrich*, vol. 3, Boston and New York: Houghton Mifflin Company, 1907.

1882. Nellie Hellis, *Rob and Ralph or a Trust Fulfilled*, London: John Shaw & Co.

1883. Samuel Langhorne Clemens, '1,002nd Arabian night', in Franklin R. Rodgers (ed.) *Mark Twain's Satires and Burlesques*, Berkeley: University of California Press, 1967, pp. 88–133.

1884. Samuel Langhorne Clemens, *The Adventures of Huckleberry Finn*, New York: Chanticleer Press.

1888a. Rudyard Kipling, 'His wedded wife' in *Plain Tales from the Hills*, Calcutta: Thacker, Spink & Co.

1888b. Sir Arthur Conan Doyle, *A Study in Scarlet*, London: Ward, Lock, & Co.

1891a. 'A Clifton masculine maid', *Modern Society*, October, pp. 1587–90.

1891b. Archibald Clavering Gunter and Fergus Redmond, *A Florida Enchantment*, New York: Hurst.

1893. *Gynecocracy, a Narrative of the Adventures and Psychological Experiences of Julian Robinson (afterwards Viscount Ladywood) under Petticoat-Rule Written by Himself,* 3 vols, Paris & Rotterdam.

1894. Samuel Langhorne Clemens, *Pudd'nhead Wilson*, London: Chatto & Windus.

1895. *Punch, Judy and Toby*, London: SPCK.

1898. Sir Arthur Conan Doyle, 'The story of the man with the watches', *The Strand Magazine*, July, vol. 16, pp. 33–43.

1900a. 'Dainty Dolly's wager', *Modern Society*, 30 June, pp. 1080–3.

1900b. 'The twins', *Modern Society*, 29 September, pp. 1946–7.

1903. C.F. de M.M., *Boy or Girl?* London: Henry J. Drane.

1907. Frank Richardson, *2835 Mayfair*, London: T. Werner Laurie.

1909. 'Velvet, female impersonator', *Photo Bits*, 11 December, pp. 12–17.

1910–11. Derk Fortescue, *Amber the Actor*, *Photo Bits*, 26 November–17 June.

1911a. Barry E.O. Pain, *An Exchange of Souls*, London: Nash.

1911b. Charles Kinross, *A Change of Sex*, London: John Long.

1911c. Rudyard Kipling, 'The honours of war', *The Family Magazine*, May. Reprinted in Rudyard Kipling, *A Diversity of Creatures*, London: Macmillan, 1917, pp. 105–28.

1912. Sir Arthur Conan Doyle, 'The fall of Lord Barrymore', *The Strand Magazine*, December, vol. 44, pp. 603–11. Reprinted in *Danger and Other Stories*, London: John Murray, 1918.

1921. B.B. (Cuthbert Morley Headlam), *A Strange Delilah*, London: John Murray.

1922. James Joyce, *Ulysses*, Paris. Page numbers from the edition of John Lane, The Bodley Head, London, 1937.

1925. A. M. Burrage, *Poor Dear Esme*, London: George Newnes.

1927a. Horace Annesley Vachell, *Miss Torrabin's Experiment*, London: Cassell & Company.

1927b. Sir Arthur Conan Doyle, 'The adventure of Shoscombe Old Place', *The Strand Magazine*, April, vol. 73, pp. 317–27. Reprinted in *The Casebook of Sherlock Holmes*, London: John Murray, 1927.

1931. Thorne Smith, *Turnabout*, Garden City, New York: Sundial Press.

1936a. Aileen Smiles, *Indian Tea*, London: Constable & Co.

1936b. Victor Wallace Germains, *Colonel to Princess*, London: Methuen & Co.

1953. Anthony Rhodes, *A Ball in Venice*, London: Arthur Barker.

1955. Nigel Dennis, *Cards of Identity*, London: Weidenfeld & Nicolson.

1966. Colin Spencer, *Poppy Mandragora and the New Sex*, London: Anthony Blond.

1968. Gore Vidal, *Myra Breckinridge*, London: Anthony Blond.

APPENDIX II
A guide to resources

The most comprehensive and detailed world-wide listings of professional and consumer organisations are to be found in:

'The Directory of Organizations & Services', *TV/TS Tapestry Journal*, IFGE Inc., P.O. Box 367, Wayland, Massachusetts, 0778–0367, USA.

1995 Who's Who & Resource Guide to the International Transgender Community, Creative Design Services, P.O. Box 61623, King of Prussia, PA 19406, USA.

The best bibliographies are:

Dallas Denny, *Gender Dysphoria: A Guide to Research*, New York: Garland Publishing, Inc., 1994.

Gilbert Demeyere, *Transvestism and Its Wider Context: A Working Bibliography*, Wijnegem, Belgium: Demeyere, 1992.

A good way to grasp the ubiquity of gender blending is to peruse:

Marjorie Garber, *Vested Interests: Cross-Dressing and Cultural Anxiety*, New York: Routledge, 1992.

and to consult the collections of transgender material housed in:

The Trans-Gender Archive, c/o Dr. Richard Ekins, University of Ulster at Coleraine, Co. Londonderry, BT52 1SA, Northern Ireland.

The Museum of International Gender Identity c/o IGTA, 1, Bank Buildings, School Green Road, Freshwater, Isle of Wight, P.O. Box 40 9AJ, England.

The National Transgender Library and Archives, AEGIS, P.O. Box 33724, Decatur, GA 30033, USA.

Professional organisations include:

American Educational Gender Information Services, Inc. (AEGIS), Dallas Denny, Executive Director, P.O. Box 33724, Decatur, GA 30033–0724, USA.

227

Harry Benjamin International Gender Dysphoria Association Inc., (HBIGDA), Alice Webb, Director, P.O. Box 1718, Sonoma, CA 95476, USA.

The Gender Centre, Projects Manager, P.O. Box 266, Petersham, New South Wales, 2049, Sydney, Australia.

National and Regional Consumer Organisations include:

International Foundation for Gender Education (IFGE), P.O. Box 367, Wayland, MA 01778, USA.

Renaissance Education Association, Inc., P.O. Box 552, King of Prussia, PA 19406, USA.

The Gender Trust, BM Gentrust, London, WC1 3XX, England.

The Beaumont Society, BM Box 3084, London, WC1N 3XX, England.

The Phoenix Society, P.O. Box 1332, Springs, 1560, Republic of South Africa.

Seahorse Society of New South Wales Inc., P.O. Box 168, Westgate, New South Wales, 2048, Australia.

Pressure Groups include:

Press for Change, BM Network, London, WC1N 3XX, England.

International Conference on Transgender Law and Employment, 5707, Firenza St, Houston, Texas, 7703-5515, USA.

BIBLIOGRAPHY

Abrams, P. (1982) *Historical Sociology*, Shepton Mallet: Open Books.

Alice, L100 (1991) 'A history of the Beaumont Society', *Beaumont Bulletin*, 23 (3): 37–9.

Apel, Karl-Otto (1977), 'The a priori of communication and the foundation of the humanities', in Fred Dallmayr and Thomas McCarthy (eds) *Understanding and Social Inquiry*, Notre Dame: University of Notre Dame Press.

Allen, C. (1954) 'Letter', *British Medical Journal*, 1 May: 1040.

Armstrong, C. N. (1958) 'The clinical diagnosis of sex', *Proceedings of the Royal Society of Medicine* 51: 23–6.

Baker, H. and Green, R. (1970) 'Treatment of transsexualism', *Current Psychiatry Therapy* 10: 88–99.

Baker, R. (1968) *Drag: A History of Female Impersonation on the Stage*, London: Triton Books.

Beaumont Society (1983) *Beaumont Society Constitution*, London: Beaumont Society.

Beigel, H. and Feldman, R. (1963) 'The male transvestite's motivation in fiction, research and reality', in H. Beigel (ed.) *Advances in Sex Research*, New York: Harper & Row.

Benjamin, H. (1953) 'Transvestism and transsexualism', *International Journal of Sexology* 7: 12–4.

—— (1954) 'Transvestism and transsexualism as psychosomatic and somato-psychic syndromes', *American Journal of Psychotherapy* 8: 219–30.

—— (1966) *The Transsexual Phenomenon*, New York: Julian Press.

—— (1967a) 'The transsexual phenomenon', *Transactions of the New York Academy of Sciences* 29: 428–30.

—— (1967b) 'Transvestism and transsexualism in the male and female', *The Journal of Sex Research* 3: 107–27.

—— (1969) 'Introduction', in R. Green and J. Money (eds) *Transsexualism and Sex Reassignment*, Baltimore: Johns Hopkins University Press.

—— (1971) 'Should surgery be performed on transsexuals?', *American Journal of Psychotherapy* 80: 74–82.

Bennetts, L. (1993) 'k.d. lang cuts it close', *Vanity Fair*, August.

Berg, A. (1982) *Creatures*, Paris: Pink Star Editions.

Berg, I., Nixon, H. and MacMahon, R. (1963) 'Change of assigned sex at puberty', *The Lancet* 12: 1216–7.

Berger, J. C., Green, R., Laub, D.R., Reynolds, C.L., Jr., Walker, P.A. and Wollman, L. (1979) *Standards of Care: The Hormonal and Surgical Reassignment of Gender Dysphoric Persons*, Galvaston, Texas: Janus Information Facility.

Berger, P. L. and Luckmann, T. (1971) *The Social Construction of Reality*, Harmondsworth: Penguin University Books.

Berry, J. (1993) Personal communication, 14 January, Emah Limited, Halcyon Associates.

Billings, D. B. and Urban, T. (1982) 'The socio-medical construction of transsexualism: an interpretation and critique', *Social Problems* 29: 266–82.

Birrell, S. and Cole, C. L. (1990) 'Double fault: Renee Richards and the construction and naturalisation of difference', *Sociology of Sport Journal* 7: 1–21.

Bishop, P. (1958) 'Discussion of Armstrong (1958)', in D. Robertson-Smith and W. M. Davidson (eds) *Symposium on Nuclear Sex*, London: Heinemann.

Blair, L. (1977) *Rhythms of Vision*, London: Paladin.

Blumer, Herbert (1971) 'Social problems as collective behavior', *Social Problems* 18: 298–306.

Bockting, W. O. and Coleman, E. (1992a) 'A comprehensive approach to the treatment of gender dysphoria', in W. O. Bockting and E. Coleman (eds) *Gender Dysphoria: Interdisciplinary Approaches in Clinical Management*, New York: The Haworth Press.

—— (eds) (1992b) *Gender Dysphoria: Interdisciplinary Approaches in Clinical Management*, New York: The Haworth Press.

Bolin, A (1994) 'Transcending and transgendering: male-to-female transsexuals, dichotomy and diversity', in G. Herdt (ed.) *Third Sex, Third Gender: Beyond Sexual Dimorphism in Culture and History*, New York: Zone Books.

Bornstein, K. (1994) *Gender Outlaw: On Men, Women and the Rest of Us*, London: Routledge.

Bowman, K. M. and Engle, B. (1957) 'Medicolegal aspects of transvestism', *American Journal of Psychiatry* 113: 583–8.

Brake, M. (1976) 'I may be a queer, but at least I am a man', in D. L. Barker and S. Allen (eds) *Sexual Divisions and Society: Process and Change*, London: Tavistock.

Bremer, J. (1959) *Asexualisation*, New York: Macmillan.

Brierley, H. (1979) *Transvestism: A Handbook with Case Studies for Psychologists, Psychiatrists and Counsellors*, Oxford: Pergamon.

Broster, L. R., Allen, C., Vines, H.W.C., Patterson, J., Greenwood, A. W., Marrian, G. F. and Butler, G. C. (1938) *The Adrenal Cortex and Intersexuality*, London: Chapman & Hall.

Bryant, C. (1977) 'Carnal behavior and social control: private patterns and commercial configurations', in C. Bryant (ed.) *Sexual Deviancy in Social Context*, New York: New Viewpoints.

Brockopp, G. and Lester, D. (1969) 'The masturbator', *Crisis Intervention* 1: 10–3.

Buckner, H. T. (1970) 'The transvestic career path', *Psychiatry* 33: 381–9.

Buhrich, N. (1976) 'A heterosexual transvestite club: psychiatric aspects', *Australian and New Zealand Journal of Psychiatry* 10: 331–5.

Buhrich, N. and McConaghy, N. (1976) 'Transvestite fiction', *Journal of Nervous and Mental Disease* 163: 420–7.

—— (1977a) 'The clinical syndromes of femmiphilic transvestism', *Archives of Sexual Behaviour* 6: 397–411.

—— (1977b) 'The discrete syndromes of transvestism and transsexualism', *Archives of Sexual Behaviour* 6: 483–95.

Bulliet, C. J. (1928) *Venus Castina. Famous Female Impersonators, Celestial and Human*, New York: Covici Friede.

Bullough, V. L. (1976) *Sexual Variance in Society and History*, New York: Wiley.

Bullough, V. L. and Bullough, B. (1993) *Cross Dressing, Sex, and Gender*, Pennsylvania: University of Pennsylvania Press.

Bullough, V. L., Bullough, L. L., Dorr Legg, W., Elcano, B. W. and Kepner, J. (1976) *An Annotated Bibliography of Homosexuality, vol. 2*, London: Garland Press.

Bunker, John P. (1970) 'Surgical manpower: a comparison of operations and surgery in the United States and in England and Wales', *New England Journal of Medicine* 282: 135–43.

Burris, B. (1971) 'The fourth world manifesto', in *Notes from the Third Year*, New York.

Butler, J. (1990), *Gender Trouble*, London: Routledge.

Cahill, S. E. (1989) 'Fashioning males and females: appearance and the social reproduction of gender', *Symbolic Interactionism* 12: 281–98.

Capra, F. (1976) *The Tao of Physics*, London: Fontana.

Carpenter, E. (1911) 'On the connection between homosexuality and divination and the importance of the intermediate sexes generally in early civilisations', *American Journal of Religious Psychology and Education* 4: 219–43.

Cauldwell, D. O. (1947a) *Why Males Wear Female Attire*, Girard, Kansas: Haldeman-Julius.

—— (1947b) *Transvestists Tell Their Stories: Confessions of Persons who Prefer to Dress Like the Opposite Sex*, Girard, Kansas: Haldeman-Julius.

—— (1949a) 'Psychopathia Transexualis', *Sexology* 16: 274–80.

—— (1949b) *Unconventional Modes of Sexual Expression*, Girard, Kansas: Haldeman-Julius.

—— (1949c) *What's Wrong with Transvestism?*, Girard, Kansas: Haldeman-Julius.

—— (1950) *Questions and Answers on the Sex Life and Sexual Problems of Transvestites*, Girard, Kansas: Haldeman-Julius.

—— (1951) *Sex Transmutation – Can One's Sex Be Changed?*, Girard, Kansas: Haldeman-Julius.

—— (1956) *Transvestism: Men in Female Dress*, New York: Sexology Corp.

Chesler, P. (1973) *Women and Madness*, New York: Avon.

Chodorow, Nancy (1978) *The Reproduction of Mothering: Psychoanalysis and the Sociology of Gender*, Berkeley: University of California Press.

—— (1979), 'Feminism and difference: gender, relation and difference in psychoanalytic perspective', *Socialist Review* 9: 51–69.

CIC (1993a) 'Girls' changing room', P.O. Box 1650, B1 lAA.

—— (1993b) 'TV dream line', P.O. Box 1650, B1 1AA.

Clarke, J., Hall, S., Jefferson, T. and Roberts, B. (1976) 'Subcultures, cultures and class', in S. Hall and T. Jefferson (eds) *Resistance Through Rituals*, London: Hutchinson.

Connell, R. W. (1987) *Gender and Power*, Oxford: Blackwell.

Conrad, P. (1975) 'The discovery of hyperkinesis: notes on the medicalization of deviant behaviour', *Social Problems* 23: 12–21.

Conrad, P. and Schneider, J. W. (1980), *Deviance and Medicalisation*, London: C. V. Mosby.

Corea, Gena (1977) *The Hidden Malpractice: How American Medicine Mistreats Women*, New York: Jove.

Cowell, R. (1954) *Roberta Cowell's Story*, London: Heinemann.

Crimson (1993) 'TV wedding belles', P. O. Box 540, CH35YU.

Cromwell, J. (1994) 'Default assumptions or the Billy Tipton phenomenon', *FTM Newsletter*, Issue 28, July: 4–5.

Dekker, R. M. and Pol, L. C. van de (1989) *The Tradition of Female Transvestism in Early Modern Europe*, Basingstoke: Macmillan.

Denny, D. (1994) *Gender Dysphoria: A Guide to Research*, New York: Garland Publishing, Inc.

Devor, H. (1987) 'Gender blending females', *American Behavioural Scientist* 31: 12–40.

—— (1989) *Gender Blending: Confronting the Limits of Duality*, Bloomington: Indiana University Press.

Dewhurst, C. J. and Gordon, R. R. (1963) 'Change of sex', *The Lancet* 12: 1213–16.

Diamond, M. (1965) 'A critical evaluation of the ontogeny of human sexual behaviour', *Quarterly Review of Biology* 40: 147–75.

—— (1982) *Sex-Watching*, London: Prion.

Dingwall, R. (1976) *Aspects of Illness*, London: Martin Robertson.

Dorenkamp, M. and Henke, R. (eds) (1994) *Negotiating Lesbian and Gay Subjects*, London: Routledge.

Driscoll, J. P. (1971) 'Transsexuals', *Transaction* – Special Supplement 8 (5–6): 28–37, 66, 68.

Dubermann, M. (1991) *About Time: Exploring the Gay Past*, New York: Penguin Books.

Dunn, C. W. (1940) 'Stilbestrol induced gynaecomastia in the male', *Journal of the American Medical Association* 115: 2263–4.

Eazee Come (1993a) 'Girls must work', P.O. Box 649, EC1U 9UU.

—— (1993b) 'So you want to be a girl – like me?', P.O. Box 649, EC1U 9UU.

Edgerton, M. (1973a) 'Introduction', in D. R. Laub and P. Gandy (eds) *Proceedings of the Second Interdisciplinary Symposium on Gender Dysphoria Syndrome*, Stanford: University Medical Center.

—— (1973b) 'Transsexualism – a surgical problem?', *Plastic and Reconstructive Surgery* 52: 74–6.

—— (1974) 'The surgical treatment of male transsexuals', *Clinics in Plastic Surgery* 1: 285–323.

Edgerton, M. T., Jacobson, W. and Meyer, E. (1960) 'Surgical-psychiatric study of patients seeking plastic (cosmetic) surgery', *British Journal of Plastic Surgery* 13: 136–45.

Edgerton, M. T., Knorr, N. J. and Callison, J. R. (1970) 'The surgical treatment of transsexual patients', *Plastic and Reconstruction Surgery* 45: 38–46.

Ehrenreich, B. and English, D. (1973) *Complaints and Disorders: The Sexual Politics of Sickness*, Old Westburg, NY: Feminist Press.

—— (1974) *Witches, Midwives and Nurses*, London: Compendium.

—— (1979) *For Her Own Good*, London: Pluto.

Eichler, M. (1980) *The Double Standard: A Feminist Critique of Feminist Social Science*, London: Croom Helm.

Ehrensaft, D. (1980) 'When women and men mother', *Socialist Review* 10: 37–73.

Ekins, R. (1988) 'News from around the world – in their own words: interview with Dr. Richard Ekins of the Trans-Gender Archive, University of Ulster', *Renaisance News* 1 (5): 4–5. [The Chrysalis Interview].

—— (1989) 'Trans-gender biography: a guide to the literature with an annotated bibliography [and wants list]', *Archive News: Bulletin of the Trans-Gender Archive* 1 (3): 12–28.

—— (1990a) 'Building a trans-gender archive: on the classification and framing of trans-gender knowledge', in A. Purnell (ed.) *Report of the First International Gender Dysphoria Conference*, London: The Beaumont Trust.

—— (1990b) 'Half-worlds between the sexes: popular press coverage of transvestism and transsexuality, 1949–1959, Part 1', *Archive News: Bulletin of the Trans-Gender Archive* 2 (1): 3–23.

—— (1992a) 'Half-worlds between the sexes: popular press coverage of transvestism and transsexuality, 1949–1959, Part 2', *Archive News: Bulletin of the Trans-Gender Archive* 3 (1): 26–8.

—— (ed.) (1992b) 'The work of Peter Farrer: women's clothes and cross-dressing with a provisional list of novels in which mention of cross-dressing is made, 1901–1950', *Archive News: Bulletin of the Trans-Gender Archive* 3 (1): 3–20.

—— (1993) 'On male femaling: a grounded theory approach to cross-dressing and sex-changing', *Sociological Review* 41: 1–29.

—— (1996) 'Screening male femaling: cross-dressing and sex-changing in the movies', *Chrysalis: The Journal of Transgressive Gender Identities* 2 (3), forthcoming.

Ellis, A. and Abarbanel, A. (1961) *The Encyclopedia of Sexual Behaviour, vol. II*, London: Heinemann.

Ellis, H. H. (1913a) 'Sexo-aesthetic inversion', *Alienist and Neurologist* 34: 156–67.

—— (1913b) 'Sexo-aesthetic inversion', *Alienist and Neurologist* 34: 249–79.

—— (1920) 'Eonism', *Medical Review of Reviews* (New York): 3–12.

—— (1928) *Studies in the Psychology of Sex, Volume 7*, Philadelphia: F.A. Davies.

Epstein, J. and Straub, K. (eds) (1991) *Body Guards: The Cultural Politics of Gender Ambiguity*, London: Routledge.

Erikson Educational Foundation (1969) 'Life begins again', *Erikson Educational Foundation Newsletter*, Spring: 1.

Fallowell, D. and Ashley, A. (1982) *April Ashley's Odyssey*, London: Jonathan Cape.

Farrer, P. (ed.) (1987) *Men in Petticoats*, Liverpool: Karn Publications Garston.

—— (ed.) (1992) *In Female Disguise: An Anthology of English and American Short Stories and Literary Passages*, Liverpool: Karn Publications Garston.

—— (ed.) (1994) *Borrowed Plumes: Letters from Edwardian Newspapers on Male Cross-dressing*, Liverpool: Karn Publications Garston.

Feinberg, L. (1993) *Stone Butch Blues*, Ithaca, New York: Firebrand Books.

Feinbloom, D. H. (1976) *Transvestites and Transsexuals: Mixed Views*, New York: Dell.

Fenichel, O. (1954) 'The psychology of transvestitism [1930]', in *The Collected Papers of Otto Fenichel, First Series*, London: Routledge & Kegan Paul.

Ferris, L. (ed.) (1993) *Crossing the Stage: Controversies on Cross-Dressing*, London: Routledge.

Fisk, N. (1973) 'Gender dysphoria syndrome (the how, what and why of a disease)', in D. R. Laub and P. Gandy (eds) *Proceedings of the Second Interdisciplinary Symposium on Gender Dysphoria Syndrome*, Palo Alto: Stanford University Press.

—— (1974) 'Gender dysphoria syndrome – the conceptualisation that liberalises indications for total gender reorientation and implies a broadly based multi-dimensional rehabilitative regimen', *Western Journal of Medicine* 120: 386–91.

Foote, R. M. (1944) 'Diethylstilbestrol in the management of psychopathological states in males', *Journal of Nervous and Mental Disease* 99: 928–35.

Forester, B.M. and Swiller, H. (1972) 'Transsexualism: review of syndrome and presentation of possible successful therapeutic approach', *International Journal of Group Psychotherapy* 22: 343–51.

Foucault, M. (1979) *The History of Sexuality*, London: Allen Lane.

Freedman, R., Green, R. and Spitzer, R. (1976) 'Reassessment of homosexuality and transsexualism', *Annual Review of Medicine* 27: 57–62.

Freidson, E. (1970) *Profession of Medicine*, New York: Harper & Row.

Gandy, P. (1973) 'Follow-up on 74 gender dysphoric patients treated at Stanford', in D. R. Laub and P. Gandy (eds) *Proceedings of the Second International Symposium on Gender Dysphoria Syndrome*, Palo Alto: Stanford University Press.

Garber, M. (1992) *Vested Interests: Cross-Dressing and Cultural Anxiety*, New York: Routledge.

Garfinkel, H. (1967) 'Passing and the managed achievement of sex status in an intersexed person', in H. Garfinkel, *Studies in Ethnomethodology*, Englewood Cliffs, N.J.: Prentice Hall.

Gilbert, O. P. (1926) *Men in Women's Guise*, London: John Lane.

—— (1932) *Women in Men's Guise*, London: John Lane.

Gillies, H. and Millard, D. R. (1957) *The Principles and Art of Plastic Surgery*, London: Butterworth.

Gitlin, T. (1979) 'Prime time ideology: the hegemonic process in television entertainment', *Social Problems* 26: 251–66.

Glaser, B. (1978) *Theoretical Sensitivity: Advances in the Methodology of Grounded Theory*, Mill Valley, Calif.: Sociology Press.

Goffman, E. (1963) *Stigma: Notes on the Management of Spoiled Identity*, Englewood Cliffs, N.J.: Prentice Hall.

—— (1968) 'The moral career of the mental patient', in E. Goffman *Asylums*, Harmondsworth: Penguin.

—— (1969) *The Presentation of Self in Everyday Life*, Harmondsworth: Penguin.

—— (1974) *Frame Analysis: An Essay on the Organisation of Experience*, New York: Harper & Row.

—— (1977) 'The arrangement between the sexes', *Theory and Society* 4: 301–31.

—— (1979) *Gender Advertisements*, London: Macmillan.

Golla, F. L. and Hodge, P. S. (1949) 'Hormone treatment of the sexual offender', *The Lancet*: 1006–7.

Goldberg, N. (1993) *The Other Side*, Manchester: Cornerhouse Publications.

Green, R. (1969) 'Childhood cross-gender identification', in R. Green and J. Money (eds) *Transsexualism and Sex Reassignment*, Baltimore: Johns Hopkins Press.

—— (1970) 'A research strategy', *International Journal of Psychiatry* 9: 269–73.

Green, R. and Money, J. (eds) (1969) *Transsexualism and Sex Reassignment*, Baltimore: Johns Hopkins University Press.

Green, R., Stoller, R. J. and MacAndrew, C. (1966) 'Attitudes toward sex transformation procedures', *Archives of General Psychiatry* 15: 178–82.

Greenberg, N. H., Rosenwald, A. K. and Nielson, P. E. (1960) 'A study in transsexualism', *Psychiatric Quarterly* 34: 203–35.

Greenberg, S. (1993) 'The next wave', *The Advocate* 633, July 13.

Grossberg, L., Nelson, C. and Treichler, P. (1992) *Cultural Studies*, New York: Routledge.

Gutheil, E. A. (1954) 'The psychological background of transsexualism and transvestism', *American Journal of Psychotherapy* 8: 231–9.

Habegger, A. (1982) *Gender, Fantasy and Realism in American Literature*, New York: Columbia University Press.

Habermas, J. (1968) *Knowledge and Human Interests*, Boston: Beacon.

—— (1973) *Theory and Practice*, Boston: Beacon.

—— (1979) *Communication and the Evolution of Society*, Boston: Beacon.

Hagberg, K. A. (1979) 'Transsexualism: is gender absolute?', *New Women's Times Feminist Review* Aug/Sept: 10–12.

Haire, N. (ed.) (1934) *Encyclopaedia of Sexual Knowledge*, London: Francis Aldor.

—— (1950) 'Change of sex', *Journal of Sex Education* 2: 200–3.

Halberstam, J. (1992) 'Skinflick: posthuman gender in Jonathan Demme's "The Silence of the Lambs"', *Camera Obscura*, 27, 9 September: 35–52.

Halcyon (1993a) 'Husband enslaved!', Emah Ltd.

—— (1993b) 'Maid for the dildo', Emah Ltd.

—— (1993c) 'Transvestite spanking!', Emah Ltd.

Hall, S. (1992) 'Cultural studies and its theoretical legacies', in L. Grossberg et al. (eds) *Cultural Studies*, New York: Routledge.

Hall, S. et al. (1978) *Policing the Crisis*, London: Macmillan.

Hamburger, C. (1953) 'The desire for changes of sex as shown by personal letters from 465 men and women', *Acta Endocrinologica* 14: 361–75.

Hamburger, C. and Sprechler, M. (1951) 'The influence of steroid hormones on the hormonal activity of the adenohypophysis in man', *Acta Endocrinologica* 12: 167–95.

Hamburger, C., Sturup, G. and Dahl-Iversen, E. (1953) 'Transvestism: hormonal, psychiatric and surgical treatment', *Journal of the American Medical Association* 152: 391–6.

Harré, R. (1979) *Social Being*, Oxford: Blackwell.

Hastings, D. W. (1966) 'Transsexualism and transvestism', *Journal of the American Medical Association* 197: 594–600.

—— (1969) 'Inauguration of a research project on transsexualism in a university medical center', in R. Green and J. Money (eds) *Transsexualism and Sex Reassignment*, Baltimore: Johns Hopkins University Press.

—— (1974) 'Postsurgical adjustment of male transsexual patients', *Plastic Surgery* 1: 335–44.

Henry, G. W. (1941) *Sex Variants: A Study of Homosexual Patterns*, New York: Paul E. Hoeber.

Herdt, G. (1981) *Guardians of the Flutes: Idioms of Masculinity*, New York: McGraw-Hill.

—— (ed.) (1994) *Third Sex, Third Gender: Beyond Sexual Dimorphism in Culture and History*, New York: Zone Books.

Hertoft, P. and Sorensen, T. (1979) 'Transsexuality: some remarks based on clinical experience', in *Sex Hormones and Behaviour*, Ciba Foundation Symposium 62 (new series), Oxford: Excerpta Medica.

Hertz, J., Tillinger, K. G. and Westman, A. (1961) 'Transvestism: report on five hormonally and surgically treated cases', *Acta Psychiatrica Scandinavica* 37: 283–94.

Hirschfeld, M. (1910) *Die Transvestiten: Eine Untersuchung uber den Erotischen Verkleidungstrieb*, Berlin: Pulvermacher. Trans. Michael Lombardi-Nash, 1991, New York: Prometheus Books.

—— (1938) *Sexual Anomalies and Perversions*, London: Encyclopaedic Press.

Hodgkinson, L. (1987) *Bodyshock: The Truth about Changing Sex*, London: Columbus Books.

—— (1989) *Michael, née Laura: The Story of the World's First Female-to-Male Transsexual*, London: Columbus Books.

Hoenig, J. (1972) 'The rationale and the myth of the surgical treatment of transsexualism', *Medical Aspects of Human Sexuality* 2: 7–13.

—— (1982) 'Transsexualism', in Granville-Grossman, K. (ed.) *Recent Advances in Clinical Psychiatry No. 4*, London: Churchill Livingstone.

—— (1985) 'Transsexualism in the arts', in B. W. Steiner (ed.) *Gender Dysphoria: Development, Research, Management*, New York: Plenum.

Hoenig, J., Kenna, J. C. and Youd, A. (1971) 'Surgical treatment for transsexualism', *Acta Psychiatrica Scandinavica* 47: 106–31.

Holloway, J. P. (1974) 'Transsexuals: legal considerations', *Archives of Sexual Behavior* 3: 33–50.

Holzner, B. and Marx, J. H. (1979) *Knowledge Application: The Knowledge System in Society*, Boston: Allyn & Bacon, Inc.

Hooker, E. (1970) 'The homosexual community', in J. Douglas (ed.) *Observations on Deviance*, New York: Random House.

hooks, bell (1994) *Outlaw Culture: Resisting Representations*, New York: Routledge.

Hoopes, J.E., Knorr, N. J. and Wolf, S. R. (1968) 'Transsexualism: considerations regarding sexual reassignment', *Journal of Nervous and Mental Disease* 147: 510–16.

Horton, C. B. and Clarke, E. K. (1931) 'Transvestism or eonism', *American Journal of Psychiatry* 10: 1025–30.

Hoyer, N. (1933) *Man into Woman*, London: Jarrolds.

Humphreys, L. (1970) *Tearoom Trade: A Study of Homosexual Encounters in Public Places*, London: Duckworth.

Hunt, D. and Hampson, J. (1980) 'Follow-up of 17 biologic male transsexuals after sex reassignment surgery', *American Journal of Psychiatry* 137: 432–8.

Ian, M. (1994) 'How do you wear your body', in M. Dorenkamp and R. Henke (eds) *Negotiating Lesbian and Gay Subjects*, London: Routledge.

ICSTIS (1993) *The Independent Committee for the Supervision of Standards of Telephone Information Services, Activity Report.*

Ihlenfeld, C. (1973a) 'Outcome of hormonal-surgical intervention on the transsexual condition: evolution and management', in D. R. Laub and P. Gandy (eds) *Proceedings of Second Interdisciplinary Symposium on Gender Dysphoria Syndrome*, Palo Alto: Stanford University Press.

—— (1973b) 'Thoughts on the treatment of transsexuals', *Journal of Contemporary Psychotherapy* 6: 63–9.

'John' (1977) 'Rebirth', *Nursing Mirror*, 24 March: 48–9.

Johns Hopkins University (1969) 'Statement on the establishment of a clinic for transsexuals at the Johns Hopkins Medical institutions', in R. Green and J. Money (eds) *Transsexualism and Sex Reassignment*, Baltimore: Johns Hopkins Press.

Johnson, C. and Brown C. with Wendy Nelson (1982) *The Gender Trap: The Moving Autobiography of Chris and Cathy, the First Transsexual Parents*, London: Proteus.

Jones, J. (1994) 'FTM cross-dresser murdered', *FTM Newsletter*, Issue 26, Feb: 3.

Jorgensen, C. (1967) *Christine Jorgensen: A Personal Autobiography*, New York: P. S. Eriksson.

Justice of the Peace and Local Government Review (1938) 'Editorial on "Masquerading"', *Justice Of The Peace and Local Government Review* 102: 135–6.

Kadushin, C. (1966) 'The friends and supporters of psychotherapy: on social circles in urban life', *American Sociological Review* 31: 786–802.

Kando, T. (1973) *Sex Change: The Achievement of Gender Identity among Feminised Transsexuals*, Springfield, Illinois: Charles C. Thomas.

Kay, B. (1976) *The Other Women*, London: Matthews Miller Dunbar.

Keeps, D. A. (1993) 'How RuPaul ups the ante for drag', *The New York Times*, July 11: H23.

Kessler, S. J. and McKenna, W. (1978) *Gender: An Ethnomethodological Approach*, New York: Wiley.

King, D. (1986) 'The transvestite and the transsexual: a case study of public categories and private identities', unpublished Ph.D. Thesis, University of Essex.

—— (1987) 'Social constructionism and medical knowledge: the case of transsexualism', *Sociology of Health and Illness* 9: 351–77.

—— (1993) *The Transvestite and the Transsexual: Public Categories and Private Identities*, Aldershot: Avebury.

Kinsey, A. C., Pomeroy, W. B. and Martin, C. E. (1948) *Sexual Behaviour in the Human Male*, Philadelphia: W. B. Saunders.

Kinsey, A. C., Pomeroy, W. B., Martin, C. E. and Gebhard, P. H. (1953) *Sexual Behaviour in the Human Female*, Philadelphia: W. B. Saunders.

Kirk, K. and Heath, E. (1984) *Men in Frocks*, London: Gay Men's Press.

Kittrie, N. (1973) *The Right to Be Different: Deviance and Enforced Therapy*, New York: Pelican Books.

Knorr, N., Wolf, S. and Meyer, E. (1969) 'Psychiatric evaluation of male transsexuals for surgery', in R. Green and J. Money (eds) *Transsexualism and Sex Reassignment*, Baltimore: Johns Hopkins Press.

Kovel, J. (1976–77) 'Therapy in late capitalism', *Telos* 30: 73–92.

Kraft-Ebbing, R. von (1894) *Psychopathia Sexualis*, 9th edn, Stuttgart: Enke.

Kubie, L. S. and Mackie, J. B. (1968) 'Critical issues raised by operations for gender transmutation', *Journal of Nervous and Mental Disease* 147: 431–43.

Kunzle, D. (1982) *Fashion and Fetishism*, Totowa, New Jersey: Rowman & Littlefield.

Laing, R. D. (1967) *The Politics of Experience and the Bird of Paradise*, Harmondsworth: Penguin.

Landers, Ann (1979) 'Sex-change operations are more than cosmetic', *The Raleigh Register*, 21 January: B–5.

Larson, M. S. (1977) *The Rise of Professionalism: A Sociological Analysis*, Berkeley: University of California Press.

Lasch, C. (1978) *The Culture of Narcissism*, New York: W.W. Norton.

Laub, D. R. and Fisk, N. T. (1974) 'A rehabilitation program for gender dysphoria syndrome by surgical sex change', *Plastic and Reconstruction Surgery* 53: 388–403.

Laub, D. R. and Gandy, P. (eds) (1973) *Proceedings of the Second Interdisciplinary Symposium on Gender Dysphoria Syndrome*, Stanford: University Medical Center.

Lemert, E. M. (1972) *Human Deviance, Social Problems and Social Control*, 2nd edn, Englewood Cliffs, N.J.: Prentice Hall.

Lester, D. (1973) 'Telephone counseling and the masturbator: a dilemma', in C. Bryant (ed.) *Sexual Deviancy in Social Context*, New York: New Viewpoints, 1988.

Levine, E. M., Shaiova, C. H. and Mihailovic, M. (1975) 'Male to female: the role transformation of transsexuals', *Archives of Sexual Behaviour* 4: 173–85.

Liebman, S. (1944) 'Homosexuality, transvestism and psychosis', *Journal of Nervous and Mental Disease* 99: 945–58.

Lindgren, T. and Pauly, I. B. (1975) 'A body image scale for evaluating transsexuals', *Archives of Sexual Behavior* 4: 640–57.

Lothstein, L. M. (1982) 'Sex reassignment surgery: historical, bioethical and theoretical issues', *American Journal of Psychiatry* 139: 417–26.

Luckenbill, D. F. and Best, J. (1981) 'Careers in deviance and respectability: the analogy's limitations', *Social Problems* 29: 197–206.

Lukacs, M. (1978) *Let Me Die a Woman: The Why and How of Sex-Change Operations,* New York: Rearguard Productions.

Lukianowicz, N. (1959) 'A survey of various aspects of transvestism in the light of our present knowledge', *Journal of Nervous and Mental Disease* 133: 346–53.

McIndoe, A. (1950) 'The treatment of congenital absence and obliterative conditions of the vagina', *British Journal of Plastic Surgery* 2: 254–67.

McIntosh, M. (1993) 'Queer theory and the war of the sexes', in J. Bristow and A. R. Wilson (eds) *Activating Theory*. London: Lawrence & Wishart Ltd.

MacKenzie, K. R. (1978) 'Gender dysphoria syndrome: towards standardised diagnostic criteria', *Archives of Sexual Behaviour* 7: 251–62.

McMullan, M. and Whittle, S. (1994) *Transvestism, Transsexualism and the Law*, London: The Beaumont Trust/The Gender Trust.

Mark, M. E. (1982) *Falkland Road*, London: Thames & Hudson.

Markland, C. (1973) 'Complications in male transsexual surgery', in D. R. Laub and P. Gandy (eds) *Proceedings of the Second Interdisciplinary Symposium on Gender Dysphoria Syndrome*, Palo Alto: Stanford University Press.

Marlowe, K. (1969) *Mr Madam*, London: Mayflower.

Marshall, G. (1981) 'Accounting for deviance', *International Journal of Sociology and Social Policy* 1: 17–45.

Marshall, G. Balfour (1913) 'Artificial vagina: a review of the various operative procedures for correcting atresia vaginae', *The Journal of Obstetrics and Gynaecology of the British Empire* 23: 193–212.

Martino, M. with Harriett (1977) *Emergence: A Transsexual Autobiography*, New York: Crown Publishers, Inc.

Mason, N. (1980a) A trans-sexual's case history', *British Journal of Sexual Medicine* 8: 60–1.

—— (1980b) 'The trans-sexual dilemma – being a trans-sexual', *Journal of Medical Ethics* 6: 85–9.

Meerloo, J. A. M. (1967) 'Change of sex and collaboration with the psychosis', *American Journal of Psychiatry* 124: 263–4.

Messerschmidt, J. W. (1993) *Masculinities and Crime: Critiques and Reconceptualisation of Theory*, Maryland: Rowman & Littlefield Publishers, Inc.

Meyer, E., Jacobson, W., Edgerton, M. and Canter, A. (1960) 'Motivational patterns in patients seeking elective plastic surgery', *Psychosomatic Medicine* 22: 193–201.

Meyer, J. K. (1973) 'Some thoughts on nosology and motivation among "transsexuals"', in D. R. Laub and P. Gandy (eds) *Proceedings of Second Interdisciplinary Symposium on Gender Dysphoria Syndrome*, Palo Alto: Stanford University Press.

—— (1974) 'Clinical variants among applicants for sex reassignment', *Archives of Sexual Behavior* 3: 527–58.

Meyer, J. K. and Hoopes J. E. (1974) 'The gender dysphoria syndromes: a position statement on so-called transsexualism', *Plastic and Reconstructive Surgery* 54: 444–51.

Meyer, J. K. and Reter, D. (1979) 'Sex reassignment', *Archives of General Psychiatry* 36: 1010–15.

Millot, C. (1990) *Horesexe: Essays on Transsexuality*, New York: Autonomedia Inc.

Miriam, K. (1993) 'From rage to all the rage: lesbian-feminism, sadomasochism and the politics of memory', in I. Reti (ed.) *Unleashing Feminism: A Collection of Radical Feminist Writings*, Santa Cruz, Calif.: Herbooks.

Money, J. (1969) 'Sex reassignment as related to hermaphroditism and transsexualism', in R. Green and J. Money (eds) *Transsexualism and Sex Reassignment*, Baltimore: Johns Hopkins Press.

—— (1972) 'Sex reassignment therapy in gender identity disorders', *International Psychiatry Clinics* 8: 198–210.

Money, J. and Gaskin, R. (1971) 'Sex reassignment', *International Journal of Psychiatry* 9: 249–69.

Money, J., Hampson, J. and Hampson, J. (1955) 'Hermaphroditism: recommendations concerning assignment of sex, change of sex, and psychologic management', *Bulletin of the Johns Hopkins Hospital* 97: 284–300.

—— (1957) 'Imprinting and the establishment of gender role', *Archives of Neurology and Psychiatry* 77: 333–6.

Money, J. and Schwartz, F. (1969) 'Public opinion and social issues in transsexualism: a case study in medical sociology', in R. Green and J. Money (eds) *Transsexualism and Sex Reassignment*, Baltimore: Johns Hopkins University Press.

Money, J. and Walker, P. A. (1977) 'Counseling the transsexual', in J. Money and H. Musaph (eds) *Handbook of Sexology*, Elsevier/North-Holland: Biomedical Press.

Money, J. and Wolff, G. (1973) 'Sex reassignment: male to female to male', *Archives of Sexual Behavior* 2: 245–50.

Morris, J. (1974) *Conundrum*, London: Faber.

National Enquirer (1979) 'Sex-change operation left me trapped between man and woman', *National Enquirer*, October 30: 1.

Newman, B. (1984) *The Ultimate Angels*, London: Hutchinson.

Newman, L. E. and Stoller, R. (1971) 'The Oedipal situation in male transsexualism', *British Journal of Medical Psychology* 44: 295–303.

—— (1974) 'Nontranssexual men who seek sex reassignment', *American Journal of Psychiatry* 131: 437–41.

Newton, E. (1979) *Mother Camp: Female Impersonators in America*, 2nd edn, Chicago: University of Chicago Press.

Norburg, M. and Laub, D. (1977) 'Review of the Stanford experience: implications for treatment'. Paper presented at the Fifth International Gender Dysphoria Symposium, Norfolk, Virginia, 12 February.

Northrup, G. (1959) 'Transsexualism: report of a case', *Archives of General Psychiatry* 1: 332–7.

Olkon, P. M. and Sherman, I. C. (1944) 'Eonism with added outstanding psychopathic features', *Journal of Nervous and Mental Disease* 99: 159–67.

Ostow, M. (1953) 'Transvestism', *Journal of the American Medical Association* 152: 1553.

Pauly, I. B. (1965) 'Male psychosexual inversion: transsexualism', *Archives of General Psychiatry* 13: 172–81.

—— (1968) 'Current status of change of sex operation', *Journal of Nervous and Mental Disease* 47: 460–71.

—— (1969a) 'Adult manifestations of female transsexualism', in R. Green and J. Money (eds) *Transsexualism and Sex Reassignment*, Baltimore: Johns Hopkins Press.

—— (1969b) 'Adult manifestations of male transsexualism', in R. Green and J. Money (eds) *Transsexualism and Sex Reassignment*, Baltimore: Johns Hopkins Press.

—— (1992) 'Terminology and classification of gender identity disorders', in W. O. Bockting and E. Coleman (eds) *Gender Dysphoria: Interdisciplinary Approaches in Clinical Management*, New York: The Haworth Press.

Pearce, F. (1981) 'The British press and the "placing" of male homosexuality', in S. Cohen and J. Young (eds) *The Manufacture of News: Deviance, Social Problems and the Mass Media*, London: Constable.

Perkins, R. (1983) *The 'Drag Queen' Scene: Transsexuals in Kings Cross*, Hemel Hempstead: Allen & Unwin.

Person, E. and Oversey, L. (1974a) 'The transsexual syndrome in males: I. Primary transsexualism', *American Journal of Psychotherapy* 28: 4–20.

—— (1974b) 'The transsexual syndrome in males: II. Secondary transsexualism', *American Journal of Psychotherapy* 28: 174–93.

Pfohl, S. J. (1977) 'The "discovery" of child abuse', *Social Problems* 24: 310–23.

Piercy, M. (1979) *Woman On The Edge Of Time*, London: Women's Press.

Plummer, K. (1975) *Sexual Stigma*, London: Routledge & Kegan Paul.

—— (1979) 'Symbolic Interactionism and Sexual Differentiation: An Empirical Investigation', final report on Grant HR 4043 to the SSRC.

Prince, C. V. (1978) 'Transsexuals and pseudotranssexuals', *Archives of Sexual Behaviour* 7: 263–72.

Radicalesbians (1971) 'Woman-identified woman', in *Notes from the Third Year*, New York.

Randell, J. B. (1959) 'Transvestism and transsexualism: a study of 50 cases', *British Medical Journal* 2: 1448–52.

—— (1960) 'Cross-dressing and the desire to change sex', unpublished MD Thesis, University of Wales.

—— (1969) 'Preoperative and postoperative status of male and female transsexuals', in R. Green and J. Money (eds) *Transsexualism and Sex Reassignment*, Baltimore: Johns Hopkins University Press.

—— (1971) 'Indications for sex reassignment surgery', *Archives of Sexual Behaviour* 1: 153–61.

Raymond, J. G. (1980) *The Transsexual Empire*, London: The Women's Press.

—— (1994), 'Introduction to the 1994 edition', in *The Transsexual Empire: The Making of the She-Male*, New York: Teachers College Press.

Rechy, J. (1964) *City of Night*, London: MacGibbon & Kee.

Rees, M. (1984) Application No. 9532/81 Mark Rees against United Kingdom, *Report of the European Commission of Human Rights*.

—— (1987) 'Time for change', *Marginal Notes* (The Registration Service Magazine) 5, December: 23–5.

—— (1993a) 'What it really means to be trans-sexual', Pamphlet, *Mothers' Union Social Concern Department*.

—— (1993b) 'He, she or it?', *Nursing Times*, 89, 10 March: 48–9.

—— (1996) *Dear Sir or Madam*, London: Cassell.

Rees Case (1986) (2/1985/88/135), 'Judgement', *European Court of Human Rights*, Strasbourg, 17 October.

Restak, R. M. (1980) 'Transsexual surgery: treatment or experiment?', *Medical News* May 5: 11.

Roazen, P. (1979) *Freud and His Followers*, Harmondsworth: Penguin.

Roberts, P. (1995) *Who's Who and Resource Guide to the International Transgender Community*, King of Prussia, PA: Creative Design Services.

Rose, E. (1978) 'Letter to the editors', *Chrysalis* 5: 6.

Rose, K. (1969) *Curzon: A Most Superior Person*, London: Weidenfeld & Nicolson.

Roth, H. N. (1973) 'Three years of ongoing psychotherapy of a transsexual patient', in D. R. Laub and P. Gandy (eds) *Proceedings of Second Interdisciplinary Symposium on Gender Dysphoria Syndrome*, Palo Alto: Stanford University Press.

Roth, M. and Ball, J. (1964) 'Psychiatric aspects of intersexuality', in C. N. Armstrong and A. Marshall (eds) *Intersexuality in Vertebrates Including Man*, London: Academic Press.

Sagarin, E. (1969) 'Transvestites and transsexuals: boys will be girls', in *Odd Man In: Societies of Deviants in America*, New York: Quadrangle Books.

—— (1978) 'Transsexualism: legitimation, amplification and exploitation of deviance by scientists and mass media', in C. Winick (ed.) *Deviance and Mass Media*, Beverly Hills: Sage.

de Savitsch, E. (1958) *Homosexuality, Transvestism and Change of Sex*, London: Heinemann.

Schneider, M. (1975) *Neurosis and Civilization: A Marxist/Freudian Synthesis*, New York: Seabury Press.

Scott, R. H. F. (1973) *The Transvestite Memoirs of Abbé de Choisy*, London: Peter Owen.

Segal, L. (1994) *Straight Sex: The Politics of Pleasure*, London: Virago.

Sieveking, P. (ed.) (1981) *Man Bites Man: The Scrapbook of an Edwardian Eccentric (George Ives)*, Harmondsworth: Penguin.

Silverstone, R. (1982) 'A structure for a modern myth: television and the transsexual', *Semiotica* 49: 95–138.

Simmel, G. (1955), *The Web of Group Affiliations*, New York: The Free Press.

Socarides, C. (1970) 'A psychoanalytic study of the desire for sexual transformation ("transsexualism"): the plaster of Paris man', *International Journal of Psycho-Analysis* 51: 341–9.

—— (1975) *Beyond Sexual Freedom*, New York: Quadrangle.

Sontag, S. (1978) *Illness as Metaphor*, New York: Farrar, Straus & Giroux.

Sorensen, T. and Hertoft, P. (1980) 'Sex modifying operations on transsexuals in Denmark in the period 1959–1977', *Acta Psychiatrica Scandinavica* 61: 56–66.

Spector, M. and Kitsuse, J. I. (1977) *Constructing Social Problems*, Menlo Park: Cummings.

Starrett, B. (1976) 'I dream in female', US pamphlet.

Steele, V. (1985) *Fashion and Eroticism*, Oxford: Oxford University Press.

Steiner, B. W. (ed.) (1985) *Gender Dysphoria: Development, Research, Management*, New York: Plenum.

Stekel, W. (1934) *Bi-Sexual Love*, New York: Physicians and Surgeons Book Co.

Stinson, B. (1972) 'A study of twelve applicants for transsexual surgery', *Ohio State Medical Journal* 68: 245–9.

Stoker, B. (1910) *Famous Imposters*, London: Sedgwick & Jackson.

Stoller, R. J. (1964a) 'A contribution to the study of gender identity', *International Journal of Psycho-Analysis* 45: 220–6.

—— (1964b) 'The hermaphroditic identity of hermaphrodites', *Journal of Nervous and Mental Disease* 139: 453–7.

—— (1967) 'Etiological factors in male transsexualism', *Transactions of the New York Academy of Sciences* 86: 431–3.

—— (1968) *Sex and Gender*, New York: Science House.

—— (1969) 'A biased view of "sex transformation" operations', *Journal of Nervous and Mental Disease* 149: 312–7.

—— (1970) 'Pornography and perversion', *Archives of General Psychiatry* 22: 490–500.

—— (1971) 'The term "transvestism"', *Archives of General Psychiatry* 24: 230–7.

—— (1972) 'Etiological factors in female transsexualism: a first approximation', *Archives of Sexual Behavior* 2: 47–64.

—— (1973a) 'Male transsexualism: uneasiness', *American Journal of Psychiatry* 130: 536–9.

—— (1973b) 'The male transsexual as "experiment"', *International Journal of Psycho-Analysis* 54: 215–25.

—— (1975) *The Transsexual Experiment*, London: The Hogarth Press.

—— (1982) 'Near miss: "sex-change" treatment and its evaluation', in M. R. Zales (ed.) *Eating, Sleeping and Sexuality: Treatment of Disorders in Basic Life Functions*, New York: Brunner/Mazel.

Stoller, R. J. and Newman, L. E. (1971) 'The bisexual identity of transsexuals: two case examples', *Archives of Sexual Behavior* 1: 17–28.

Stone, S. (1991) 'The *empire* strikes back: a posttranssexual manifesto', in J. Epstein and K. Straub (eds) (1991) *Body Guards: The Cultural Politics of Gender Ambiguity*, London: Routledge.

Strauss, A. L. (1977) *Mirrors and Masks*, London: Martin Robertson.

Sturup, C. (1976) 'Male transsexuals: a long-term follow-up after sex reassignment operations', *Acta Psychiatrica* 53: 51–63.

Sturup, G. K. (1969) 'Legal problems related to transsexualism and sex reassignment in Denmark', in R. Green and J. Money (eds) *Transsexualism and Sex Reassignment*, Baltimore: Johns Hopkins University Press.

241

Sulloway, F. (1980) *Freud, Biologist of the Mind*, London: Fontana.

Talamini, J. T. (1982) *Boys will be Girls: The Hidden World of the Heterosexual Male Transvestite*, Washington D.C.: University Press of America.

Talmey, B. S. (1914) 'Transvestism', *New York Medical Journal* 99: 362–8.

Tappan, P. (1951) 'Treatment of the sex offender in Denmark', *American Journal of Psychiatry* 108: 241–9.

Taussig, M. T. (1980) 'Reification and the consciousness of the patient', *Social Science Medicine* 14: 3–13.

Telfer, J. B. (1885) *The Strange Career of the Chevalier D'Eon de Beaumont*, London: Longmans, Green.

Thompson, C. J. S. (1938) *Mysteries of Sex: Women who Posed as Men and Men who Impersonated Women*, London: Hutchinson.

Thompson, J. B. (1988) 'Mass communication and modern culture: contribution to a critical theory of ideology', *Sociology* 22: 359–83.

TIC (1994) 'True TV experiences', *Exchange and Mart*, December: 22–8.

Tiefer, L. and Zitrin, A. (1977) 'A follow-up of operated transsexuals: a survey of the literature and unpublished experience', paper presented at the Fifth International Gender Dysphoria Symposium, Norfolk, Virginia, 12 February.

Tsur, H., Borenstein, A. and Seidman, D. S. (1991) 'Letter', *The Lancet* 338: 945–6.

Tully, B. (1992) *Accounting for Transsexualism and Transhomosexuality*, London: Whiting and Birch.

Van Buren, A. (1977) 'Male athlete would rather be a woman', *Paris News* (Paris, Kentucky), 10 November: A–10.

Van Putten, T. and Fawzy, I. (1976) 'Sex conversion surgery in a man with severe gender dysphoria: a tragic outcome', *Archives of General Psychiatry* 33: 751–3.

Vizetelly, E. A. (1895) *The True Story of the Chevalier D' Eon*, London: Tylston and Edwards.

Volkan, V. and Bhatti, T. (1973) 'Dreams of transsexuals awaiting surgery', *Comprehensive Psychiatry* 14: 269–79.

Walker, K. M. and Fletcher, P. (1955) *Sex and Society*, London: Frederick Muller.

Walker, K. M. and Strauss, E. B. (1939) *Sexual Disorders in the Male*, London: Hamish Hamilton.

Walter, A. (ed.) (1980) *Come Together: The Years of Gay Liberation*, London: Gay Men's Press.

Walworth, J. (1994) 'Michigan womyn's music festival 1994: transsexual protesters allowed to enter', *Cross-Talk*, Issue 61: 27–9.

Watson, L. (1974) *Supernature*, London: Coronet.

Weeks, J. (1977) *Coming Out: Homosexual Politics in Britain from the 19th Century to the Present*, London: Quartet Books.

—— (1981) *Sex, Politics and Society*, Harlow, Essex: Longmans.

—— (1990) *Coming Out: Homosexual Politics in Britain from the 19th Century to the Present*, revised edition, London: Quartet Books.

Wheelwright, J. (1989) *Amazons and Military Maids: Women who Dressed as Men in the Pursuit of Life, Liberty and Happiness*, London: Pandora Press.

Wiederman, G. H. (1953) 'Transvestism', *Journal of the American Medical Association* 152: 1167.

Wilden, A. (1972) *System and Structure: Essays in Communication and Exchange*, London: Tavistock.

Wise, T. N. and Meyer, J. K. (1980) 'Transvestism: previous findings and new areas for inquiry', *Journal of Sex and Marital Therapy* 6: 116–28.

Woodhouse, A. (1989) *Fantastic Women: Sex, Gender and Transvestism*, Basingstoke: Macmillan.

Woolgar, S. and Pawluch, D. (1985) 'Ontological gerrymandering: the anatomy of social problems explanations', *Social Problems* 32: 214–27.

Worden, F. G. and Marsh, J. T. (1955) 'Psychological factors in men seeking sex transformation', *Journal of the American Medical Association* 157: 1292–8.

Yawger, N. S. (1940) 'Transvestism and other cross-sex manifestations', *Journal of Nervous and Mental Disease* 92: 41–8.

INDEX

Notes: 1. Major page references are indicated by **bold** figures; 2. Most references are to transsexualism and transvestism, which are therefore generally omitted as qualifiers; 3. Most references are to Britain unless otherwise specified